# YOUR VOICE
# AND MINE 1

# YOUR VOICE AND MINE 1

*Joan M. Green*
*Natalie Little*
*Brenda Protheroe*

HOLT, RINEHART AND WINSTON OF CANADA, LIMITED

ISBN: 03-921794-9

Executive Editor: Maggie Goh
Developmental Editor: David Friend
Production Editor: Lisa Collins
Art Director: Mary Opper
Designer: Jolene Cuyler
Mechanicals: Julie Russel
Cover Illustrator: Shelley Browning

Holt, Rinehart & Winston of Canada, Limited is grateful
for the evaluations and suggestions of these educators:

Sheila A. Brooks
Dartmouth District School Board
Dartmouth, Nova Scotia

Coralie Bryant
Winnipeg School Board, Division #1
Winnipeg, Manitoba

Heather Croil
London Senior Secondary School
Richmond, British Columbia

Nigel Gough
Perth County Board of Education
Stratford, Ontario

Clare Henderson
Halton Board of Education
Acton, Ontario

Joanne K.A. Peters
Winnipeg School Board, Division #2
Winnipeg, Manitoba

Ina M. Remenda
Central Collegiate Institute
Regina, Saskatchewan

Don Stone
Windsor Board of Education
Windsor, Ontario

Printed in Canada

1 2 3 4 5   91 90 89 88 87

Joan M. Green, Superintendent, Toronto Board of
  Education
Natalie Little, Vice-Principal, Yorkdale Secondary School,
  North York Board of Education
Brenda Protheroe, Assistant Head of English, Vaughan
  Road Collegiate Institute, York Board of Education

**Canadian Cataloguing in Publication Data**
Green, Joan M. (Joan Marie), 1947–
  Your voice and mine 1

For use in high schools
ISBN 0-03-921794-9

1. English literature – 20th century.  2. Canadian
literature (English) – 20th century.*  3. Readers
(Secondary).  I. Little, Natalie.  II. Protheroe, Brenda.  III.
Title.

PE1121.G73 1986     820'.8     C86-093123-4

# TABLE OF CONTENTS

## YOUR VOICE AND MINE 1

# ACKNOWLEDGMENTS

**THE HUSBAND WHO STAYED AT HOME:** From THE MAID OF THE NORTH: FEMINIST FOLK TALES FROM AROUND THE WORLD retold by Ethel Johnston Phelps. Copyright © 1981 by Ethel Johnston Phelps. Reprinted by permission of Holt, Rinehart and Winston, Publishers.

**DR. JAMES BARRY:** From ROGUES, REBELS AND GENIUSES: THE STORY OF CANADIAN MEDICINE by Donald Jack. Copyright © 1981 by Pierre Berton and Martin M. Hoffman, M.D.. Reprinted by permission of Doubleday & Company, Inc.

**HOW SEX-STEREOTYPED TOYS SEX STEREOTYPE CHILDREN:** CO-ED Magazine.

**A SPECIAL GIFT:** Adapted from the teleplay by Durrell Royce Crays. Produced by Martin Tahse Productions. Based on the book A SPECIAL GIFT by Marcia L. Simon. Used by permission. All rights reserved.

**LAKE OF BAYS:** Reprinted from COLLECTED POEMS OF RAYMOND SOUSTER by permission of Oberon Press.

**DANCER CARTOON FROM *PICK OF THE PUNCH*:** © 1980 by Punch Publications Ltd. Reprinted with permission. Los Angeles Times Syndicate.

**CAREFUL, OR YOU MIGHT GET SCRATCHED:** By Joan Dash. Reprinted from SEVENTEEN ® Magazine. Copyright © 1985 by Triangle Communications Inc. All rights reserved.

**MASK:** By Melanie Harrison.

**CIRCLE:** By Toni Weston, reprinted by permission of Toni Weston.

**ON THE SIDEWALK BLEEDING:** From HAPPY NEW YEAR HERBIE AND OTHER STORIES, © 1957 by Evan Hunter.

**WHAT ABOUT FRIENDSHIPS?:** Reprinted by permission from LISTEN Magazine, © 1985.

**THE MOUNTAIN AND THE VALLEY:** By Ernest Buckler, reprinted by permission of McClelland and Stewart Ltd., The Canadian Publishers.

**HOW WELL DO YOU KNOW YOUR CHILDREN?:** Copyright 1985: KNT (Tribune Media Services) Reprinted with permission — The Toronto Star Syndicate.

**FROM MOTHER ... WITH LOVE:** By Zoa Sherburne. Permission granted by ANN ELMO AGENCY, INC.

**SISTER:** By Carol Shields. By permission Borealis Press Ltd, 1985.

## PHOTOGRAPHS

## ILLUSTRATIONS

# YOUR VOICE AND MINE 1

## Why Is the Book Called *Your Voice and Mine?*

People use their voices to speak to each other about their thoughts and emotions. When speaking isn't convenient, people often voice their opinions in writing, or in films, television shows, drawings, and so on. You will encounter many kinds of voices as you read this book. Some of the voices belong to the authors, speaking to you through the writing collected here. Some are those of your classmates, who will be telling you their reactions to what they have read or viewed and about their own knowledge and experience. Another voice in this book is yours. You'll get to share your views with your classmates and your teacher, in speech, in writing, and in a variety of other forms. Each voice, yours included, is unique and has something special to say.

## What Will I Find in This Book?

*Your Voice and Mine* is full of opportunities for you to read, observe, listen, think, speak, and write. It contains short stories, plays, poems, cartoons, comic strips, and articles from newspapers and magazines. The book is divided into ten clusters. The selections in each cluster speak about the same topic, although they may say very different things. In addition to the selections, there are many activities for you and your classmates to work on together.

## What Kinds of Activities Will I Do?

Like a photographer taking a picture, you will begin by trying to see things clearly. Each cluster opens with some Focussing activities. You and your classmates will share your ideas and experiences so you can see how much you already know about the topic of the cluster. You may also want to gather some resource materials, like magazines, books, videos, and movies. Your teacher can suggest interesting places to look.

After you read a selection, the Close Up activities will help you to see the piece of writing in detail so you can understand it better. The Wide Angle activities have a broader focus and encourage you to explore new directions using the knowledge you have just gained.

A kaleidoscope is an instrument that lets you create an enormous number of shapes and patterns. Kaleidoscope activities ask you to think about what you have encountered in the selections in the cluster and then to rearrange the ideas in new patterns. Kaleidoscope activities also ask you to think about how the topic you have examined is related to other topics. With your new insights, you can go on to answer your own questions.

## How Many Activities Will I Do?

You may choose to do several or a few, depending on the objectives set by you and your teacher.

## Why Do I Work on the Activities with Other People?

Your goal is not just to learn, but to help other people learn by telling them what you know. In the same way, other people can help *you* learn. Explaining your ideas so that others can understand them will help you figure things out, as well. Also, when you are working to polish your writing, a partner can assist you by making observations and suggestions.

## How Do I Find Out about Activities I've Never Done Before?

You may not know how to write a script or a cinquain poem. When an activity is unfamiliar to you, look for a definition in Formats (Student Handbook, p. 186). If you can't find a definition there, ask your classmates or your teacher for help.

## How Will I Organize My Work?

Most of your work will be kept in your writing folder. It contains three writing files (Work in Progress, Private, Polished), each of which holds a different kind of written work. Also in the writing folder are three checklists and two record sheets. They will help you revise your work and keep track of your corrections and accomplishments. In addition to your writing folder, you will also keep a journal, in which you can note your ideas, feelings, observations, and questions. You can use your journal to record the events of your life, too. The Student Handbook gives a full description of the writing folder (pp. 180-84) and the journal (p. 174).

## Can I Use a Computer in My Work?

Some of the activities ask you to use a computer. You can be as creative with a computer as you can be with a pen and paper. Applying the Computer (Student Handbook, pp. 184-86) provides brief explanations of some of the different ways you can learn with computers and put them to work for you. Probably you will have your own ideas about how to use computers with the activities. Tell your teacher about your ideas so other people can try them too.

## Am I Going to Like This Book?

If you enjoy talking with others, if you are curious about other people's experiences, and if you are interested in communicating your ideas well, then this book is for you.

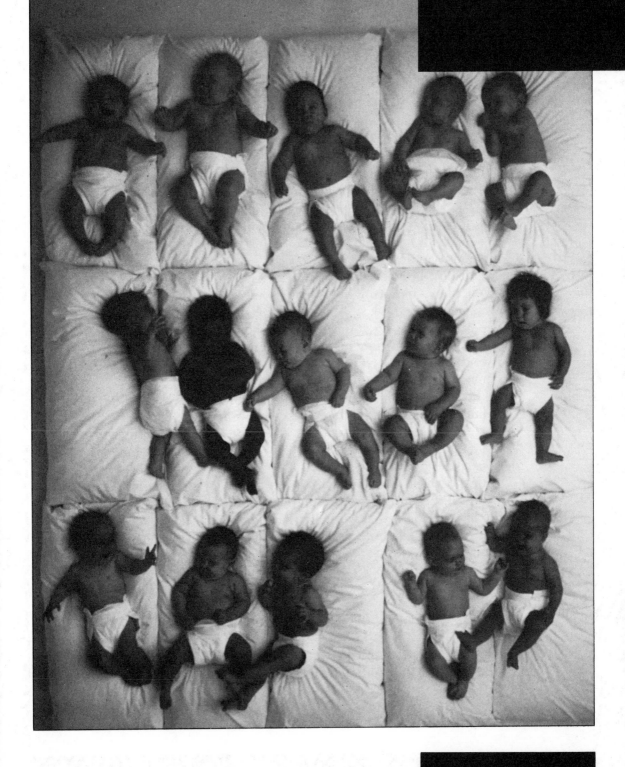

# THE HUSBAND WHO STAYED AT HOME

*A Norwegian Tale*

ONCE UPON a time there was a man so cross and bad-tempered that he thought his wife never did anything right in the house.

So one evening during the haymaking time, when he came home scolding and complaining, his wife said, "You think you could do the work of the house better than I?"

"Yes, I do," growled the husband. "Any man could!"

"Well, then, tomorrow let's switch our tasks. I'll go with the mowers and mow the hay. You stay here and do the housework."

The husband agreed at once. He thought it a very good idea.

Early the next morning his wife took a scythe over her shoulder and went out to the hayfield with the mowers; the man stayed in the house to do the work at home.

He decided first to churn the butter for their dinner. After he had churned awhile, he became thirsty; he went down to the cellar to tap a pitcher of ale. He had just taken the bung out of the ale barrel and was about to put in the tap when overhead he heard the pig come into the kitchen.

With the tap in his hand, he ran up the cellar steps as fast as he could, lest the pig upset the butter churn. When he came up to the kitchen, he saw that the pig had already knocked over the churn. The cream had run all over the floor and the pig was happily slurping it.

He became so wild with rage that he quite forgot the ale barrel in the cellar. He ran after the pig, slipped, and fell facedown into the cream.

When he scrambled to his feet, he caught the pig running through the door and gave it such a kick in the head that the pig dropped dead.

All at once he remembered the ale tap in his hand. But when

he ran down to the cellar, every drop of ale had run out of the barrel.

There was still no butter for their dinner, so he went into the dairy to look for more cream. Luckily there was enough cream left to fill the churn once more, and he again began to churn butter.

After he had thumped the churn for a while, he remembered that their milking cow was still shut up in the barn. The poor cow had had nothing to eat or drink all morning, and the sun was now high in the sky.

He had no time to take the cow down to the pasture, for the baby was crawling about in the spilt cream, and he still had to clean up the floor and the baby. He thought it would save time if he put the cow on the top of their house to graze. The flat roof of the house was thatched with sod, and a fine crop of grass was growing there.

Since the house lay close to a steep hill at the back, he thought that if he laid two planks across the thatched roof to the hill, he could easily get the cow up there to graze.

As he started out the door he realized he should not leave the churn in the kitchen with the baby crawling about. "The child is sure to upset it!" he thought.

So he lifted the churn onto his back and went out with it.

"I had best give the cow some water before I put her on the roof to graze," he said to himself. He took up a bucket to draw water from the well, but as he leaned over the well to fill the bucket, all the cream ran out of the churn, over his shoulders, and down into the well.

In a temper, he hurled the empty churn across the yard and went to water the cow. Then he searched for two planks to make a bridge from the hill to the roof of the house. After a great deal of trouble, he persuaded the cow to cross the planks onto the sod roof.

Now it was near dinnertime and the baby was crying. "I have no butter," he thought. "I'd best boil porridge."

So he hurried back to the kitchen, filled the pot with water, and hung it over the fire. Then he realized the cow was not tied; she could easily fall off the roof and break her legs.

Back he ran to the roof with a rope. Since there was no post to tie her to, he tied one end of the rope around the cow, and the other end he slipped down the hole in the roof that served as a chimney. When he came back to the kitchen he tied the loose end around his knee.

The water was now boiling in the pot, but the oatmeal still had to be ground for the porridge. He ground away and was just throwing the oatmeal into the pot when the cow fell off the roof.

As she fell, the rope on the man's knee jerked, and he was pulled up into the air. The pot of water was knocked over, putting the fire out, and the man dangled upside down above the hearth. Outside, the poor cow swung halfway down the house wall, unable to get up or down.

In the meantime, the wife had mowed seven lengths and seven breadths of the hayfield. She expected her husband to call her home to dinner. When he did not appear, she at last trudged off to their home.

When she got there, she saw the cow dangling in such a queer place that she ran up and cut the rope with her scythe. As soon as the rope was cut, the man fell down the hearth.

His wife rushed into the house to find her husband in the hearth, covered with ashes, the floor slippery with clots of cream and ground oatmeal, and the baby wailing.

When they had cleaned up the house and taken the cow out to pasture and hung up the pig for butchering, they sat down to eat stale bread without butter or porridge.

The wife said to him, "Tomorrow you'll get the right way of it."

"Tomorrow!" he sputtered. "You'll not be going out with the mowers tomorrow!"

"And why not? You agreed to it," said she. "Do you think the work of the house too hard?"

This the husband would not admit. "No indeed! If you can do it, I can do it!" he growled.

"Well, then!" said his wife.

They argued the rest of the day over who should mow and who should mind the house. There seemed no way to settle it until at last the husband agreed that he would work in the fields three days a week and work in the house three days; his wife would take his place in the fields for three days, and take care of the house the other days.

With this compromise they lived quite peaceably, and neither the husband nor the wife complained very much at all.

# FOCUSSING

1. In groups of three or four, brainstorm the meanings of the following words and phrases:
   - roles;
   - traditional roles;
   - traditional roles of mothers and of fathers;
   - changing work roles;
   - non-traditional jobs;
   - stereotyping;
   - sexism.

   To clarify some meanings, you may wish to look up some of the words in the dictionary. Appoint someone to write a list of the group's definitions. Combine the lists of all the groups into one list that the whole class can use. If you have a computer you can use it to save your word lists in a data file. A word processing program will allow you to "merge" the group lists into one class list.

2. Interview two people older than 35 (you may wish to start with one of your parents) and two people under 20. By comparing the responses of the two age groups, you can discover how the interests and expectations of boys and girls have changed over the years. Tape your interviews and play your results back to your group. Work with a partner to develop some questions for your interview in the following areas:
   - career goals;
   - family plans;
   - special interests.

3. For one week, keep track of the re-run and current television programs you watch. Set up a chart so you can record information under the following headings:
   - name of the show;
   - current or re-run;
   - roles of the mother/the father/the children;
   - problems of the children;
   - jobs of the women/jobs of the men;
   - children supervised by mother/father/brothers or sisters/helper/other;
   - types of families (i.e., single-parent family, two-parent family, foster family, extended family).

   After compiling the information identify, in a small group, how the families shown on television have changed over the years. Discuss whether the changes have been positive or negative.

# DR. JAMES BARRY
## by Donald Jack

D R. BARRY'S origins were mysterious. He would never admit the date of his birth, though it was later estimated as being somewhere between 1790 and 1795. It is still not known who brought him up after his parents died shortly after his birth; except that he appeared to have been placed in the care of a personage of considerable means. In those days an independent income was essential for an army officer, to enable him to keep up a fashionable front. James Barry's career was well financed; but who his patron was, nobody knew.

There were other mysterious influences on Dr. Barry's life. He rose through the army hierarchy like a Congreve rocket. The first promotion was understandable enough. Two years after joining up, six months after the Battle of Waterloo, he was made assistant surgeon. But after all, he was an Edinburgh M.D., and thus thoroughly qualified for the post. If anything, the promotion was overdue.

But from then on his rise, at a time when an army officer might remain at one level for fifteen or even twenty years, went at an accelerated pace that his qualities did not appear to warrant. His promotions were even harder to understand because he was often in trouble with his superiors over breaches of discipline. He was an extraordinarily difficult person, pretentious and almost pathologically sensitive to the slightest hint of disrespect. Unfortunately it was difficult for people meeting him for the first time to suppress their amusement or disdain, for the doctor was an even more absurd sight than General Wolfe had been.

He was thin and undersized, but wore ridiculously large spurs and the longest, sharpest sword in the army. To match the sword he had a sharp voice, which he used on his subordinates in a rancorous way. He challenged to a duel at least two adversaries who had not been warned about the choleric medic. One of them paid for a verbal blunder with his life.

By the time Dr. Barry arrived in Montreal in 1857, he was inspector-general of the Canadian military hospitals. He was thought to have occupied a house at the corner of Durocher and Sherbrooke Street, and his physician was a Dr. Campbell who, though he got to know Barry quite well, could not have been overly perceptive.

The inspector-general soon became a familiar if not particularly popular figure around the hospitals, and in Montreal and Quebec military circles.

Even then, Barry's rise in the hierarchy did not falter. Within two years of his appointment in Montreal he became head of the entire army medical service, which confirmed in the minds of those who had never seen any intrinsic cause for Barry's success that his patron was very high up indeed. How else could he have got on so well when he had so often been guilty of breaches of discipline on account of his fiery temper and neurotic sensitivity? Of course, there was no doubt that he was a first-class medical officer, but since when had superior ability guaranteed success in the army? Was he perhaps the illegitimate son of a duke, perhaps even of the Prince Regent himself? And there was another strange thing about Barry, a contradiction that deepened the mystery of his background: although he had often shown bravery in the field,

during his service he never received the military decorations that were his due. It was almost as if not one but two influences were at work on his behalf, and in conflict with each other.

It wasn't until James Barry's death in London in 1865 that one of the mysteries, at least, was cleared up, when a woman in the sickroom where he died became, so far as is known, only the second person in nearly half a century to see the unclad form of James Barry, and found it to be that of a woman. The finding was confirmed (as if confirmation were needed), by the autopsy that was ordered by an astounded War Office.

The only other direct witness, it seems, was the surgeon-general, Sir Thomas Longmore, who had attended Barry in Trinidad in 1844. She had been too sick to prevent a complete examination. Longmore had subsequently been sworn to secrecy.

The reason for the forty-six year impersonation has never been determined, though it was surmised that it may have originated in a love affair with the person who helped her to skip many of the rungs in the promotional ladder, a man of influence but of illogical standards, who could allow her to fool the entire army; but who could not bring himself to permit decorations for valour to be awarded to a woman.

Perhaps he was the father of her child. There were unsubstantiated reports that the autopsy had revealed that she had once given birth to a child. It is just as possible that James Barry had a spirit that could not be satisfied in any other way except through a life of adventure in the army. Whatever the explanation the experience must have caused an enormous strain on her personality. One writer speculates that, "some at least of her physical peculiarities were assumed in order to conceal her identity, and that the asperity which she showed to subordinates was a necessary part of the role she played."

She may have had to force herself, for forty-six years, to act tempestuously and temperamentally, for the opinion of those who knew her well suggested that her Wolfe-like qualities were not natural to her. That in reality she was quite an agreeable person.

# CLOSE UP

1. Write a chronological chart of the life of James Barry, with brief comments. You will find an example of a completed chronological chart on p. 171. Begin with the following line:
   **1790-1795 Birth of James Barry; exact date unknown.**
   Draw a sketch of Dr. Barry to accompany your chart.
2. This selection was taken from a book called *Rogues, Rebels, and Geniuses*. Discuss with a partner why each word in the title applies to James Barry.
3. List all the words and phrases that are used to describe Dr. Barry. Beside each, write a definition in your own words. Create a crossword puzzle using the words in your list. You can rework the definitions into clues—be sure to make them tricky! If you have a computer in your class, find out if your teacher has a program that will help you make the puzzle and print it out. Form a small group and try to solve each other's puzzles.
4. You are a reporter who has just heard the results of the autopsy performed on Dr. Barry. Write three headlines: one for an article that would appear in a tabloid, one for a weekly newsmagazine, and one for a community paper in Canada West in 1865. If there is a word processor available, use it to draft and print your headlines. (Remember that each publication would use different kinds of words and typefaces in its headlines.)

# WIDE ANGLE

1. You are Dr. James Barry and you know you are soon going to die. Write to Sir Thomas Longmore, telling him the secret story of who you are, why you did what you did, and how you felt about pretending to be a man for so many years.
2. Form a small group and go to the library to find out about three other women who had to pretend to be men in order to practise their professions. Make point-form notes on the women, and tell their stories to another group.
3. With a partner, produce a *Witness to Yesterday* television program in which one of you plays the role of a reporter from your own time and the other plays Dr. James Barry. The reporter interviews Dr. Barry about her adventures and about the role of women in the 1800s. Use a video cassette recorder to tape the interview and play it back for the class.

# HOW TOYS SEX STEREOTYPE CHILDREN

*by Barbara Horner*

CHILDREN'S toys are big business. Last year (1983) the toy industry racked up $9 billion in retail sales.

But toys are more than big business. They say a lot about how we define the sex roles of boys and girls, too.

Little girls are still playing with "girl" toys—baby dolls, glamorous dress-up dolls, miniature cribs, baby carriages, and kitchens. And little boys are still playing with "boy" toys—miniature cowboys and Indians, soldiers, guns, tanks, and other war paraphernalia. But why? Do parents and relatives push boys and girls in different directions? Or do boys and girls actually think so differently they choose these toys themselves?

## HOW SEXISM BEGINS

The fact is, little boys and little girls are different—and they know it! When given a choice, by the age of one boys usually pick out so-called "boy" toys and girls usually pick out "girl" toys.

"There are girl toys and boy toys, and I think that can be good. Males and females lead different kinds of adult lives. For instance, men don't bear children," says Susan Laber, a child development expert and consultant to International Games Company.

But knowing what sex you are is different from being locked into a stereotype. Most "girl" toys still reflect a woman's role as taking care of the house and kids—at a time when almost half of all mothers work outside the home. So, the National Association of Female Executives suggest manufacturers make toys that provide "a positive role model for the woman"—like toy briefcases, typewriters, and offices. And at least one toy company—Mattel—has been complying. "Our Barbie doll got an astronaut's outfit in 1965—almost two decades before Sally Ride became America's first woman in space. And, while other dolls were nurses, Barbie got a doctor's outfit in 1973," says a spokesperson from Mattel. Yet, Barbie's best-selling outfit is still the bridal gown.

Some feminists see Barbie as a harmful sex stereotype. "She tells little girls that all they need for success is a pretty face, perfect figure and fashionable clothes," says a member of the National Organization for Women (NOW). But others don't see Barbie's glamour as the problem. "There's nothing really wrong with Barbie," says Laber. "She's pretty and has a lot of clothes and that's not bad. It's only bad if it's taken as a sole judgment."

Barbie dolls aren't the only toys that place girls in traditional roles. Just on the market is a toy microwave, which promotes the notion of cooking for the family. Toy kitchens, baby dolls that wet, cry, and can be dressed in cute clothes, doll houses, and makeup kits are also big sellers.

But playing with these toys hasn't stopped little girls from growing up to be doctors, lawyers, astronauts, and politicians. These

toys may have given little girls a one-sided vision of what their adult life will be—wife, mother, and homemaker—but in the meantime they've also given girls practice in being caring, compassionate, and creative people.

## WHAT BOY TOYS SAY

Boys aren't as lucky. When it comes to sex-stereotyping in toys, boys get the short end of the stick. "Boy toys appeal to what some think of as masculine traits," Laber points out. "Computer games—where usually one critter devours or zaps another—and GI Joes are all aggressive. At least girls' toys are friendly. But in boys' toys there's a preoccupation with death and violence."

Sales figures show the increasingly violent direction boys' toys are taking. In the late 1970s, the GI Joe series and similar war toys were discontinued. "Probably because of the negative effects of the Vietnam War," said one toy manufacturer spokesperson. But sales of toy guns and rifles doubled between 1979 and 1982 to $72 million.

And GI Joe was brought back from furlough last year to become a top-seller. Experts say it's partly because of a surge of patriotism in the U.S. The sale of guns and other war paraphernalia, Star Wars characters and gear, and battle-oriented video games are all an extension of the feeling that strength and aggression are okay.

And then there's the influence of television. On TV, guns are a frequently used method of getting what you want. But on TV the consequences of using the gun—blood, pain, and possible retaliation—are not explored.

Many parents give in to their kids' wish for guns partly because they feel the child can tell the difference between make-believe and reality. But aiming a finger and shouting "you're dead" isn't nearly as harmful as actually holding a toy—but realistic-looking—gun. Giving a child a toy gun implies that guns are okay. In two different studies, children holding toy guns showed much more aggression in their play than those who did not have a gun.

## A NEW TREND IN SEX STEREOTYPING

The fact is that little boys do play with different toys than little girls do. But there are choices. Today there are many new toys that aren't sex-stereotyped—toy offices, bicycles, cars, erector sets and building blocks, to name a few.

And for good and bad, many of the traditionally stereotyped toys have changed to appeal to both boys and girls. For example, the GI Joe series has included girl fighters since 1982.

The merchandising of toys has changed, too. Just take a look at the new packaging of toy kitchens, Star Wars, Legos and science kits. They all show both boys and girls playing with them.

"The trend in packaging has definitely been towards equalizing the appeal of toys to both sexes," said a spokesperson for the Toy Manufacturers of America.

Advertising also reflects this trend. On TV girls are now seen playing baseball and boys are seen cooking on a miniature oven.

This new image of toys is having its effect on sales. Cabbage Patch reports that both boys and girls play with their dolls. One mother from Seattle, Washington said, "My three-year-old son loves the toy kitchen we bought him. Maybe that's because it's daddy who cooks all the meals." But another mother from New Jersey commented, "I bought my son a baby doll, but he doesn't like playing with it. He likes his toy fire engine better. I don't know why."

Why do boys choose one toy while girls choose another? Is it parents who decide? Is it the toy makers? Or is it a genetically based choice? Are boys born more aggressive? Are girls born more nurturing? So far no one knows for sure. But certainly if boys are continually given guns and girls are continually given dolls—the message of what toy is for a girl or boy is clear. Be aware of what toys are saying about sex stereotyping. And when it comes time for you to buy toys for children—keep that in mind.

# CLOSE UP

1. In groups of four, write a title for each paragraph in the article. Divide the task among group members and share the results.

2. Pretend you have just arrived on Earth from a different planet. You see all the children playing with objects, which someone tells you are *toys*. You notice that the girls play with one kind of toy and the boys with another kind of toy. Role-play a discussion in which your partner, taking the part of the author of the article, explains to you what "boys' toys" and "girls' toys" are and the reasons some people think there should be a difference.

3. Write a pamphlet about sexist toys that a principal in an elementary school could send to parents. The pamphlet should define "stereotyping," "sexism," and "traditional roles." (See the definitions the class wrote for Focussing #1.) The pamphlet should also explain why it is harmful to give boys one kind of toy and girls another kind.

# WIDE ANGLE

1. Look back on memories of your childhood and write a journal entry entitled "Toys in My Life." If your journal is a disc rather than a notebook (see Keeping a Journal, p. 174), write your entry on a word processor and save it in a separate file on your journal disc.

2. Collect advertisements for childrens' toys and categorize them as either sexist or non-sexist. Choose a toy (e.g., a skipping rope) and write and illustrate a non-sexist advertisement that implies both girls and boys would enjoy using the toy.

3. You are visiting a day-care centre and you see a little girl playing with a fighter jet and a little boy playing with a doll in a carriage. A worker changes the toys, saying, "Girls play with dolls, and boys play with jets." Share your reaction with a partner, discussing any differences of opinion. Write a letter to the day-care centre, expressing your opinion of the worker.

4. a) Work in a group of four or five, and visit a day-care centre, a kindergarten class, and a playground. Interview several children of various ages about their favourite toys. You will have to make up questions appropriate for each age group. You will want to look at

   - the toys children choose at different ages. Why do they make those choices? Have they been influenced by television advertisements, brothers and sisters, friends, or parents?
   - the language children use around their toys. Do they have conversations with their dolls? Do they make the sounds of the things their toys represent (like spaceship sounds or car sounds)?
   - the characteristics that certain toys encourage. Do the children form teams to use their toys? Do they share their toys or play by themselves?
   - how often girls and boys play with the same kinds of toys. Do boys and girls play together?

   b) After you have gathered your information, discuss the results and draw conclusions. Write a report to the author of "How Toys Sex Stereotype Children," saying whether your results support or contradict her article.

# A SPECIAL GIFT

*adapted from the teleplay by*
*Durrell Royce Crays*

## CHARACTERS

PETER HARRIS,
*a basketball player
and ballet dancer*

GEORGE,
*his friend and teammate*

DALTON,
*another teammate*

CARL HARRIS,
*Peter's father*

GRACE HARRIS,
*Peter's mother*

ELIZABETH HARRIS,
*Peter's younger sister*

LISA,
*a ballet dancer*

JOHN LESTER,
*a ballet dancer*

COACH SANFORD,
*the basketball coach*

JACK CORBIN,
*a professional dancer*

BOB PEARSON,
*Carl Harris' friend*

MR. WATKINS,
*Peter's boss*

MADAME IVANOVA,
*a ballet teacher*

DR. SCHULTZ,
*a doctor at a hospital*

*Fade in on the gym of Wheaton High School. Wheaton is a small town not far from Los Angeles. The basketball team has just finished a tough practice session. The team members head for the locker room. Peter and George are walking together.*

**GEORGE:** Let's go and get a burger after we shower.

**PETER:** I can't. My mom's going to pick me up and drive me . . . (*He doesn't finish the sentence.*)

**GEORGE** (*surprised*): I thought you worked in the hardware store on Thursdays.

**PETER:** Yeah. I mean, I do. (*He grins. George looks confused.*)

(*Cut to a ballet studio. Madame Ivanova watches a group of girls doing ballet exercises. Peter's sister Elizabeth is one of them. On the other side of the room, Peter does his exercises. He is the only boy in the class. When the music stops, Madame Ivanova makes an announcement.*)

**MADAME IVANOVA:** We have no class next week. Instead, we will have tryouts here for the Los Angeles Ballet Company. They are looking for young people for a production they'll be putting on. (*The students look excited.*) I must warn you that students from all over the city will try out. (*She looks at Peter.*) But I think some of you have a very good chance. (*Peter and Elizabeth grin at each other.*)

(*Cut to the hardware store. George comes in and talks to Mr. Watkins, the owner.*)

**GEORGE:** Hi, Mr. Watkins, I stopped by to say hello to Peter, if it's okay with you.

**MR. WATKINS:** It's fine with me, except Peter isn't here.

**GEORGE** (*confused*): He left early?

**MR. WATKINS:** No. Peter never works on Thursdays.

(*Cut to the Harris farm. Peter's father, Carl, is feeding the cattle. Bob Pearson, another farmer, drives up.*)

**PEARSON:** Howdy, Carl. I just came from the feed store. If the price of feed goes up any more, I'll have to start eating it myself.

**CARL:** That's the truth, all right.

*Peter*

*(Carl's wife, Grace, drives up in a pickup truck. She, Elizabeth, and Peter get out. Elizabeth and Grace wave and go toward the house. Peter walks toward his father and Pearson. He is carrying his ballet bag. A ballet slipper hangs out of it.)*

**PEARSON:** How are you doing, Pete? *(He reaches for the ballet slipper.)* I always wanted to look at one of those things. Does Elizabeth really walk around on her toes in them?

**PETER** *(without thinking)*: No, the girls wear toe slippers. These are . . . *(He looks at his father uneasily.)* These are mine.

*(Pearson laughs. Then he sees the angry look on Carl's face. He realizes it wasn't a joke, and he stops laughing.)*

**PETER:** Well, it isn't so strange. One of the pro football teams had some of their guys take ballet to help their game.

**PEARSON** *(uncomfortably)*: I thought you were a basketball player.

**PETER:** I am. I just take ballet lessons, that's all.

**PEARSON:** What do the guys on the team think of that?

**PETER:** They don't think anything about it. I never told them. *(He looks at his father, who starts feeding the cattle again.)* I'll go change my clothes and help out. *(He leaves.)*

**PEARSON:** I always thought Pete was just one of the guys. But ballet dancing?

**CARL:** I'd appreciate it if you didn't spread it around, Pearson.

**PEARSON:** Sure thing.

*(Cut to the Harris dinner table. The whole family is there.)*

**GRACE:** Peter and Elizabeth have a chance to try out for a real ballet.

**CARL** *(looking at his food)*: I need help around the farm. This ballet thing could interfere with basketball practice or schoolwork.

**PETER:** Yeah. I guess I'm pretty tied up with things to do. *(Carl nods.)* It would be great to be in a real ballet, though. I'd like to perform with professional dancers, instead of just kids.

**CARL** *(sternly)*: When I was your age, I was working full time. I didn't have time for school, much less dancing.

**PETER:** I have homework to do. *(He leaves the room.)*

**GRACE:** He really wants to try out, Carl.

**ELIZABETH:** He talked about it all the way home.

**CARL:** I've never stopped him from taking those lessons.

**GRACE:** But you're against it. Why don't you object to Elizabeth's dancing?

CARL: Elizabeth's a girl. If she wants to keep dancing, fine. But Peter's 14 now. Boys play basketball. Girls dance. That's just the way things are.

(Cut to a study hall. George and Peter are sitting next to each other.)

GEORGE: Do you see that new girl, Lisa? She keeps looking at you.

PETER: Come on, will you?

GEORGE: She does. Hey, where were you Thursday? I stopped by the store looking for you.

PETER (angrily): What did you do that for?

GEORGE: Hey, calm down. I just thought you worked on Thursdays.

PETER: I do—sometimes.

(George doesn't believe him.)

(Cut to the ballet studio. Jack Corbin, a professional dancer, watches all the students try out. There are several boys there, including John Lester. Of the boys, Peter and John are the best. Peter is a little better. After the tryouts, Peter and Elizabeth wait outside for their mother.)

Lisa

ELIZABETH: Guess who thinks you're really good.

PETER: Who?

ELIZABETH: Lisa, that new girl in our school. She was trying out today, too. (Peter looks upset.) What's the matter?

PETER: I guess I liked it better when it was just you and me from our school.

ELIZABETH: Peter, you can't keep it a secret forever.

PETER: Who's keeping it a secret? Look, maybe I don't tell everybody I dance ballet! But I don't run around telling everybody I play basketball, either!

(Cut to the school hallway. Peter and George are at their lockers. Lisa comes up behind them.)

LISA: Peter, I got in! The letter came yesterday!

GEORGE: In what?

LISA: The Los Angeles Ballet Company's next show. (To Peter) How about you? Did you hear yet?

PETER (turning to his locker): No.

GEORGE: What are you two talking about?

LISA: The ballet! Peter, Elizabeth, and I tried out.

GEORGE (smiling): Ballet? You mean all that flitting stuff? (He turns to Peter and stops smiling.) You're kidding. Do you really do that?

PETER (quietly): Yeah, I dance ballet. So what?

GEORGE: Uh—nothing. I've got to get to class. (He hurries off.)

LISA (realizing what has happened): Peter, I'm sorry.

PETER: Why didn't you put up a sign, so everybody would

know? *(He walks away, angry. She stares after him.)*

*(Cut to the team locker room. Coach Sanford is talking to the players.)*

**SANFORD:** The first game is a week from Saturday at 10 a.m. This is the only Saturday game on our schedule. If you miss it, I'd better be able to visit you in the hospital. Understand?

*(Cut to the hardware store. Peter and Mr. Watkins are behind the counter. George comes in. He avoids looking at Peter.)*

**GEORGE:** Mr. Watkins, my father needs a bolt like this one.

*(Mr. Watkins looks at Peter, then at George. They are avoiding each other. Watkins gets the bolt and takes the money from George. Then George leaves.)*

**MR. WATKINS:** I thought you and George were best friends. Is something wrong?

**PETER:** Can I take a few minutes off, Mr. Watkins?

**MR. WATKINS:** Sure.

*(Peter runs out and catches up with George.)*

**PETER:** Okay, so I dance ballet.

**GEORGE** *(shrugging his shoulders)*: It doesn't matter to me.

**PETER:** Yeah, it does.

**GEORGE:** No . . . really.

**PETER:** Sure. When are you going to tell Dalton and the other guys?

**GEORGE:** Why would I tell them? Look, my dad's waiting for me. I'll see you. *(He turns and walks away.)*

*(Cut to the Harris home. Peter has just read a letter. It tells him he's been accepted for the dance company. He looks excited – then unhappy. He doesn't know how to tell his father. He goes out to shoot baskets on the side of the barn. His father joins him. They talk as they play basketball.)*

**CARL:** Listen, Peter. Everything that goes on in Los Angeles isn't—well,—acceptable in a small town like this.

**PETER:** You mean like ballet?

**CARL** *(after a long pause)*: What about when you grow up, get married, and have a family? How do you plan to support them? By dancing?

**PETER:** I don't know. But what's wrong with dancing for a living? *(Carl stops playing.)*

**CARL:** Is that what you want to do?

**PETER:** I'm not sure. Maybe. If I thought I was good enough, I think I'd like to try. You always told us to try to be the best at whatever we did.

**CARL:** Well, this ballet thing has never been my cup of tea.

*George*

PETER: Dad—I got the part.

*(Carl stares at him. Then he tosses him the ball. The game goes on, but their talk is over.)*

*(Cut to the ballet studio. As Peter is getting ready for practice, John comes in.)*

JOHN: Hey, congratulations!

PETER: You, too. I knew you'd make it, but I wasn't sure about myself.

JOHN: Come on! You were good! Is this your first show?

PETER: Yeah. Yours, too?

JOHN: No. I was in a show at my school last year.

PETER: You danced at your *school*?

JOHN: Yeah. Why?

PETER: How did everybody act?

JOHN *(grinning)*: You mean, did my friends give me a bad time about dancing? *(Peter nods.)* A little. Let's go. Corbin's ready to start.

CORBIN: I want to congratulate all of you on being chosen for the company. I hope you're all ready to work hard. Are there any questions about rehearsals?

JOHN: Are all the rehearsals after school?

CORBIN: No. When we move to the theatre, there will be Saturday rehearsals, too.

*(Peter starts to raise his hand. He wants to say something about the Saturday basketball game. Then he changes his mind.)*

CORBIN: Can everybody make it on Saturdays? Good. Is everybody excited to be chosen? *(They all grin at him.)* Well, enjoy it now. By the time we're finished, you may wish you hadn't been chosen.

*(We see a series of short scenes of hard work. First, John and Peter are doing muscle-straining exercises, while Corbin watches. Then Peter is going through a tough practice session with the basketball team. Then he's helping his father toss large bales of hay onto a truck. Then he's back in the studio for more hard work. After a practice session, Elizabeth, Peter, Lisa, and John lie on the floor, exhausted.)*

CORBIN: It's been tough. But I warned you, and I'm proud of you. You've worked like real professionals. John, you're going to be the understudy for a starring role. Peter, you'll be dancing the starring role.

ELIZABETH: That's great!

CORBIN: If you think you've worked hard so far, wait! The worst part hasn't started yet. Starting Saturday, we move rehearsals to the theatre. I want you there and warmed up for whatever time we need you.

PETER: Not this Saturday! I can't! It's the first basketball

Corbin

game. If I miss it, I'm off the team.

**CORBIN:** I'm sorry, Peter. But if you miss a rehearsal, you can't dance a starring role.

**PETER:** What'll I do?

**CORBIN:** I don't know. But remember, you didn't get this role by luck. It took years of hard work, and you earned it. Even more important, you have talent. You have a special gift. I hope you decide to use it. John, if Peter can't make it, you'll be dancing the role.

*(Cut to the Harris farm, Saturday morning. Carl is fixing a fence. Grace comes out to talk to him.)*

**GRACE:** Carl, you know why he's playing in that game today.

**CARL:** Nobody told him he has to.

**GRACE:** He knows how you feel.

**CARL:** I just never thought he'd carry this ballet business this far. It was okay for him to take lessons when he was eight or nine.

**GRACE:** Carl, he'd give anything to be in that show.

**CARL:** Grace, if he was to be in that show, the whole town would know about it. How would his friends act if they knew? You don't understand, Grace. Boys can be cruel.

**GRACE:** Are you really worried about his friends, Carl—or yours? *(She turns and walks to the house.)*

*(Cut to the high school entrance. Grace drives up. Peter gets out with his basketball gear.)*

**GRACE:** Do you think the game will be over by noon? *(Peter shrugs.)* Your father or I will be back to pick you up.

*(She drives off. Peter meets George on the way into the school.)*

**PETER:** You don't have to talk to me.

**GEORGE:** Look, we've been friends for years. You could have told me about this ballet stuff.

**PETER:** Would it have made any difference?

**GEORGE:** I don't know. Maybe. You have to admit ballet's kind of weird.

**PETER:** Is that what you think I am? Weird?

**GEORGE:** I didn't say that. But, you know the other guys. I mean, how would guys like Dalton act if they knew?

**PETER:** So that's it. Whatever Dalton thinks, you'll think.

**GEORGE:** I didn't say that!

**PETER:** You didn't have to! *(He walks away.)*

*(We see another series of short scenes. At the theatre, dancers are rehearsing. Backstage, John is getting ready to do Peter's role. Then we see Peter at the game. He plays without much interest, and the coach puts him on the bench. Peter is more interested in the time than in the score of the game. Back at the theatre, a news pho-*

*Grace*

*tographer takes pictures of the dancers. At the game, the coach turns to talk to Peter. Peter is gone. Then we see him backstage at the theatre with Elizabeth and John.)*

**PETER** *(to Elizabeth)*: Just don't let Dad know. I'll have to figure out a way to tell him.

**JOHN**: You're not going to dance now! You aren't warmed up!

**PETER**: Look, John, I'm sorry about this. I know how much you wanted the part.

**JOHN**: That isn't it! I saw you come in just now. You aren't warmed up! You know what can happen if you try to dance without exercising first!

**CORBIN**: Peter! On stage!

**PETER**: I'll be okay, John.

*(As Peter dances, the photographer takes pictures. Peter goes into a difficult leap. Because his muscles aren't warmed up, he lands the wrong way. He falls to the floor in pain and grabs his ankle.)*

*(Cut to a hospital waiting room. Grace is sitting in a chair. Carl is angrily pacing back and forth.)*

**CARL**: He said he was playing basketball. That's what I expected him to be doing. No one gave him permission to take the bus into Los Angeles!

*(Dr. Schultz comes in.)*

**DR. SCHULTZ**: Mr. and Mrs. Harris? I just examined your boy.

**GRACE**: Is he going to be all right?

**DR. SCHULTZ**: He'll be fine. In two or three days, he'll be as good as new. You've got quite an athlete there, Mr. Harris.

**HARRIS**: Athlete? He was hurt dancing!

**DR. SCHULTZ**: Ballet dancers are some of the best athletes. Believe me. I've treated them all. I'd say ballet is as dangerous a sport as any ever invented.

**CARL**: There will be no more dancing!

*(Cut to the school hallway. Dalton and some of the other team members come up to Peter.)*

**DALTON**: We want you off the team, Harris.

**PETER**: Why? Because my picture was in the paper? Because I dance?

**DALTON**: We don't need anybody in skirts on the team.

**LISA** *(joining them)*: You're really a jerk, Dalton!

**DALTON**: Well, wouldn't you know it? He needs a girl to protect him. I guess girls stick together.

*(Peter punches him in the jaw. Dalton falls to the floor, and Peter walks away.)*

*(Cut to the farmyard. Carl is fixing the tractor. Peter comes home from school.)*

**PETER:** You were right.

**CARL:** Is that so? About what?

**PETER:** About what people would think. But it doesn't make any difference anymore. My whole life's ruined anyway.

**CARL:** Does it have anything to do with this? *(He takes a newspaper photo from his pocket. It shows Peter leaping during the ballet practice.)*

**PETER:** Because of that, the guys don't want me on the team anymore. That's what you've always been afraid of, isn't it? That's why you *forbid* me to dance anymore. Well, I don't care anymore! You can stop me now. But someday I'm going to dance. And you'll just have to be ashamed of me!

*(Carl is silent for a long time. Then he starts walking toward the barn.)*

**CARL:** You can walk along, if you want to. *(Peter joins him.)* When I was a kid—10 or 11 years old—I used to sing in the church choir.

**PETER:** You? You sang in a choir?

*Carl*

**CARL:** I used to tell my friends that my mother made me do it. But I really liked it—even though I sang soprano. *(Peter looks surprised.)* It's true. My voice hadn't changed yet. Anyway, there was this Christmas concert coming up. I was going to sing a solo. It was an important thing to me. I practised for months. *(He pauses.)* After the concert, these boys were waiting outside for me. I've never forgotten how much it hurt. Some of the names they called me. It didn't matter that they weren't true. They hurt anyway. And I've never sung a note since. I never wanted that to happen to you.

**PETER:** I didn't know.

**CARL:** I guess this ballet dancing means a lot to you.

**PETER:** That's what I've always tried to tell you, Dad.

**CARL:** Then I was wrong to forbid it. And I apologize for it. The decision isn't mine. The decision is yours, Peter.

*(Cut to the breakfast table, the next morning. The whole family is there.)*

**GRACE:** It might be better if Peter didn't go to school today.

**CARL:** You can help around the farm today, Peter. Give it a day to cool down.

**PETER:** Since I'm going to dance, I'd better learn to handle people like Dalton. Besides, there's a dress rehearsal after school.

**GRACE:** Are you sure your ankle is all right?

**PETER:** Good as new.

**CARL:** I have to go to Inglewood this afternoon to pick up some parts. I might as well drive you to Los Angeles.

*(Cut to the school hallway. The team members are waiting at Peter's locker.)*

**DALTON:** Hey, guys, the ballerina's back. How about doing a little dance for us, Harris?

**PETER:** You'll have to buy a ticket like everyone else, Dalton.

**DALTON:** Who'd want to go watch a bunch of—

**GEORGE:** Shut up, Dalton. Peter, I'm sorry. I've talked to some of the guys. We don't think you ought to quit.

**DALTON:** If he comes back on the team, I quit!

**GEORGE:** Go ahead. The rest of us are staying. *(Dalton storms down the hall.)* Peter, look, I'm sorry.

**PETER:** Forget it.

**GEORGE:** Let me say it, will you? I apologize for going along with Dalton. I guess I was afraid if they thought you were weird, they'd think I was, too.

**PETER** *(with a small grin)*: Then you don't think I'm weird anymore?

**GEORGE** *(grinning)*: Yeah, a little—but not the way they thought.
*(Cut to the entrance to the theatre. Carl is dropping off Lisa, Elizabeth, and Peter.)*

**PETER:** Dad, it's dress rehearsal. I thought maybe you'd like to come and watch for a while.

**CARL** *(uncomfortable)*: I really have to get to Inglewood. Maybe some other time.

**PETER** *(with a smile)*: I know. Ballet isn't your cup of tea. I'll see you when I get home.
*(Peter goes inside and puts on his costume. Corbin comes in.)*

**CORBIN:** How's the ankle?

**PETER:** Good.

**CORBIN:** Don't ever try it again without warming up. *(He notices Peter's scraped knuckles.)* You didn't get that from dancing.

**PETER:** In a way, I did.

**CORBIN:** Did you get into a fight because you dance? *(Peter nods.)* Welcome to the club. I've seen dancers that could have been great. But they couldn't handle the name calling. I'm glad you're going to stick it out. *(Corbin goes out and stands in the empty theatre. As the dance begins, he watches, enjoying what he sees. Then he turns and sees Carl staring at the stage.)*

**CORBIN** *(whispering)*: Can I help you with something?

**CARL:** That's Peter. *(He sounds as though he's in a trance.)* He's good.

**CORBIN:** He's better than that. Do you know him?

**CARL** *(smiling proudly)*: He's my son.

THE END

# CLOSE UP

1. With a partner, identify each decision that Peter makes about his dancing, from the beginning when he lies to George about working on Thursdays through to the final decision when he tells his father "Ballet isn't your cup of tea."

2. The characters in the teleplay have very strong feelings about Peter's dancing. For each of the following characters, state how they felt at the beginning and at the end of the teleplay:

| Name of Character | Feelings at Beginning of Teleplay | Feelings at End of Teleplay |
|---|---|---|
| Peter | | |
| Carl | | |
| Grace | | |
| George | | |
| Lisa | | |
| Elizabeth | | |
| Dalton | | |

3. On the printed program for the ballet Peter performs in, there are short histories of all the dancers. Discuss with someone else the details that should be included in the biographical sketch about Peter, then write a one-paragraph sketch.

# WIDE ANGLE

1. Imagine that the teleplay continues. On the way back from the dress rehearsal, Carl meets his friend Pearson. Work with a partner and role-play the discussion between the two men. Write the conversation in the form of another scene of the teleplay. If you compose the conversation on a word processor, you can make a print-out that looks like a published teleplay. Refer to *A Special Gift* to see what a printed teleplay should look like.

   **or**

   Peter makes decisions that reveal he is braver than most of the other people in the teleplay, including Carl. With a partner, role-play a discussion between Peter and his father after the performance in Los Angeles. The morning after the conversation, Peter records it in his diary. Write Peter's entry, remembering to mention how Peter now feels about his dancing and his father.

2. In the library, research famous male dancers to discover whether they encountered the same kind of prejudices as Peter did. Combine your research with the research of three other people. Make a booklet that has illustrations and descriptions of the dancers. Laminate it, if you wish, and place it in your school library.

3. Ask your physical education teacher to help you find the fitness level of dancers compared with that of other athletes, such as skaters and football players. Make a poster of this information, including illustrations of the various sports.

4. Like Carl, parents often try to protect their children from being hurt in ways that they were hurt when they were children. Ask your father, mother, or guardian whether this has happened in your family. Write a summary of his or her comments and your response, and put it with the other work in your Private Writing File.

5. Sometimes people are criticized and left to themselves when they break stereotypes. (If you are unsure what *stereotypes* means, refer to the class dictionary from Focussing #1.) Interview a person in your school or community who has done something that isn't traditional. Find out how he or she overcame any resulting prejudice. Write an article on this person to be included in your school newsletter or yearbook.

# LAKE OF BAYS
## *by Raymond Souster*

"Well, I'm not chicken . . . "
that skinny ten-year-old girl
balanced on the crazy-high railing
of the Dorset bridge:
                      suddenly let go
down
fifty feet into the water.

"That one will never grow up
to be a lady," my mother said
as we walked away.

but I'll remember
her brown body dropping like a stone
long after I've forgotten
many many ladies . . .

# CLOSE UP

1. In order to describe vividly the girl's jump into the water, the poet uses
   a) words that appeal to the sense of sight, and
   b) lines of different lengths.
   Read the poem aloud for your partner and listen carefully while your partner reads it for you. Find examples of the two techniques and explain how they work. Make a sketch of the picture the poet creates.
2. The mother and the narrator are both looking at the same scene—the girl jumping into the water—yet they have quite different feelings about it. Discuss with a partner what their two viewpoints are, then write a sentence to describe the mother's feelings and a sentence to describe the narrator's feelings.

# WIDE ANGLE

1. You are the girl in "Lake of Bays." In a poem, describe the sensations you have as you make the jump. (You may wish to begin your poem with the line "Well, I'm not chicken. . . .") A word processor can help you write poetry. Enter several descriptive words and then move them around to form new combinations. When you are pleased with the phrases you have made, write the poem around them. You can save your poem on a disc, or print out a draft copy to share with others.
2. Show the sketch you made in Close Up #1 to your father, mother, or guardian, and ask if he or she would let
   a) a ten-year-old girl jump from the bridge, and
   b) a ten-year-old boy make the jump.
   Jot down the responses and share them with four or five partners. (You may wish to read "Lake of Bays" to the person who answered your questions.)

# KALEIDOSCOPE

1. With a partner, investigate the expectations your school has for males and females. Consider looking at
   - the courses students enrol in;
   - discipline (Are the consequences for boys different from those for girls?);
   - the number of boys and the number of girls who are involved in sports;
   - the marks obtained by boys and by girls in various courses;
   - the tasks given by teachers to girls and to boys;
   - the number of male and female department heads and administrators;
   - the number of male and female teachers in each department.

   Bring your findings back, draw conclusions, and report to your class. You may wish to discuss some of your findings with the principal.

2. Collect as many cartoons as you can that depict how roles are changing. Here is an example of such a cartoon.

The Pick of the Punch – Los Angeles Times Syndicate

*"If she doesn't make it as a ballet dancer, she wants to be a dentist."*

   Make a collage of the cartoons you find and display it in your classroom, or ask the teacher if it could be posted in a more public part of the school.

3. Find comics, cartoons, newspaper clippings and head-lines, magazine articles, quotes, and pictures that rein-force traditional stereotypes. Post them on a bulletin board with the heading, "What's Wrong with This?"

Pin blank cards beside each item for other students to write in what is wrong in the item. After one week, have a classmate collect the comment cards and read them aloud for everyone.

4. a) In the library find five fairy tales. For each tale, write a brief note on
   - the sex of the hero;
   - the sex of the villain;
   - the heroic deed; and
   - the villainous deed.

   Discuss the tales you read with a classmate, paying special attention to the stereotyped role of each of the characters.

   b) Write a modern fairy tale that does not present men and women in traditional roles. You may wish to read *The Paper Bag Princess* by Robert Munsch as an example. Using the strategies in Checking on Your Own (p. 180), revise your work. You may wish to illustrate your tale and visit an elementary class to read your story to the children.

# CAREFUL, OR YOU MIGHT GET SCRATCHED

*by Joan Dash*

"R EADY to order?" I said to the two middle-aged women in Ultrasuede dresses. They were so busy talking, they hardly heard, so I went on to a single, a hippie type who wanted carob-chip cookies and Red Zinger tea. I'd have gone to the next table, only I caught certain words from the Ultrasuedes that came at me like a cold wind.

One woman was saying, "They're simply sick over it, the Beckwiths. The girl has no ambition, no interest in education . . . They feel the boy is throwing himself away."

The second woman, while putting her glasses on and picking up the menu: "I wonder what he sees in her . . . I think an omelet."

First woman: "They thought once Bryan went away to college, he'd forget all about her, but he came back for Easter break, and they took up right where they left off . . . Be sure to try the croissants. They have marvelous croissants here."

The door burst open. More people came in, and from behind the counter, I saw Avery, my boss, lift the brown beret he wore winter and summer, slap it back on so it tilted over one eyebrow, and wiggle his other eyebrow at me. But I was still frozen in place. My mouth had gone dry; my tongue felt too large for it. Finally, I pulled myself away from the women, took two more orders, and went to the counter.

Avery said, "What's with you, Crystal?"

"Skip it. I need two hash browns, one eggs sunny-side up . . ." I tore the orders off my pad and started back.

"First, the raccoons," Avery said, "then you—some way to start a morning." In the mirror behind him, I saw a girl who looked a little like me—short, with short, straight blond hair and a drowned look in her eyes. The girl Bryan Beckwith was throwing himself away on . . . I turned my back on her and pushed myself in the direction of the Ultrasuedes. The first one, the big talker, was still at it: "It's been going on for a year and a half," she was saying.

*Seven months*, I said inside my head. "Ready now?"

Bigmouth, with a false smile, said, "One omelet, espresso for two, two croissants, and some of that blackberry jam."

"We're out," I snapped. (We were not—we had gallons of blackberry jam, which I'd made from the bushes out back.) "There's grape jelly. Welch's."

They'd have straight butter instead. I took other orders and went to the counter with them, returning with food. More orders, more food. Refills on coffee. My stomach had tied itself into knots like hard little fists.

Ten forty-five. Breakfast rush was over, which meant we had a breathing space before the lunch crowd started in. Avery and I were on the couch opposite the counter. It was covered with fuzzy blue plush, and its springs sagged way down. Crazy to have such a beat-up couch in the middle of a café, but we did. Avery said it was like an old friend, and he didn't believe in putting a friend out to pasture because of arthritis and sag.

He lit a cigarette and pulled off the beret in order to run a hand through his frizzy brown hair. "You look like you're coming down with malaria," he said.

"Forget it. Hey, give me a puff."

"You're too young for nasty habits." (Avery was only four years older.) He slouched back, folded his arms, and stared up at the ceiling—a skinny little slip of a guy with a narrow face that was always half smiling at the world, as if everything he saw was half sad and half humorous. Maybe that was why his café was such an oddball place, with neat blue checked curtains and tablecloths and terrific food along with that broken-down couch and many customers who were ditto.

He said, "Well, it looks like the dinner special had better be the zucchini lasagna. Not because it's so hot, but because it's almost the only thing left. That and the Vegetarian Fantasy."

"Raccoons did it again, huh?"

"You betcha. Cleaned out my meat loaf—all they left was the pan. They also got my handmade sausages. I could have bawled. I'm going to have that alley bulldozed—raccoons, blackberry bushes—the works."

He'd said it loads of times before, so I paid no attention. Inside my head, I was back at the table with the Ultrasuedes. "Sick." The Beckwiths were sick over it . . . I'd known all along that

Bryan's parents weren't exactly crazy about me—but sick over it?

"Coffee, Crystal?" Mrs. Beckwith said.

"Thank you, I'd love some." (She made lousy coffee.)

"Coffee for you, Bryan?"

Bryan shrugged, pushing away his dish of fruit salad. "Maybe milk," he said. "I don't feel like coffee."

"I'm afraid there isn't more than half a glass of milk left, dear."

"Never mind, then," Bryan said, leaning toward his dad. "We thought we'd head out for Matthews Beach. Lie on the sand awhile, feed the ducks—do a lot of nothing . . ."

We were going biking that Saturday, the two of us, and the Beckwiths had invited me for brunch; I was, therefore, very busy inspecting their faces, watching for signs of how they felt about me. Which wasn't easy. They were both so polite, the Beckwiths. Nice people, really nice, and with class—Mr. B. was a college professor. You never walked into that house without hearing Mozart or Bach on the stereo, and the place was loaded with books. But polite people don't want to let on how they feel about you; you have to read between the lines, pick up clues from what they *don't* say.

Bryan, meanwhile, was not eating. He was dying to get out, get going, feel fresh air on his face. He sat with one arm around my shoulder, his fingers tap-tapping on the back of my chair. He had a certain nervousness that went with being so thin—tall, dark-haired, with big dark eyes under shiny black brows. Intense, that's how I thought of him.

Mr. B., dabbing at the edges of his mouth with a napkin, said, "Better stoke up then, Bryan. You haven't touched your plate; biking's hard work."

"Not really hungry. Anyhow, Crystal packed a big lunch."

But I held out my plate for seconds on quiche and fruit, feeling sorry about all that uneaten food. "A small slice of coffee cake, too," I said, "if that's okay." Mrs. B., looking absentminded, gave me seconds on everything. The four of us breathed at each other for a while, and on their faces was nothing at all. Just good-humoured smiles—maybe real, maybe fake, you couldn't tell.

Then Mrs. B. stood up and left the room, and there were only the three of us. Mr. B. said, "How's that job of yours, Crystal?"

"Great," I said, as Bryan shifted in his chair, his fingers tapping harder. He knew how they felt about the job, the waitressing . . . their brilliant son, who'd gotten into a top engineering school back east, going with this lightweight that he'd met while lifeguarding at the Myrtle Edwards Pool. Dozens of lovely college-bound girls around, and look who he chooses . . . Bryan and I rarely discussed it. Why pour salt on the wounds?

"It's really interesting," I said. "I mean, one of these days, I wouldn't mind owning a place like that. A café, with people from the neighbourhood dropping in. I'm a fairly good cook, and I do most of the bookkeeping . . . "

Mr. B's eyebrows shot way up, but before he could get a word out, Mrs. B. came back from the kitchen. She was slightly out of breath.

"Here's your milk, Bryan," she said. "I went next door and borrowed a quart."

Bryan jumped to his feet. "Thanks a lot, Mom, but I think we'd better get moving." He was pulling my chair back . . . Throat-clearings, handshakes. Polite thank-yous and everything-tasted-so-greats from me.

Mrs. B. still had Bryan's glass of milk; she held it out to him. "Save it for tomorrow," he said. And then we were going out the door.

Bryan got his bike from the garage; I pulled mine from against the wall of the house, where I'd left it. And just as I was about to climb on, he came over to me, leaned his cheek against mine, and whispered in my ear, "Alone at last, Princess. I thought we'd never get out." And he kissed me, his dark eyes shining.

From the front window, I caught a sudden glimpse of his mother—still holding the glass of milk—watching us. And then I knew, because her mouth was tight, her nostrils flared, her chin seemed to wobble . . . She was sick over it, all right.

Part of me felt like yelling out to her, "I'm not dumb, you hear? Different from you, okay, but I've got hopes and dreams of my own, and I'm not dumb. Don't you forget that!" Only the hot sun was on my face, and Bryan was at my side, and I felt too good for yelling. At anyone.

Later that week, I almost got up the courage to mention it to him. He'd walked to the café to hang out with me in the prelunch lull. We were setting tables. "Over here, right in this chair," I said, "a friend of your mom's was having breakfast . . . "

"Yeah?" He straightened a paper napkin, then lined up the knife and fork.

"She was talking to this other woman. I couldn't help overhearing."

Silence. Bryan's head bent close to mine.

"She said your parents—"

He breathed out, or else it was a sort of laugh. He shook his head, as if to shake away whatever I was going to say about his parents, then blew on a knife handle and started polishing it. A car honked outside.

Through the front window, we saw the Beckwiths' car, with Mr. B. inside it, smiling in our direction. Bryan dropped the knife, turning as if to go—then suddenly, impulsively, he grabbed me and hugged me so hard I could barely breathe. Then he kissed me—a light, sweet kiss. "Don't eavesdrop, Princess," he whispered. "I love you very much, that's all that counts."

Then he marched out the front door, climbed into the car beside his dad, and waved good-bye to Avery. They were off, to who-knows-where, Bryan's father looking straight ahead now, not smiling, hunched over the wheel and businesslike.

I turned to Avery. "What next? Tables are set. You want me to heat up that mushroom soup?"

"Sure, kid."

"Why are you staring at me?"

He shrugged. "Why not?" He was standing behind the counter, his hands jammed in his pockets, and just staring with his half-sad eyes.

"You look like you feel sorry for me or something," I said.

"Oh really? Is that how I look?" Avery blinked and turned away . . . Why? What went on under that idiotic beret? Why did he stare at me so often nowadays and always with that sorrowful expression?

The door opened, letting in a whoosh of warm spring air and two old ladies talking a mile a minute. One was tall and straight but so thin, she looked like she'd been pressed between the covers of a book. The other was bent over and tiny. Both wore blond wigs and clothes they must have picked out at a rummage sale while blindfolded. They sat at a window table, holding up the menu with shivery fingers. "One amaretto ice cream," the small one said. "And two spoons, please."

"I very strongly advise the Buddha's Delight," Avery said. "It has six different vegetables. Buy a couple of ice creams, and I'll throw in a Buddha for free."

They frowned, bent their wigs together, and discussed his offer. The tall one looked up at him. "Do we have to?" she asked.

"You betcha," Avery said, shifting the beret till it tilted over his ear. "No ice cream for senior citizens without some veggies—it's a rule of the house."

The little one giggled. Avery winked at me and went to the counter. I headed for the kitchen, where I took the lid off a big stockpot of mushroom soup. I breathed in the wonderful smell. Through the window over the stove, I saw the alley—blackberry bushes, spider webs, all sorts of wild and tangled things. This was the hiding place of the famous raccoons, which you couldn't see now, in the daylight. But they were in there somewhere. Sleeping behind their masks. Even in the daytime, the back alley had a mysterious look to it, full of shadows and secrets. Bulldoze the whole thing? I hoped Avery wouldn't. I loved the place. To me, it was just as much a part of the café as the couch and Avery's brown beret. Besides, I needed those bushes: Every summer, since I'd first come to work at Avery's, I'd made the jam; I usually made so much that it lasted till the new crop came in . . .

Which brought me right back to the Ultrasuede women. I climbed on a high stool and in my head continued the conversation with Bryan: *You think it doesn't matter how your parents feel about me, and maybe you're right. It's your life and all that jazz. But listen, they're paying your bills, they deserve a little—*

I had to stop, though. I had to ask myself what, and how much, they deserved. This is a rough world we live in, getting rougher every day, so if you find someone you really love, are you supposed to just forget that person—because of your parents?

From the doorway, I heard Avery's voice. "You think I should bulldoze?"

"Huh?"

"Or maybe just leave the whole thing as it is and set out the traps . . . I don't know. I like the alley. You like the alley. I've seen you out there in the mornings—"

"Avery, will you kindly let me alone a couple of minutes more?"

He had the beret in his hands and was twisting it. "Remember last summer? Remember how we picked blackberries by the pailfuls?"

"Will you just flake off, Avery?"

A moment of silence, then the beret was back on his head. "You've got a sharp tongue there, kid. I was simply asking your opinion."

"All right, I'm sorry."

"If I were you, I'd watch that tongue."

"I said I was sorry. Look, you're not the only one who has worries."

He came up behind me and put his hand on my shoulder, patting me the way you pat a child. "There are times when you definitely remind me of those blackberry bushes," he said. "A person's got to be careful around you, or they might get scratched."

"Yeah. Well. We bushes have to protect ourselves any way we can."

He came over and stood in front of me, leaning across the stove to look out the window. "We'd lose the spider webs, that's another thing. They look so great on summer mornings when they're full of dew."

"Quit kidding yourself, Avery, you'll never bulldoze. You'll just go right on griping about the raccoons, till you maybe move to another place, a place without an alley."

He laughed a little. "You don't know me, kid. I don't give up that easy. When I find a place I like, I stick with it, raccoons or no raccoons."

There were noises from inside now. We went out to face the midday rush. After that came the slow trickle of people in for dessert: mothers with toddlers, old people from the neighbourhood, middle-aged women on the way home from downtown, their arms full of fancy shopping bags. At one point, a pair of kids holding hands walked in, sat at a small table, and stared so hard into each other's eyes, I was afraid if I spoke to them it would be like waking sleepwalkers.

I stomped up to Avery. "You wait on those two; I'm taking my break now."

"What break? Who takes a break at a quarter past four, when she goes off duty at five?"

"I do," I said and threw myself onto the blue couch, trying not to watch the lovebirds but watching them, feeling homesick for the way they were. So wrapped up in each other. So uncaring about the rest of the world. That's how it ought to be . . . except sometimes, the rest of the world comes and plunks itself down in front of you and sticks its clammy hands between you. I shut my eyes to shut out the two kids and went back in my mind to the talk I was maybe going to have with Bryan: *Let's cool it. If we're as much in love as I think we are, it won't hurt if we try going out with other people. You can go out with the type of girl your parents like, I can go out with—well, anyone. Meanwhile, your folks will have a breather, you'll have a breather—*

Something touched my cheek. My eyes shot open. "Bryan— what are you doing here?"

He lowered himself onto the couch beside me, listening with interest to the twangs and moanings of the springs. Then, his hand on my chin, he turned my face toward his. "Got something to tell you, Princess. Something wonderful."

I saw that his eyes were sparkling—even his eyebrows seemed

to glisten—but I told him to go wait at our usual table, because I had to work another half hour. When I got off at five, Avery's brother came on; the two of them did the dinner rush between them. "Will it keep half an hour?" I asked Bryan.

"It'll keep," he said with that glow on his face. Then as we pulled ourselves off the blue couch, I saw Avery waving, meaning he'd run the show by himself for a while. I could take the half hour as a gift.

So·I said to Bryan, "Looks like we won't have to wait." We headed for our table, passing a fat girl who was stuffing her face with double-chocolate cupcakes, then the smooching couple, then a giant philodendron, with late afternoon sun filtering in through its leaves. Behind it was our special corner. Bryan sat; I sat. We reached for each other's hands beneath the table.

He said, "I got a letter from the U. They said it's okay for me to transfer here."

I blinked, dumbfounded.

"No more letter-writing. No more long-distance calls. We'll have time together—all the time in the world." He held my hand between both of his now, and on his face was that certain look he got when he was excited. Like a runner, waiting for the starter's signal and straining to take off.

Only I couldn't share Bryan's excitement. We'd been through this whole thing before, we'd talked it all out during Christmas vacation and finally agreed it didn't make sense—the U wasn't nearly so good in engineering as the place he'd handpicked.

"Say something, Crystal."

And when I didn't, just sat there, hating to spoil it for him but dead sure we'd been right to begin with, he whispered, "Don't you want me here?"

"Of course I do. Okay, I do, and I don't. Bryan, listen. You're not being fair to yourself, and you're not being fair to your parents."

He stiffened a little. "Come off it. If the U is good enough for my dad to teach in, it's good enough for me to go to."

"He'll hate it. They'll both hate it. They'll realize why you switched, and—"

"It's none of their business!" The words shot out. Bryan dropped my hand and turned his head away from me.

I said, "Bryan, don't you think you owe them something?"

At that, he shoved his long legs out in the direction of the table across from ours, the one with the lovebirds. He looked at them with annoyance, but they didn't look at him or see him, because if the place burned down, they wouldn't know it; they were forehead-to-forehead now . . . Bryan never thought much of kids who went all lovesick in public places. He turned away from them to face me: "You know something, Crystal? I am bored out of my skull by the whole subject of my parents." His thumb was beating against the table edge.

At which point, Avery pulled up a chair. "Hi, Bryan," he said.

"Hi, Avery, how's it going?"

I said, "Listen, we're talking now, Avery."

Avery said to Bryan, "It's going okay, old pal, except for certain problems. Certain serious environmental problems."

"Avery!" I said.

"Flake off, Crystal," he said. "I want to get a third opinion here. I want to hear what Bryan thinks about these problems."

I groaned. "What problems?" Bryan asked.

Avery told him about the alley, the bushes, the raccoons. How he couldn't figure out how they got in. "I'm thinking of having it all bulldozed. Let them go hide in someone else's bushes and steal someone else's food."

"So? Go ahead and bulldoze," Bryan said. Meanwhile, those same ladies in wigs were back, walking toward their table. One of them put an oversize purse in front of her, holding onto it with both hands.

When she caught Avery's eye, she said, "We'll have two coffees."

"Okay, you can get them yourself," he said. "Feel free; just step right up to the machine at the counter."

She tottered to her feet—the tall, skinny one. The other one kept a firm grip on the handbag. Avery said, "Trouble is, I sort of like the alley. Some of my friends like it, too, just the way it is. Come on, I'll show you."

"I've already seen it," Bryan said.

The old lady was back with two coffees. She put them on the table. The other one took a fat sandwich wrapped in waxed paper out of the handbag, unwrapped it, and pushed half of it toward her partner.

Bryan said, "To tell the truth, Avery, I'd get rid of them, too— that weird couch, the mess in the alley, and these deadbeats who are taking up space they don't pay for. You asked me, I'm giving you my considered opinion."

Avery said, "Thank you for your opinion, Bry, I appreciate it." He got up, touched me lightly on the shoulder, and disappeared in the direction of the kitchen. The two ladies set to work on their sandwich, and Bryan shook his head at me.

"Who's the boss around here—Avery or his customers?"

I said, "Tell me the real reason you want to switch schools."

"What?"

"It's because it will make your parents mad, isn't it?" I said. "Isn't that why you started going with me in the first place—to needle them?"

His mouth fell open. "What the heck is going on here, Princess?"

I didn't know how to answer him or at what exact minute the information fell into place in my brain—it had something to do with the smooching couple. With the way Bryan never went in for that kind of stuff in public. Except when that public happened to be his folks. He didn't love me, he probably didn't even like me very much. How could he, when I was an oddball. I was full of thorns, stubborn and tough like the blackberry bushes, and an offbeat person. Like those women in their wigs.

The one great thing about me was, I made his parents sick. I said, "You've been using me, Bryan."

"What kind of crazy talk is this? All of a sudden, out of the clear blue sky—"

"I think you'd better go. I don't feel like talking to you anymore, not just now. So go. I'll see you tomorrow. Or next week. Or never. Go on, Bryan, please. Do us both a favour."

"Not without a better explanation!"

"Never mind the explanation. Just go!" Suddenly, I didn't want Bryan around anymore, didn't like his smile or his dark good looks or his calling me Princess or anything else about him. Not one thing. How come it took me so long to figure it all out? How come I cared about his parents' feelings when he didn't care? And wouldn't he end up treating me the same way—someday?


Nine forty-five, and I was still at the café, working behind the counter with Avery. Cleaning up, while his brother finished off the dishes in the kitchen. I said to Avery, "You never liked him, did you?"

"No. Never. I think he's spoiled rotten."

I'd been crying before, running in and out of the ladies' room to bawl in private, and my eyes were all puffy now.

"Come on," Avery said. "Let's go out in the alley and mooch around for a while. The raccoons might turn up. We can . . . scare them away or something." He took off his beret and stuck it on my head.

"I thought you were after their hides," I said.

"Nah. I like them. I like all wild things. That's why I'll never bulldoze." He took my hand and led me toward the kitchen, the beret still on my head, warming it.

"So what will you do—about the raccoons?"

Avery shrugged. "Just play it by ear. See how it goes, and just . . . you know. Things'll work out."

There were no raccoons in the alley, none we could see, but there was a sliver of moon, fireflies under the blackberry bushes, and, from the other side of the ravine, the sound of frogs. We stood there taking it all in, Avery looking at me from time to time . . . his hands in his pockets, his legs far apart. He seemed to be watching me the way you watch a person who's wobbly from being sick, checking for signs of health, for their breathing to improve or the colour to come back in their face.

It wouldn't be easy, though. It wouldn't happen overnight. It leaves a big hole inside you, having somebody just torn away like that.

There was a sudden noise at our feet, a little jump, then the sounds of scurrying. Avery bent forward to look, moving close up against the bushes. "Careful," I whispered. "Watch out for the thorns."

But whatever it was had disappeared by now. Avery stood up, reached out, and tugged the beret so it sat way back on my head, then stepped back to admire the effect. He nodded twice; he smiled at me. The frogs chug-chugged, the fireflies winked, the bushes breathed their fruity smells at us, watching us as if we were the wild things, as if our world was the dark, mysterious one, full of secrets.

Then Avery said, "Don't worry, Crystal. I'm not afraid of thorns."

# FOCUSSING

1. Working in a small group, brainstorm a list of characteristics that a good friend should have. Choose the five characteristics you think are most important and write a sentence about each one. Put your sentences on a poster to remind yourself of how to be a good friend.
2. Write a poem about friendship that you could use when you sign your friends' yearbooks.
3. Find a picture of yourself and a friend taken when you were in elementary school. Write a memoir recalling the experience in the photograph. If you give your memoir to your friend, be sure to keep a copy for your Private Writing File (see p. 181).
4. Writing letters is a good way to keep in touch with friends when they move away. Write a letter to a friend of yours who no longer lives in your town or city. Proofread it carefully before you mail it to your friend. Keep a copy of your letter for your writing folder; if you get a reply, clip it to the draft and file them together.
5. Write a journal entry that you could put away to look up in five years' time. Writing one paragraph for each person; describe three people (one older than you, one younger than you, and one approximately your own age) who are very important in your life right now, and say why they are important.

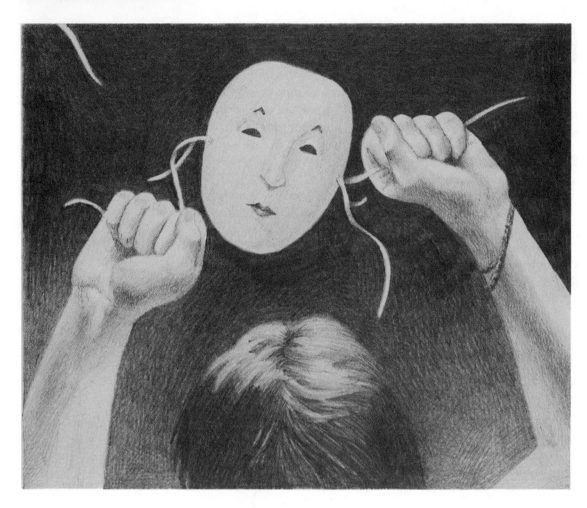

## MASK
### *by Melanie Harrison*

there you sat
with your expressionless mask
my fingers curled
around its edges
"take it off!" I shrieked

you shook your head
and remained expressionless

but then
I pulled it off

and you were grinning

# CLOSE UP

1. Make two drawings for the poem. The first one should show the face before the mask is removed, and the second should show the results after it is pulled off.
2. After you have discussed "Mask" in a small group, write a one- or two-sentence definition of the phrase *mask your feelings*.
3. In your own words, rewrite "Mask" as a paragraph that you could give to someone who was having difficulty understanding the poem.

# WIDE ANGLE

1. Sometimes when we care about someone and they don't seem to be communicating with us, we feel like crying out: "Tell me what you are thinking!" Tell a partner about a time when you felt someone was hiding her or his real feelings from you. Write a journal entry describing your experience and telling whether or not you ever found out what the other person was thinking.
2. Add another line or two to the end of "Mask," starting with the word "because . . . ".

## CIRCLE
### by Toni Weston

I thought it would be hard
breaking up with you.
That is why I hung on.

Today I woke with a happy feeling.
I knew I could do it without a second thought.

I said goodbye so easily . . .

Now I am choking on the silence.

# CLOSE UP

1. "Circle" describes some of the feelings that the poet experienced when she broke up with her boyfriend. Complete the following sentences with a word or words that describe each stage of her feelings:

   First I was  _____;

   then I felt  _____;

   and then I was  _____.

2. Looking at your answer to #1, write one or two sentences explaining why the poem has the title "Circle."

# WIDE ANGLE

1. Saying goodbye is often very hard. Interview five people who have parted with someone for whom they cared a great deal (a boyfriend, a girlfriend, a family member, a schoolmate who moved away). Make a chart that summarizes some of the experiences of the people you interviewed. A sample chart is shown below.

| Person's First Name | Relationship to Person Leaving | Feelings When Saying Goodbye | What Helped the Person Feel Better |
|---|---|---|---|
|  |  |  |  |

# ON THE SIDEWALK BLEEDING

*by Evan Hunter*

THE BOY lay bleeding in the rain. He was sixteen years old, and he wore a bright purple silk jacket, and the lettering across the back of the jacket read THE ROYALS. The boy's name was Andy, and the name was delicately scripted in black thread on the front of the jacket, just over the heart. *Andy*.

He had been stabbed ten minutes ago. The knife had entered just below his rib cage and had been drawn across his body violently, tearing a wide gap in his flesh. He lay on the sidewalk with the March rain drilling his jacket and drilling his body and washing away the blood that poured from his open wound. He had known excruciating pain when the knife had torn across his body, and then sudden comparative relief when the blade was pulled away. He had heard the voice saying, "That's for you, Royal!" and then the sound of footsteps hurrying into the rain, and then he had fallen to the sidewalk, clutching his stomach, trying to stop the flow of blood.

He tried to yell for help, but he had no voice. He did not know why his voice had deserted him, or why the rain had become so suddenly fierce, or why there was an open hole in his body from which his life ran redly, steadily. It was 11:30 P.M., but he did not know the time.

There was another thing he did not know.

He did not know he was dying. He lay on the sidewalk, bleeding, and he thought only: *That was a fierce rumble. They got me good that time*, but he did not know he was dying. He would have been frightened had he known. In his ignorance, he lay bleeding and wishing he could cry out for help, but there was no voice in his throat. There was only the bubbling of blood from between his lips whenever he opened his mouth to speak. He lay silent in his pain, waiting, waiting for someone to find him.

He could hear the sound of automobile tires hushed on the muzzle of rainswept streets, far away at the other end of the long alley. He lay with his face pressed to the sidewalk, and he could see the splash of neon far away at the other end of the alley, tinting the pavement red

and green, slickly brilliant in the rain.

He wondered if Laura would be angry.

He had left the jump to get a package of cigarettes. He had told her he would be back in a few minutes, and then he had gone downstairs and found the candy store closed. He knew that Alfredo's on the next block would be open until at least two, and he had started through the alley, and that was when he'd been ambushed. He could hear the faint sound of music now, coming from a long, long way off, and he wondered if Laura was dancing, wondered if she had missed him yet. Maybe she thought he wasn't coming back. Maybe she thought he'd cut out for good. Maybe she'd already left the jump and gone home. He thought of her face, the brown eyes and the jet-black hair, and thinking of her he forgot his pain a little, forgot that blood was rushing from his body. Someday he would marry Laura. Someday he would marry her, and they would have a lot of kids, and then they would get out of the neighbourhood. They would move to a clean project in the Bronx, or maybe they would move to Staten Island. When they were married, when they had kids. . . .

He heard footsteps at the other end of the alley, and he lifted his cheek from the sidewalk and looked into the darkness and tried to cry out, but again there was only a soft hissing bubble of blood on his mouth.

The man came down the alley. He had not seen Andy yet. He walked, and then stopped to lean against the brick of the building, and then walked again. He saw Andy then and came toward him, and he stood over him for a long time, the minutes ticking, ticking, watching him and not speaking.

Then he said, "What'sa matter, buddy?"

Andy could not speak, and he could barely move. He lifted his face slightly and looked up at the man, and in the rain-swept alley he smelled the sickening odour of alcohol and realized the man was drunk. He did not feel any particular panic. He did not know he was dying, and so he felt only mild disappointment that the man who had found him was drunk.

The man was smiling.

"Did you fall down, buddy?" he asked. "You mus' be as drunk as I am." He grinned, seemed to remember why he had entered the alley in the first place, and said, "Don' go way. I'll be ri' back."

The man lurched away. Andy heard his footsteps, and then the sound of the man colliding with a garbage can, and some mild swearing, and then the sound of the man urinating, lost in the steady wash of the rain.

He waited for the man to come back.

It was 11:39.

When the man returned, he squatted alongside Andy. He studied him with drunken dignity.

"You gonna catch cold here," he said. "What'sa matter? You like layin' in the wet?"

Andy could not answer. The man tried to focus his eyes on Andy's face. The rain spattered around them.

"You like a drink?"

Andy shook his head.

"I gotta bottle. Here," the man said. He pulled a pint bottle from his inside jacket pocket. He uncapped it and extended it to Andy. Andy tried to move, but pain wrenched him back flat against the sidewalk.

"Take it," the man said. He kept watching Andy. "Take it." When Andy did not move, he said, "Nev' mind, I'll have one m'self." He tilted the bottle to his lips, and then wiped the back of his hand across his mouth. "You too young to be drinkin', anyway. Should be 'shamed of yourself, drunk an' layin' in a alley, all wet. Shame on you. I gotta good minda calla cop."

Andy nodded. Yes, he tried to say. Yes, call a cop. Please. Call one.

"Oh, you don't like that, huh?" the drunk said. "You don' wanna cop to fin' you all drunk an' wet in a alley, huh? Okay, buddy. This time you get off easy." He got to his feet. "This time you lucky," he said. He waved broadly at Andy, and then almost lost his footing. "S'long, buddy," he said.

*Wait*, Andy thought. *Wait, please, I'm bleeding.*

"S'long," the drunk said again. "I see you aroun'," and then he staggered off up the alley.

Andy lay and thought: *Laura, Laura. Are you dancing?*

The couple came into the alley suddenly. They ran into the alley together, running from the rain, the boy holding the girl's elbow, the girl spreading a newspaper over her head to protect her hair. Andy lay crumpled against the pavement, and he watched them run into the alley laughing, and then duck into the doorway not ten feet from him.

"Man, what rain!" the boy said. "You could drown out there."

"I have to get home," the girl said. "It's late, Freddie. I have to get home."

"We got time," Freddie said. "Your people won't raise a fuss if you're a little late. Not with this kind of weather."

"It's dark," the girl said, and she giggled.

"Yeah," the boy answered, his voice very low.

"Freddie . . . ?"

"Um?"

"You're . . . you're standing very close to me."

"Um."

There was a long silence. Then the girl said, "Oh," only that single word, and Andy knew she'd been kissed, and he suddenly hungered for Laura's mouth. It was then that he wondered if he would ever kiss Laura again. It was then that he wondered if he was dying.

*No*, he thought, *I can't be dying, not from a little street rumble, not from just getting cut. Guys get cut all the time in rumbles. I can't be dying. No, that's stupid. That don't make any sense at all.*

"You shouldn't," the girl said.

"Why not?"

"I don't know."

"Do you like it?"

"Yes."

"So?"

"I don't know."

"I love you, Angela," the boy said.

"I love you, too, Freddie," the girl said, and Andy listened and thought: *I love you, Laura. Laura, I think maybe I'm dying. Laura, this is stupid but I think maybe I'm dying. Laura, I think I'm dying!*

He tried to speak. He tried to move. He tried to crawl toward the doorway where he could see the two figures in embrace. He tried to make a noise, a sound, and a grunt came from his lips, and then he tried again, and another grunt came, a low animal grunt of pain.

"What was that?" the girl said, suddenly alarmed, breaking away from the boy.

"I don't know," he answered.

"Go look, Freddie."

"No. Wait."

Andy moved his lips again. Again the sound came from him.

"Freddie!"

"What?"

"I'm scared."

"I'll go see," the boy said.

He stepped into the alley. He walked over to where Andy lay on the ground. He stood over him, watching him.

"You all right?" he asked.

"What is it?" Angela said from the doorway.

"Somebody's hurt," Freddie said.

"Let's get out of here," Angela said.

"No. Wait a minute." He knelt down beside Andy. "You

cut?" he asked.

Andy nodded. The boy kept looking at him. He saw the lettering on the jacket then. THE ROYALS. He turned to Angela.

"He's a Royal," he said.

"Let's . . . what . . . what do you want to do, Freddie?"

"I don't know. I don't want to get mixed up in this. He's a Royal. We help him and the Guardians'll be down our necks. I don't want to get mixed up in this, Angela."

"Is he . . . is he hurt bad?"

"Yeah, it looks that way."

"What shall we do?"

"I don't know."

"We can't leave him here in the rain." Angela hesitated. "Can we?"

"If we get a cop, the Guardians'll find out who," Freddie said. "I don't know, Angela. I don't know."

Angela hesitated a long time before answering. Then she said, "I have to get home, Freddie. My people will begin to worry."

"Yeah," Freddie said. He looked at Andy again. "You all right?" he asked. Andy lifted his face from the sidewalk, and his eyes said: *Please, please help me*, and maybe Freddie read what his eyes were saying, and maybe he didn't.

Behind him, Angela said, "Freddie, let's get out of here! Please!" There was urgency in her voice, urgency bordering on the edge of panic. Freddie stood up. He looked at Andy again, and then mumbled, "I'm sorry," and then he took Angela's arm and together they ran toward the neon splash at the other end of the alley.

*Why, they're afraid of the Guardians*, Andy thought in amazement. *But why should they be? I wasn't afraid of the Guardians. I never turkeyed out of a rumble with the Guardians. I got heart. But I'm bleeding.*

The rain was soothing somehow. It was a cold rain, but his body was hot all over, and the rain helped to cool him. He had always liked rain. He could remember sitting in Laura's house one time, the rain running down the windows, and just looking out over the street, watching the people running from the rain. That was when he'd first joined the Royals. He could remember how happy he was the Royals had taken him. The Royals and the Guardians, two of the biggest. He was a Royal. There had been meaning to the title.

Now, in the alley, with the cold rain washing his hot body, he wondered about the meaning. If he died, he was Andy. He was not a Royal. He was simply Andy, and he was dead. And he wondered suddenly if the Guardians who had ambushed him and knifed him had ever once realized he was Andy? Had they known that he was Andy, or had they simply known that he was a Royal wearing a purple silk jacket? Had they stabbed *him*, Andy, or had they only stabbed the jacket and the title, and what good was the title if you were dying?

*I'm Andy,* he screamed wordlessly. *I'm Andy, I'm Andy!*

An old lady stopped at the other end of the alley. The garbage cans were stacked there, beating noisily in the rain. The old lady carried an umbrella with broken ribs, carried it with all the dignity of a queen. She stepped into the mouth of the alley, a shopping bag over one arm. She lifted the lids of the garbage cans delicately, and she did not hear Andy grunt because she was a little deaf and because the rain was beating a steady relentless tattoo on the cans. She had been searching and foraging for the better part of the night. She collected her string and her newspapers, and an old hat with a feather on it from one of the garbage cans, and a broken footstool from another of the cans. And then she delicately replaced the lids and lifted her umbrella high and walked out of the alley mouth with queenly dignity. She had worked swiftly and soundlessly, and now she was gone.

The alley looked very long now. He could see people passing at the other end of it, and he wondered who the people were, and he wondered if he would ever get to know them, wondered who it was on the Guardians who had stabbed him, who had plunged the knife into his body.

"That's for you, Royal!" the voice had said, and then the footsteps, his arms being released by the others, the fall to the pavement. "That's for you, Royal!" Even in his pain, even as he collapsed, there had been some sort of pride in knowing he was a Royal. Now there was no pride at all. With the rain beginning to chill him, with the blood pouring steadily between his fingers, he knew only a sort of dizziness, and within the giddy dizziness, he could only think: *I want to be Andy.*

It was not very much to ask of the world.

He watched the world passing at the other end of the alley. The world didn't know he was Andy. The world didn't know he was alive. He wanted to say, "Hey, I'm alive! Hey, look at me! I'm alive! Don't you know I'm alive? Don't you know I exist?"

He felt weak and very tired. He felt alone and wet and feverish and chilled, and he knew he was going to die now, and the knowledge made him suddenly sad. He was not frightened. For some reason, he was not frightened. He was only filled with an overwhelming sadness that his life

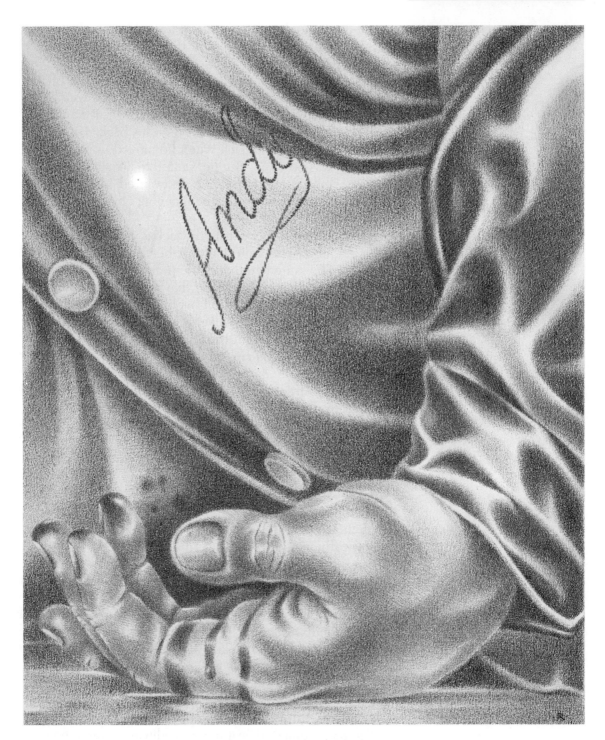

would be over at sixteen. He felt all at once as if he had never done anything, never seen anything, never been anywhere. There were so many things to do and he wondered why he'd never thought of them before, wondered why the rumbles and the jumps and the purple jacket had always seemed so important to him before, and now they seemed like such small things in a world he was missing, a world that was rushing past at the other end of the alley.

*I don't want to die*, he thought. *I haven't lived yet.*

It seemed very important to him that he take off the purple jacket. He was very close to dying, and when they found him, he did not want them to say, "Oh, it's a Royal." With great effort, he rolled over onto his back. He felt the pain tearing at his stomach when he moved, a pain he did not think was possible. But he wanted to take off the jacket. If he never did another thing, he wanted to take off the jacket. The jacket had only one meaning now, and that was a very simple meaning.

If he had not been wearing the jacket, he would not have been stabbed. The knife had not been plunged in hatred of Andy. The knife hated only the purple jacket. The jacket was a stupid meaningless thing that was robbing him of his life. He wanted the jacket off his back. With an enormous loathing, he wanted the jacket off his back.

He lay struggling with the shiny wet material. His arms were heavy, and pain ripped fire across his body whenever he moved. But he squirmed and fought and twisted until one arm was free and then the other, and then he rolled away from the jacket and lay quite still, breathing heavily, listening to the sound of his breathing and the sound of the rain and thinking: *Rain is sweet, I'm Andy.*

She found him in the alleyway a minute past midnight. She left the dance to look for him, and when she found him she knelt beside him and said, "Andy, it's me, Laura."

He did not answer her. She backed away from him, tears springing into her eyes, and then she ran from the alley hysterically and did not stop running until she found the cop.

And now, standing with the cop, she looked down at him, and the cop rose and said, "He's dead," and all the crying was out of her now. She stood in the rain and said nothing, looking at the dead boy on the pavement, and looking at the purple jacket that rested a foot away from his body.

The cop picked up the jacket and turned it over in his hands.

"A Royal, huh?" he said.

The rain seemed to beat more steadily now, more fiercely.

She looked at the cop and, very quietly, she said, "His name is Andy."

The cop slung the jacket over his arm. He took out his black pad, and he flipped it open to a blank page.

"A Royal," he said.

Then he began writing.

# CLOSE UP

1. With a partner, discuss what information you think a reporter would be able to find about Andy's murder. Imagine that you are the reporter, and write the story. If you write it using a word processor, there are computer programs that will allow you to print your article exactly the way it would look in a newspaper.
2. Before he died, Andy wanted to be known as an individual, not a Royal. In Laura's voice, write an obituary for Andy to appear alongside the reporter's account of Andy's death. The leader of the Royal gang would remember Andy differently. Write another obituary in the leader's voice.
3. The Royal jacket took on a new meaning for Andy as he lay dying. After discussion with a partner, in one or two sentences explain why his attitude toward it changed.
4. In a small group, role-play one of the following situations:
   - Freddie and Angela telling close friends about their decision to leave the wounded boy;
   - the drunk telling someone about the guy he found lying in the street;
   - Laura telling her closest friend or family member about finding Andy;
   - the police officer telling his sergeant about the latest street rumble.

# WIDE ANGLE

1. Imagine that Andy was rescued. Discuss with a partner whether or not the stabbing would change Andy's life. Write your ideas in a letter that Andy would send to Laura while he recovered in a hospital.
2. Read the play *West Side Story*. Working with at least one other person, draw a mural that illustrates all the relationships in the play, with the ending of the play as the final scene of the mural. Do a similar mural that starts with Laura and Andy at the dance and ends with the police officer and Laura standing over Andy's body.
3. Ask your history teacher or librarian to help you find out about couples in history who were separated by the violent death of one or the other or both. Tape one of the stories as you tell it in your own words. (You may want to rehearse it first.) Play your tape for a small group and listen to the stories they have recorded.

# WHAT ABOUT FRIENDSHIPS?

*by Eve R. Wirth*

EVERYONE needs one or two very close friends from whom he or she can derive the sort of understanding that is different from that of parents or teachers. What are the things that you enjoy about your best friend? Do you confide to him or her the things that you wouldn't dream of telling anyone else? Do you discuss the things that cause you anxiety or that make you happy or sad? Do you enjoy a good, hearty laugh together over the same joke or situation? Above all, can you trust this friend with your innermost secrets? Can you trust him or her not to let you down when you find yourself in a sticky predicament? If you answer honestly, you'll find that you probably don't have this warm, intimate relationship with more than one or two people.

*The very same things that make your friend so important to you, make you important to him or her.*

What then are the real secrets of a friendship? And if at this particular time you don't have a true friend, what can you do about it?

The very first thing to realize is that friendships are made. They don't just happen. They must be cultivated. If you really want a friend, you'll have to give yourself a push and go out and make one.

How do you go about doing that? If you hide in your house, your chances of making a friend are slimmer than a pencil. Your plan should be to go where the people are and be with them. Try to think of a few people whom you enjoy being with or think you'd enjoy being with and then *be* with them.

Of course, it's much simpler to make friends with someone who likes the same things or activities that you do. It stands to reason that if you're the type of person who enjoys art, you'll probably have more in common with another art aficionado.

Here are some hints that will help you to develop a close friend:

- Be a good listener.
- Show the other person that you are concerned and interested. Show understanding and sympathy for his or her feelings, interests, and ways of thinking.
- Let the person know that he or she can count on you for a helping hand.
- Be yourself. Don't put on false pretenses. A close relationship can never be built on false premises.

Remember that it takes time to develop a close friendship. Shared experiences and trust are not acquired overnight. You may meet someone you think you have a lot in common with, only to find out later that that's not the case. However, you may also meet a person whom you initially think you could not enjoy, only to find that when you give the relationship more time to develop and ripen, a real friendship emerges. The key here is not to make rash judgments.

Once you have discovered that beautiful feeling of having found a person with whom you can joyfully share activities, thoughts, and life itself, you have found a precious jewel. You would be careful to protect a precious gem from damage or loss. The same care should be shown with a friendship. It is a rare something to be treasured.

# CLOSE UP

1. Make a poster that highlights the suggestions this writer offers about developing friendships. You may wish to decorate or illustrate your poster with drawings or pictures from a magazine.

   **or**

   In the comic strip below, Snoopy has found an interesting way to cheer up Peppermint Patty. Take one of the hints about making friends presented by the author of "What about Friendships?", and draw your own cartoon illustrating her point.

# WIDE ANGLE

1. Think about a friend who means a lot to you. Consider the following questions:
   a) How did you and your friend first meet?
   b) What drew you to your friend?
   c) What experience(s) made you realize that this person is a special friend?
   Respond to the questions in a journal entry.
2. You have been asked to write a sequel to "What about Friendships?" In a small group, discuss the ways you keep good friends once you've made them. Your notes from the discussion can be the basis of your article.

# KALEIDOSCOPE

1.  "What are the three most important things you look for in a good friend?" Ask the above question to
    a) five people aged 4–12;
    b) five people aged 13–19;
    c) five people over 20.
    Summarize the results of your survey of each age group in a chart like the one below.

| Age Group | Important Characteristics Looked for in Friends |
|---|---|
| 4 – 12 | |
| 13 – 19 | |
| Over 20 | |

    You can use a computer data base or a word processor to prepare your chart. Next, combine the results of your survey with the work of others in the class to identify any common patterns in the data.
    (*Data* is the information in your chart.)

2.  With help from your teacher and librarian, find five poems that deal with being in touch with friends. Copy each poem and paste it on its own page (or pages). Under each poem write a comment on why you chose the poem, including the following points:
    (i) what you think the poem's message is; and
    (ii) what lines you especially like and why.
    You may wish to draw an illustration to accompany some of the poems.

3.  "All successful romantic relationships are based on friendship." Discuss the statement in a small group, and then debate for or against the claim with someone from another group. Two people, one from each of the two groups, can act as the judges of the debate. The judges should take notes during the arguments, and then work together to write a one-paragraph decision saying who convinced them.

# OUR CLOSE RESEMBLANCE

*from*

# THE MOUNTAIN AND THE VALLEY

*by Ernest Buckler*

THERE WERE the three days: the day before Christmas, the day of Christmas, and the day after. Those three days lamplight spread with a different softness over the blue-cold snow. Faces were all unlocked; thought and feeling were open and warm to the touch. Even inanimate things came close, as if they had a blood of their own running through them.

On the afternoon of the first day the cold relaxed suddenly, like a frozen rag dipped in water. Distances seemed to shrink. The dark spruce mountain moved nearer, with the bodies of the trees dark as before rain.

Martha had done up all her housework before noon, and the afternoon had the feel of Saturday. It was a parenthesis in time— before the sharp expectancy began to build with the dusk and spark to its full brightness when the lamp was lit. There were so many places it was wonderful to be that afternoon that David was scarcely still a minute.

He went outside and made a snowman. The snow was so packy it left a track right down to the grass roots. It was a perfect day to be alone with, the only confidant of its mysteries. Yet it was equally nice to be with people. The claim of their ordinary work was suspended today, no one's busyness was any kind of pushing aside.

He went inside and sat close to his grandmother. He asked her a string of questions; not for information, but because he was young and she was old. To let her feel that she was helping him get things straight was the only way he knew to give her some of the splendid feeling he had so guiltily more of.

He went out again where Chris was sawing wood. How could Chris *stand* there like that, today. His shoulders moved so patiently, the saw sank with such maddening slowness. Yet because he did, he was somehow wonderful. When a block fell, David would thrust the stick ahead on the saw-horse with such a prodigal surge of helpfulness beyond what the weight of the wood asked for that Chris would have to push it back a little before he made the next cut.

He went back into the house and stood at the table where his mother was mixing doughnuts.

Everything was clean as sunshine. The yellow-shining mixing bowl in the centre of the smooth hardwood bread board; the circles of pure white where the sieve had stood; the measuring cup with the flour-white stain of milk and soda on its sides; and the flat yellow-white rings of the doughnuts themselves lying beside the open-mouthed jug that held the lard, drift-smooth at the centre and crinkled like pie crust along the sides. His mother carried the doughnuts to the stove, flat on her palm, and dropped them one by one into the hot fat. He followed her, watching. They'd sink to the bottom. Then, after a fascinating second of total disappearance, they'd loom dark below the surface, then float all at once, brown and hissing all over. It had never been like this, watching her make doughnuts before.

He went into the pantry and smelled the fruit cakes that lay on the inverted pans they'd been cooked in. He opened the bag of nuts and rolled one in his palm; then put it back. He put his hand deep down into the bag and rolled all the nuts through his fingers: the smooth hazelnuts that the hammer would split so precisely: the crinkled walnuts with the lung-shaped kernels so fragile that if he got one out all in one piece he'd give it to Anna: the flat black butternuts whose meat clove so tightly to the shell that if you ever got one out whole you saved it to the very last.

Then he leaned over and smelled the bag of oranges. He didn't touch it. He closed his eyes and smelled it only. The sharp, sweet, reminding, fulfilling, smell of the oranges was so incarnate of to-morrow it was delight almost to sinfulness.

He went out and sat beside Anna. She was on her knees before the lounge, turning the pages of the catalogue. They played "Which Do You Like the Best?" with the coloured pages. Anna would point to the incredibly beaded silk dress that the girl wore standing in a great archway with the sunlight streaming across it, as her choice. He'd say, "Oh, I do, too." And as his hand touched Anna's small reaching hand and as he looked at her small reaching face, he almost cried with the knowing that some Christmas Day, when he had all that money he was going to have, he'd remember every single thing that Anna had liked the best. She'd find every one of them beneath the tree when she got up in the morning.

He went out where his father was preparing the base for the

tree. All the work-distraction was gone from his father today, and David knew that even if so few pieces of board were to be found as to defeat anyone else, his father would still be able to fix something that was perfect.

Joseph lay one crosspiece in the groove of the other. He said to David, "Think you could hold her just like that, son, till I drive the nails?"

"Oh yes," David said, "yes." He strove with such intense willingness to hold them so exactly that every bit of his strength and mind was soaked up. He touched the axe that would cut the tree. The bright cold touch of it shone straight through him.

He ran in to tell Anna it was almost time. He waited for her to button her gaiters. He was taut almost to pallor when Joseph stepped from the shop door, crooked the axe handle under one arm, and spat on the blade for one final touch of the whetstone.

"Chris," he called, "we're *goin!*"

"All right," Chris said. "You go on. I guess I'll finish the wood."

How *could* Chris stay here? How could anyone *wait* anywhere today? It was almost impossible to be still even in the place where the thing was going on.

Joseph walked straight toward the dark spruce mountain. David and Anna would fall behind, as they made imprints of their supine bodies in the snow; then run to catch up. They would rush ahead, to simulate rabbit tracks with their mittens—the palms for the parallel prints of the two back feet, the thumb the single print where the front feet struck together; then stand and wait. Their thoughts orbited the thought of the tree in the same way their bodies orbited Joseph's.

"Anna, if anyone walked right through the mountain, weeks and weeks, I wonder where he'd come out . . . "

"Dave, hold your eyes almost shut, it looks like water . . . "

"There's one, there's one . . . " But when they came to it the branches on the far side were uneven.

Joseph himself stopped to examine a tree.

"Father, the best ones are way back, ain't they?" David said quickly. This *was* a good tree, but it wouldn't be any fun if they found the perfect tree almost at once.

"There's one . . . " But it was a cat spruce.

"There's one . . . " But the spike at the top was crooked.

"There's one, Father . . . " But a squirrel's nest of brown growth spoiled the middle limbs.

Joseph found the perfect fir, just short of the mountain. The children had missed it, though their tracks were all about. He went to it from the road, straight as a die. The bottom limbs were ragged, but those could be cut off; and above them, the circlets of the upward-angling branches were perfect. The trunk was straight and round. The green of the needles was dark and rich, right to the soft-breathing tip.

"How about this one?" Joseph said.

The children said nothing, looking at the lower limbs.

"From here up," Joseph said. He nicked the bark with his axe.

"Yes, oh yes," they cried then. "That's the best tree anyone could find, ain't it, Father?" The ridiculous momentary doubt of their father's judgement made them more joyous than ever.

They fell silent as Joseph tramped the snow about the base of the tree, to chop it. David made out he was shaking snow from his mitten. He took off Anna's mitten too, pretending to see if there was any snow in hers. He stood there holding her mitten-warmed hand, not saying anything, and watched his father strike the first shivering blow.

The tree made a sort of sigh as it swept through the soft air and touched the soft snow. Then the moment broke. The children came close and touched the green limbs. They thrust their faces between them—into the dark green silence. They smelled the dark green, cosy, exciting smell of the whole day in the balsam blisters on the trunk.

Joseph stood and waited: the good kind of waiting, with no older-hurry in him. Then he lifted the tree to his shoulders, both arms spread out to steady it at either end.

The twins walked close behind him. They let the swaying branches touch their faces. They walked straight now, because the first cast of dusk had begun to spread from the mountain. The first dusk-stiffening of the snow and a shadow of the first night-wonder were beginning. Now the things of the day fell behind them; because all that part of the day which could be kept warm and near was in the tree, and they were taking the tree home, into the house, where all the warm things of afterdark belonged.

Anna whispered to David, "I got somethin' for you, Dave."

And he whispered, "I got somethin' for you, too."

"What?"

"Oh, I can't tell."

Then they guessed. Each guess was made deliberately small, so there'd be no chance that the other would be hurt by knowing that his present was less than the vision of it. Each of them felt that whatever they had for each other all their lives would have something of the magic, close-binding smell of the fir boughs somewhere in it, like the presents for each other of no other two people in the world.

Martha had huddled the furniture in the dining room together, to clear a corner for the tree.

"Aw, Mother," David said, "you said you'd wait!"

His mother laughed. "I just moved the sofa and mats a little," she said. "I didn't touch the trimmings. Do you think it's too late to put them up before supper?"

"No," David cried, "no. I'm not a bit hungry."

"I suppose if supper's late it'll make you late with your chores, won't it?" she said to Joseph.

"Well," Joseph said, "I suppose I *could* do em before supper." He hesitated. "Or do you want me to help you with the trimmin'?"

"Oh, yes," David said. "Help us."

He wanted everyone to be in on it. Especially his father. It was wonderful when his father helped them with something that wasn't work, *inside* the house.

David fanned open the great accordion-folding bell (because of one little flaw his mother had got it—it didn't seem possible—for only a quarter). He tied the two smaller bells on the hooks of the blinds. Then he and his father and Chris took off their boots. They stood on chairs in their stocking feet and hung the hemlock garlands Ellen had made; around the casings and from the four ceiling corners of the room to a juncture at its centre, where the great bell was to be suspended.

Someone would say, "Pass the scissors?" and David would say, "*Sure*," beating with gladness to do them any small favours. Martha would stand back and say, "A little lower on that side," and they'd say, "Like that? Like that? More still?" all full of that wonderful patience to make it perfect. Everyone would laugh when someone slipped off a chair. His father would say, "Why wouldn't some red berries look good in there?" and to hear his *father* say a thing like that filled the room with something really splendid. Sometimes he'd step on Anna's toe as they busied back and forth. He'd say, "Oh, Anna, did that hurt?" and she'd laugh and say, "No, it didn't hurt." He'd say, "Are you *sure*?" and just that would be wonderful.

The dusk thickened and the smell of the hemlock grew soft as lamplight in the room. The trimming was done and the pieces swept up and put into the stove.

Then Joseph brought in the tree, backward through the door so the limbs wouldn't break. No one spoke as he stood it in the space in the corner. It just came to the ceiling. It was perfect. Suddenly the room was whole. Its heart began to beat.

They ate in the dining room that night. David smelled the roast spare ribs that had been kept frozen in the shop. He felt now how hungry he'd been all the time.

The room was snug with the bunching of the furniture and the little splendour of eating there on a weekday. And when Martha held the match to the lamp wick, all at once the yellow lamplight soft-shadowed their faces (with the blood running warm in them after being out in the cold) like a flood and gathered the room all in from outside the windows. It touched the tree and the hemlock and the great red bell with the flaw no one could even notice, like a soft breath added to the beating of the room's heart: went out and came back with a kind of smile. The smell of the tree grew suddenly and the memory of the smell of the oranges and the feel of the nuts. In that instant suddenly, ecstatically, burstingly, buoyantly, enclosingly, sharply, safely, stingingly, watchfully, batedly, mountingly, softly, ever so softly, it was Christmas Eve.

# FOCUSSING

1. There are many different kinds of families: single-parent families, families with many children or one, foster families, blended families, adoptive families, nuclear families, and extended families. Ask your school librarian or family studies teacher to help you find definitions of the different types of families. Share your definitions in a small group and draw a diagram of each type of family, with a sentence stating what is unique about that kind of family. Post the diagrams on the bulletin board.

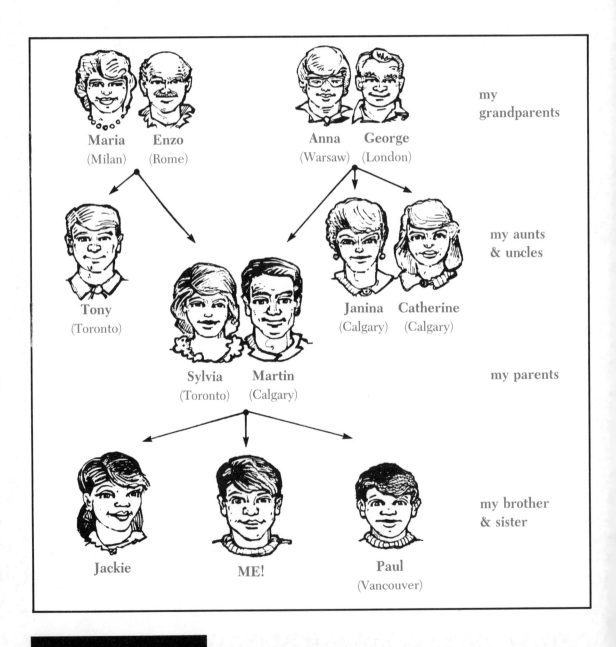

**Maria** (Milan)  **Enzo** (Rome)     **Anna** (Warsaw)  **George** (London)     my grandparents

**Tony** (Toronto)     **Janina** (Calgary)  **Catherine** (Calgary)     my aunts & uncles

**Sylvia** (Toronto)  **Martin** (Calgary)     my parents

**Jackie**   **ME!**   **Paul** (Vancouver)     my brother & sister

2. Ask your mother, father, or guardian to help you do a "family tree." Include your grandparents, aunts, uncles, parents, cousins, sisters, brothers (and nieces and nephews, if you have any). Make sure you indicate their names and places of birth. Share your family tree with others in your class and determine

a) whose grandparents were born the farthest from where you live; and

b) how many males and females there are in each family. Post the family trees on the bulletin board. Perhaps you could distribute copies of your family tree among the members of your family.

3. a) Give the following quiz to your father, mother, or guardian, and then discuss the answers with him or her. In your journal, write about what you think your parent or guardian learned about you. Share your journal entry with a partner.

---

**How Well Do You Know Your Children?**
**by Betsy Lammerding**
1. Who is your child's best friend?
2. What colour would he/she like his/her room to be?
3. Who is your child's greatest hero?
4. What embarrasses him/her most?
5. What is his/her biggest fear?
6. In gym, would your child rather play basketball, do exercises, or run relays?
7. What is his/her favourite kind of music?
8. What person outside the family has most influenced your child's life?
9. What are his/her favourite and least favourite subjects in school?
10. Of what accomplishment is your child proudest?
11. What is your child's biggest complaint about the family?
12. What is his/her favourite television show?
13. What sport does your child most enjoy?
14. If you could buy your child anything in the world, what would be his/her first choice?
15. Who is your child's favourite teacher?
16. What really makes your child angry?
17. Does your child feel liked by children at school?
18. What would your child like to do when he/she grows up?
19. What has been the biggest disappointment in your child's life this year?

20. Does your child feel too small or too big for his/her age?
21. What gift from you does your child cherish most?
22. What would your child's choice be for a vacation: a camping trip, a visit to a big city, or a boat trip.
23. Which of these chores does your child dislike most: drying dishes, cleaning his/her room, or taking out the trash?
24. What non-school book has your child most recently read?
25. What is his/her favourite family occasion?
26. What foods does your child like or dislike most?
27. What nicknames is your child called at school?
28. When does your child prefer to do homework: right after school, after supper, before bed, or in the morning before school?
29. Which would your child prefer to have as a pet: a cat, dog, bird, or fish?
30. What is your child's most prized possession?

If you score between 25–30, you are a top-notch observer and listen well to the likes and needs of your children. Scoring between 14–25 means you know quite a bit about your children, but could improve. Between 0–14 means you and the children haven't been communicating as much as you could.

If you're unhappy with your score, it's never too late to take time to know your children—and let them know you, too.

3. b) Work with your partner to write a similar quiz, called "How Well Do You Know Your Parent(s) or Guardian?" Make up ten questions that are different from the ones in the quiz above. If you compose the quiz on a word processor, it will be easy to print out several identical copies. Do the quiz yourself, then administer it to two friends of yours who are in other classes. You and your friends will have to check with your guardian, mother, or father to see if you answered correctly. Compare your score with the scores of your two friends.

4. Think of something special that happened between you and a sister or brother (or a cousin or friend if you are an only child). Tell your story to two partners, and then listen to their stories.

# FROM MOTHER . . . WITH LOVE

*by Zoa Sherburne*

I T BEGAN like any other Saturday, with Minta lying
in bed an extra hour. Breakfast was always lazy and
unhurried on Saturday mornings. The three of them
in the breakfast room—Minta's father engrossed in
his paper; her mother flying around in a gayly coloured housecoat, mixing waffles and frying bacon; Minta
setting the table.

They talked, the casual happy talk of people who love
each other and don't have to make conversation. About
neighbourhood doings . . . about items in the paper . . .
about the clothes Minta would need when she went to
school in a couple of weeks.

It was after the dishes were finished that Minta's father
asked her if she would like to go down to the beach for a
little while. They started walking up the beach slowly, not
toward the group of people digging clams, but in the other
direction, toward the jagged pile of rocks that jutted out
into the bay.

She heard a strange voice, her own voice.

"I thought . . . I thought you wanted to talk to me about
school, but it isn't that, is it, Father?"

His fingers tightened around hers. "In a way it is . . .
about school."

And then, before the feeling of relief could erase the
fear, he went on. "I went to see Dr. Morton last week,
Minta. I've been seeing him pretty regularly these last few
months."

She flashed a quick frightened look up at him. "You aren't
ill?"

"No." He sighed and it was a heartbreaking sound. "No.
It isn't me. It's your mother."

She broke off and stopped walking and her hand was
steady on his arm. "Tell me," she said quietly.

The look was back in his eyes again but this time Minta
scarcely noticed it. She was aware only of his words, the
dreadful echoing finality of his words.

Her mother was going to die.

Her mother.

To die, the doctor said. Three months, perhaps less . . .

Her mother who was scatterbrained and more fun than anyone else in the world. Her mother who could be counted on to announce in the spring, that she was going to do her Christmas shopping early this year, and then would leave everything until the week before Christmas.

She wasn't ever sick—except for the headaches and the operation last year which she had laughingly dismissed as a rest cure.

"I shouldn't have told you." Her father was speaking in a voice that Minta had never heard from him before.

"Of course you had to tell me." she said steadily. "Of course I had to know." And then—"Three months, but Dad, that's Christmas."

He took her hand and tucked it under his arm and they started walking again.

Just before they reached home he reached over and took her hand in a tight hurting grip.

"We can't tell her, Minta. The doctor left it up to me and I said not to tell her. We have to let her have this last time . . . this last little time . . . without that hanging over her. We have to go on as if everything were exactly the same."

It seemed impossible that life could go on exactly as before but Minta and her father knew that they must try.

The small private world peopled by the three of them was kept as snug and warm and happy as though no shadow had touched them.

They watched television and argued good-naturedly about the programs. Minta's friends came and went and there was the usual round of parties and dances and games. Her father continued to bowl two evenings a week and her mother became involved in various pre-holiday pursuits.

"I really must get at my Christmas shopping," she mentioned the day she was wrapping trick-or-treat candy for Halloween.

Minta shook her head and sighed gustily.

Her mother started this "I must-get-at-my-Christmas-shopping" routine every spring, but she never actually got around to it until two or three days before Christmas.

It was amazing that Minta could laugh and say, "Oh, you . . . " the way she did year after year.

That night she wakened in the chilly darkness of her room and began to cry softly, her head buried in the curve of her arm. At first it helped, loosening the tight bands about her heart, washing away the fear and the loneliness, but when she tried to stop she found that she couldn't. Great wracking sobs shook her until she could no longer smother them against her pillow. And then the light was on and her mother was there bending over her, her face concerned, her voice soothing.

"Darling, what is it? Wake up, baby, you're having a bad dream."

"No . . . no, it isn't a dream," Minta choked. "It's true . . . it's true."

The thin hand kept smoothing back her tumbled hair and her mother went on talking in the tone she had always used to comfort a much smaller Minta.

She was aware that her father had come to the doorway. He said nothing, just stood there watching them while Minta's sobs diminished into hiccupy sighs.

Her mother pulled the blanket up over Minta's shoulder and gave her a little spank. "The idea! Gremlins, at your age," she said reprovingly. "Want me to leave the light on in case your spook comes back?"

Minta shook her head, blinking against the tears that crowded against her eyelids, even managing a smile.

She never cried again.

Not even when the ambulance came a week later to take her mother to the hospital. Not even when she was standing beside her mother's high white hospital bed, holding her hand tightly, forcing herself to chatter of inconsequential things.

"Be sure that your father takes his vitamin pills, won't you, Minta? He's so careless unless I'm there to keep an eye on him."

"I'll watch him like a beagle," Minta promised lightly. "Now you behave yourself and get out of here in a hurry, you hear?"

Not even at the funeral . . .

The friends and relatives came and went and it was as if she stood on the sidelines watching the Minta who talked with them and answered their questions. As if her heart were encased in a shell that kept it from breaking.

She went to school and came home afterwards to the empty house. She tried to do the things her mother had done but even with the help of well-meaning friends and neighbours it was hard. She tried not to hate the people who urged her to cry.

"You'll feel better, dear," her Aunt Grace had insisted and then had lifted her handkerchief to her eyes and walked away when Minta had only stared at her with chilling indifference.

She overheard people talking about her mother.

"She never knew, did she?" they asked.

And always Minta's father answered, "No, she never knew. Even at the very last, when she was waiting for the ambulance to come she looked around the bedroom and said, 'I must get these curtains done up before Christmas.' "

One night Minta's father came to the door of her room where she was studying.

"I wonder if you'd like to go through those clothes before your Aunt Grace takes them to the church bazaar," he began haltingly. And then when she looked up at him, not understanding, he went on gently, "Your mother's clothes. We thought someone might as well get some good out of them."

She stood up and closed the book and went past him without another word, but she closed the door behind her when she went into her mother's room.

At the very back of the closet were the two pieces of matched luggage that had been her mother's last birthday gift from her father. They were heavy when she tried to move them—too heavy.

She brought them out into the room and put them side by side on her mother's bed. Her breath caught in her throat when she opened them.

Dozens and dozens of boxes, all tied with bright red ribbon, the gift tags written out in her mother's careful script. Gayly coloured Christmas stickers, sprigs of holly.

To Minta from Mother and Dad . . . to Grace from Mary . . . to John from Mary . . . to the Kelly Gremlins from Aunt Mary . . . to Uncle Art from the Hawley family . . .

"So you knew," Minta whispered the word. "You knew all the time."

She looked down in surprise as a hot tear dropped on her hand and she dashed it away almost impatiently.

She picked up another package and read the tag. To Minta from Mother . . . with love.

She put all the other packages back in the suitcase and carried the cases back into the closet.

Poor Dad, she thought.

"She never knew," she could hear him saying. "Not even at the last."

Minta opened the box beside the bed and took out a sweater and pale green slip.

She brushed the tears away and went down the stairs and out into the cheerless living room.

"I'd like to keep these things, Dad," she said in her most matter-of-fact voice, and she showed him the sweater and slip. "The slip is a little big but I'll grow into it. It . . . it looks like her, I think."

She went around the room, snapping on the lamps, turning on the television that had been silent for so long. She was aware that his eyes followed her, that he could hardly avoid noticing the tear stains on her cheeks.

"I think I'll have an apple," she said. "Want one?"

He nodded. "Sure. Bring me one as long as you're making the trip."

It was natural. It was almost like old times, except that the blue chair by the fireplace was vacant.

She went out into the kitchen hurriedly.

"I'll tell him that I pestered Mother to do her shopping early this year," she told herself as she got the apples from the refrigerator. "I'll tell him that it was my idea. She wanted him to believe that she didn't know."

The vitamin pills were pushed back on a shelf. She took them out of the refrigerator and put them on the window sill where she would be sure to see them in the morning.

When she came back into the living room she noticed that a light in a Christmas wreath was winking on and off in the Kellys' window across the street.

"I guess we should start thinking about Christmas, Dad." She tossed him an apple as she spoke and he caught it deftly.

She hesitated for just a moment and then walked over and sat down in the blue chair by the fire, as if she belonged there, and looked across at her father, and smiled.

# CLOSE UP

1. Discuss with a partner Minta's feelings about her mother and her mother's death. Imagine that you are Minta and write an entry in your diary for one of the following days:
   - the day your father told you about your mother's illness;
   - the day of your mother's funeral; or
   - the day you discovered the Christmas packages.

   Try to describe the emotions Minta would feel. Share your diary entry with a partner, who will help you add to it and then will proofread your final copy for you.

2. Work with a partner to complete the following:
   a) Minta's father kept telling people her mother never knew she was dying because _____
   b) We know that Minta's mother knew she was dying because _____
   c) Minta's mother did not want her husband to know she knew the truth because _____

   Compare your responses to those of another pair of students.

# WIDE ANGLE

1. Write in your journal about an experience of yours or of someone close to you that is similar to Minta's loss of her mother. The loss may involve a friend or close relative or perhaps even a parent or brother or sister. If you wish to, share your piece of writing with a class-mate or your teacher.

2. "Doctors have an obligation to tell their patients of all the details and dangers of an illness."
   a) In a small group, talk over the statement and choose a position. Write an argument for the side you choose, and challenge a group that holds the opposite view to a debate.
   b) After the debate, hold a vote in class to see whether most people think Dr. Morton was right or wrong in telling Minta's father, rather than Minta's mother, about the disease. Discuss whether he would have told Minta's mother first if it had been Minta's father who was going to die.
   c) Have two people from the class explain the story to a doctor and ask for her or his opinion about Dr. Morton's conduct. The students should report to the class what they find.

# THE TWINS
### by Henry S. Leigh

In form and feature, face and limb,
  I grew so like my brother,
That folks got taking me for him,
  And each for one another.
It puzzled all our kith and kin,
  It reached a fearful pitch;
For one of us was born a twin,
  Yet not a soul knew which.

One day, to make the matter worse,
  Before our names were fixed,
As we were being washed by nurse,
  We got completely mixed;
And thus, you see, by fate's decree,
  Or rather nurse's whim,
My brother John got christened me,
  And I got christened him.

This fatal likeness even dogged
  My footsteps when at school,
And I was always getting flogged,
  For John turned out a fool.
I put this question, fruitlessly,
  To everyone I knew,
"What would you do, if you were me,
  To prove that you were you?"

Our close resemblance turned the tide
  Of my domestic life,
For somehow, my intended bride
  Became my brother's wife.
In fact, year after year the same
  Absurd mistakes went on,
And when I died, the neighbours came
  And buried brother John.

# CLOSE UP

1. Describe the ways in which the twins got mixed up, using a separate sentence for each confusion. Compare your sentences with a partner's, and make any revisions that can improve your work.

# WIDE ANGLE

1. Working with a partner, write a short story about identical twins who switch roles to play a trick on their friends, their teachers, their parents, or their dates. You and your partner may want to share a word processor to write your story. You can revise your work together on screen, using the computer to make changes neatly.

## SISTER
### by Carol Shields

Curious
the way our mother's
gestures survive
in us.

When she was alive
we never noticed
but now in the dark
opening up
since her sudden
leaving, we are more aware.

A thousand miles away in
a similar kitchen
you pause
to lift a coffee cup.

And here
my smaller identical wrist
traces the same arc,
precise in mid-morning air,

linking us together,
reminding us
exactly who she was,
who we are.

# RÉGINE
## by Sylvia Tyson

Sister Régine was the pretty one
She never was lonely for long
And I was poor Ellen the plain one
Who never did anything wrong

Our mother died when we were both young
And I learned to cook and clean
Father died slowly of cancer and care
And always he talked of Régine

Chorus:
Régine walks like a Queen
Loves like a child, lives in a dream
Régine what have you done
You took all the love and left me with none

Régine left the farm at seventeen
She had children with two different men
And as she bore them she brought them to me
And I was a mother to them

I was near thirty when I married Carl
And I know that he married the land
But he's steady and he's kind and he's good to the girls
And I know the place needed a man

Chorus.

My sister's two daughters are like night and day
And my heart is caught in between
For one of them's pretty and one of them's plain
And the pretty one looks like Régine

For sister Régine was the pretty one
Who carried herself like a queen
And I am poor Ellen the plain one
Who wishes that she were Régine

# CLOSE UP

1. "Sister" and "Régine" are both about two sisters. With a partner, talk about the sisters in "Régine," finding lines in the poem that hint at their relationship. Do the same with the sisters in "Sister." Compare the relationships in both poems, and write a sentence or two that summarizes what you talked about.

# WIDE ANGLE

1. Write down in point form how you resemble (or don't resemble) other members of your family. Ask someone older than you in your family to answer the same question about you. Compare lists to see if there are similarities in viewpoints. Share with three or four partners the results of your investigation.
2. In both poems, family patterns are repeated from one generation to the next. Write another verse to "Régine" in which one of Régine's daughters talks about her experiences. Before you write, decide whether the same pattern will happen all over again, or whether things will change.
3. Working with a partner, write a script that shows Ellen and Régine meeting and confiding what they admire and dislike about each other.

*from*

# YOU'RE A GOOD MAN, CHARLIE BROWN

*by Clark Gesner*

## CHARACTERS

LUCY
LINUS

**LUCY:** Oh, Linus, I'm glad you're here. I'm conducting a survey and there are a few questions I'd like to ask you.

**LINUS:** Sure, go ahead.

**LUCY:** The first question is: on a scale of zero to one hundred, with a standard of fifty as average, seventy-five as above average and ninety as exceptional, where would you rate me with regards to crabbiness?

**LINUS** (*Slowly turns his head to look at her, then turns back to the TV*): You're my big sister.

**LUCY:** That's not the question.

**LINUS:** No, but that's the answer.

**LUCY:** Come on, Linus, answer the question.

**LINUS** (*Getting up and facing Lucy*): Look, Lucy, I know very well that if I give any sort of honest answer to that question you're going to slug me.

**LUCY:** Linus. A survey that is not based on honest answers is like a house that is built on a foundation of sand. Would I be spending my time to conduct this survey if I didn't expect complete candour in all the responses? I promise not to slug you. Now what number would you give me as your crabbiness rating?

**LINUS** (*After a few moments of interior struggle*): Ninety-five.

(*Lucy sends a straight jab to his jaw which lays him out flat.*)

**LUCY:** No decent person could be expected to keep her word with a rating over ninety.

YOU'RE A GOOD MAN, CHARLIE BROWN. Reprinted by permission of

# FOR BETTER OR FOR WORSE

*by Lynn Johnston*

# CLOSE UP

1. Transform the script about Lucy and Linus into a comic strip. (You may wish to look at some *Peanuts* comics featuring Lucy and Linus to see how Charles Schulz, creator and cartoonist of *Peanuts*, draws them.)
2. With a partner, look closely at the *For Better or For Worse* comic. Note ways in which the cartoonist expresses what is going on. (For example, in the first frame, the exclamation marks show that the brother and sister are having an argument.) Trade notes among groups and compare observations.

# WIDE ANGLE

1. In your reading of *Peanuts* comics in Close Up #1, you may have noticed that Lucy bullies or bothers not only her brother, but also every other character in her neighbourhood. Continue the script so that Linus finally gets even, with the help of Charlie Brown, Snoopy, and other friends. Role-play the scene for the class.
2. The scene portrayed in *For Better or For Worse* is familiar to everyone who has watched young brothers and sisters playing together. Usually there is a parent, guardian, or some other adult nearby to break up children's battles. Imagine what would happen if children had to keep things under control when adults quarrel childishly over their possessions. In a small group, talk about possible situations where that could happen and write a description of one of them. Read your work aloud for another group, and work with them to brainstorm an amusing title.

# THE FIRST DAY OF SCHOOL

*by R.V. Cassill*

THIRTEEN bubbles floated in the milk. Their pearl transparent hemispheres gleamed like souvenirs of the summer days just past, rich with blue reflections of the sky and of shadowy greens. John Hawkins jabbed the bubble closest to him with his spoon, and it disappeared without a ripple. On the white surface there was no mark of where it had been.

"Stop tooling that oatmeal and eat it," his mother said. She glanced meaningfully at the clock on the varnished cupboard. She nodded a heavy, emphatic affirmation that now the clock was boss. Summer was over, when the gracious oncoming of morning light and the stir of early breezes promised that time was a luxury.

"Audrey's not even down yet," he said.

"Audrey'll be down."

"You think she's taking longer to dress because she wants to look nice today?"

"She likes to look *neat*."

"What I was thinking," he said slowly, "was that maybe she didn't feel like going today. Didn't feel *exactly* like it."

"Of course she'll go."

"I meant she might not want to go until tomorrow, maybe. Until we see what happens."

"Nothing's going to happen," his mother said.

"I know there isn't. But what if it did?" Again John swirled the tip of his spoon in the milk. It was like writing on a surface that would keep no mark.

"Eat and be quiet. Audrey's coming, so let's stop this here kind of talk."

He heard the tap of heels on the stairs, and his sister came down into the kitchen. She looked fresh and cool in her white dress. Her lids looked heavy. She must have slept all right—and for this John felt both envy and a faint resentment. He had not really slept since midnight. The heavy traffic in town, the long wail of horns as somebody raced in on the U.S. highway holding the horn button down, and the restless murmur, like the sound of a celebration down in the courthouse square, had kept him awake after that. Each time a car had passed their house his breath had gone tight and sluggish. It was better to stay awake and ready, he had told himself, than to be caught asleep.

"Daddy gone?" Audrey asked softly as she took her place across the table from her brother.

"He's been gone an hour," their mother answered. "*You* know what time he has to be at the mine."

"She means, did he go to work today?" John said. His voice had risen impatiently. He met his mother's stout gaze in a staring contest, trying to make her admit by at least some flicker of expression that today was different from any other day. "I thought he might be down at Reverend Specker's," John said. "Cal's father and Vonnie's and some of the others are going to be there to wait and see."

Maybe his mother smiled then. If so, the smile was so faint that he could not be sure. "You know your father isn't much of a hand for waiting," she said. "Eat. It's a quarter past eight."

As he spooned the warm oatmeal into his mouth he heard the rain crow calling again from the trees beyond the railroad embankment. He had heard it since the first light came before dawn, and he had thought, Maybe the bird knows it's going to rain, after all. He hoped it would. *They won't come out in the rain,* he had thought. Not so many of them, at least. He could wear a raincoat. A raincoat might help him feel more protected on the walk to school. It would be a sort of disguise, at least.

But since dawn the sun had lain across the green Kentucky trees and the roofs of town like a clean, hard fire. The sky was as clear as fresh-washed window glass. The rain crow was wrong about the weather. And still, John thought, its lamenting, repeated call must mean something.

His mother and Audrey were talking about the groceries she was to bring when she came home from school at lunch time. A five-pound bag of sugar, a fresh pineapple, a pound of butter. . . .

"Listen!" John said. Downtown the sound of a siren had begun. A volley of automobile horns broke around it as if they meant to drown it out. "*Listen* to them."

"It's only the National Guard, I expect," his mother said calmly. "They came in early this morning before light. And it may be some foolish kids honking at them, the way they would. Audrey, if Henry doesn't have a good-looking roast, why then let it go, and I'll walk out to Weaver's this afternoon and get one there. I wanted to have something a little bit special for our dinner tonight."

So . . . John thought . . . she wasn't asleep last night

either. Someone had come stealthily to the house to bring his parents word about the National Guard. That meant they knew about the others who had come into town, too. Maybe all through the night there had been a swift passage of messengers through the neighbourhood and a whispering of information that his mother meant to keep from him. Your folks told you, he reflected bitterly, that nothing is better than knowing. Knowing whatever there is in this world to be known. That was why you had to be one of the half dozen kids out of some nine hundred blacks of school age who were going today to start classes at Joseph P. Gilmore High instead of Webster. Knowing and learning the truth were worth so much they said—and then left it to the hooting rain crow to tell you that things were worse than everybody had hoped.

Something had gone wrong, bad enough wrong so the National Guard had to be called out.

"It's eight twenty-five," his mother said. "Did you get that snap sewed on right, Audrey?" As her experienced fingers examined the shoulder of Audrey's dress they lingered a moment in an involuntary, sheltering caress. "It's all arranged," she told her children, "how you'll walk down to the Baptist Church and meet the others there. You know there'll be Reverend Chader, Reverend Smith, and Mr. Hall to go with you. It may be that the white ministers will go with you, or they may be waiting at school. We don't know. But now you be sure, don't you go farther than the Baptist Church alone." Carefully she lifted her hand clear of Audrey's shoulder. John thought, Why doesn't she hug her if that's what she wants to do?

He pushed away from the table and went out on the front porch. The dazzling sunlight lay shadowless on the street that swept down toward the Baptist Church at the edge of the black section. The street seemed awfully long this morning, the way it had looked when he was little. A chicken was clucking contentedly behind their neighbour's house, feeling the warmth, settling itself into the sun-warmed dust. Lucky chicken.

He blinked at the sun's glare on the concrete steps leading down from the porch. He remembered something else from the time he was little. Once he had kicked Audrey's doll buggy down these same steps. He had done it out of meanness—for some silly reason he had been mad at her. But as soon as the buggy had started to bump down, he had understood how terrible it was not to be able to run after it and stop it. It had gathered speed at each step and when it hit the sidewalk it had spilled over. Audrey's doll had smashed into sharp little pieces on the sidewalk below.

His mother had come out of the house to find him crying harder than Audrey. "Now you know that when something gets out of your hands it is in the Devil's hands," his mother had explained to him. Did she expect him to forget—now—that that was always the way things went to smash when they got out of hand? Again he heard the siren and the hooting, mocking horns from the centre of town. Didn't his mother think *they* could get out of hand?

He closed his eyes and seemed to see something like a doll buggy bump down long steps like those at Joseph P. Gilmore High, and it seemed to him that it was not a doll that was riding down to be smashed.

He made up his mind then. He would go today, because he had said he would. Therefore he had to. But he wouldn't go unless Audrey stayed home. That was going to be his condition. His bargaining looked perfect. He would trade them one for one.

His mother and Audrey came together onto the porch. His mother said, "My stars, I forgot to give you the money for the groceries." She let the screen door bang as she went swiftly back into the house.

As soon as they were alone, he took Audrey's bare arm in his hand and pinched hard. "You gotta stay home," he whispered. "Don't you know there's thousands of people down there? Didn't you hear them coming in all night long? You slept, didn't you? All right. You can hear them now. Tell her you're sick. She won't expect you to go if you're sick. I'll knock you down, I'll smash you if you don't tell her that." He bared his teeth and twisted his nails into the skin of her arm. "Hear them horns," he hissed.

He forced her halfway to her knees with the strength of his fear and rage. They swayed there, locked for a minute. Her knee dropped to the porch floor. She lowered her eyes. He thought he had won.

But she was saying something and in spite of himself he listened to her almost whispered refusal. "Don't you know anything? Don't you know it's harder for them than us? Don't you know Daddy didn't go to the mine this morning? They laid him off on account of us. They told him not to come if we went to school."

Uncertainly he relaxed his grip. "How do you know all that?"

"I listen," she said. Her eyes lit with a sudden spark that seemed to come from their absolute brown depths. "But I don't let on all I know the way you do. I'm not a . . . . " Her last word sunk so low that he could not exactly hear it. But if his ear missed it, his understanding caught it. He knew she had said "coward."

He let her get up then. She was standing beside him, serene and prim when their mother came out on the porch again.

"Here, child," their mother said to Audrey, counting the dollar bills into her hand. "There's six, and I guess it will be all right if you have some left if you and Brother get yourselves a cone to lick on the way home."

John was not looking at his sister then. He was already turning to face the shadowless street, but he heard the unmistakable poised amusement of her voice when she said, "Ma, don't you know we're a little too old for that?"

"Yes, you are," their mother said. "Seems I had forgotten that."

They were too old to take each other's hand, either, as they went down the steps of their home and into the street. As they turned to the right, facing the sun, they heard the chattering of a tank's tread on the pavement by the school. A voice too distant to be understood bawled a military command. There were horns again and a crescendo of boos.

Behind them they heard their mother call something. It was lost in the general racket.

"What?" John called back to her. "What?"

She had followed them out as far as the sidewalk, but not past the gate. As they hesitated to listen, she put her hands to either side of her mouth and called to them the words she had so often used when she let them go away from home.

"Behave yourselves," she said.

# CLOSE UP

1. "The First Day of School" focuses on John's fears about going to a new school. Working with a partner, make a list of the ways John shows his fears. Write two or three sentences that describe what John most fears.

2. "I wanted to have something a little bit special for our dinner tonight because . . . " In the mother's voice, finish the statement in a way that would explain to an outsider why today is so significant for your family.

3. You are the director of a movie or video version of "The First Day of School." Write a one-paragraph memo to the actor who will play the mother, describing the feelings and attitudes she should try to portray. Do the same for the actors who will play Audrey and John. Start by making a list with a partner of the things each person must be thinking about in this situation. Below is the format for a memo:

> **To:** Genevieve
> **From:** Tina
> **Subject:** Audrey's Character
>
> **When you play Audrey you might want to consider . . .**

If you compile your list on a word processor, you can transform your notes into sentences and then redraft your sentences in the memo format without having to write things over and over by hand.

4. Near the end of the story, John grabs his sister's arm and tries to hurt her. In your own words, summarize the conflict between John and Audrey and explain why the conflict ends. You might write down your summary or simply tell it to a partner.

# WIDE ANGLE

1. Ask your history teacher or librarian to help you locate some information on the integration of black children in the schools of the southern United States. Write a newspaper report about one particular incident. Read your story aloud for a partner and listen to his or her story.

2. In a small group, brainstorm all the possible events that could occur as John and Audrey set off for school. Choose a conclusion to the story from the possibilities you have discussed, and draw a storyboard that captures the events of this selection scene by scene. You may wish to extend your illustrations to include Audrey and John's return home that evening.

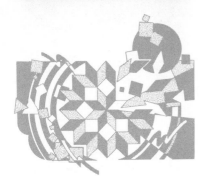

# KALEIDOSCOPE

1. Write a memoir about one or more of the following:
   - what I admire most about my family, and what bothers me most about my family;
   - a typical day in my family;
   - mealtime in my family;
   - our happiest family times;
   - what the people I live with mean to me;
   - a family I admire.

Watch three television programs that feature families and complete the following chart. A sample entry has been provided:

| Program | Main Characters | Occupations | Kind of Family | Relationship |
|---------|-----------------|-------------|----------------|--------------|
| *The Cosby Show* | father mother five children | doctor lawyer | nuclear | close, loving |

Compare your chart with those made by four other people and decide
a) which family you like best and why;
b) which family is best at resolving its conflicts and why;
c) which is the most unusual family and why;
d) which families (if any) are like the families you know in your own life;
e) which family you would least like to belong to and why.

Report on your decisions to the class.

3. Work in a group of six. Three members of the group discuss and list the advantages of having brothers and sisters, and three do the same for the disadvantages. Choose a partner from the other group, exchange lists, and see if you can add to what your partner has written. If word processors are used to draft the lists, the groups' list files can be joined together and edited into a master list of advantages and disadvantages.

# WOMAN WITH-OUT FEAR

*by Daniel P. Mannix*

FIRST HEARD of Grace Wiley when Dr. William Mann, former director of the National Zoological Park in Washington, D.C., handed me a picture of a tiny woman with a gigantic king cobra draped over her shoulders like a garden hose. The snake had partly spread his hood and was looking intently into the camera while his mistress stroked his head to quiet him. Dr. Mann told me: "Grace lives in a little house full of poisonous snakes, imported from all over the world. She lets them wander around like cats. There's been more nonsense written about 'snake charming' than nearly any other subject. Grace is probably the only non-Oriental who knows the real secrets of this curious business."

Looking at the picture of that deadly creature, I knew what a famous writer meant when he described a snake as a "running brook of horror." Still, I like snakes and when my wife, Jule, and I moved into our Malibu house, I made it a point to call on Grace Wiley.

She was living near Cypress, outside Los Angeles, in a small three-room cottage surrounded by open fields. Behind the cottage was a big, ramshackle barn where the snakes were kept. Grace was cleaning snake boxes with a hose when I arrived. She was a surprisingly little lady, scarcely over five feet tall, and probably weighed less than a hundred pounds. Although Grace was sixty-four years old, she was as active as a boy and worked with smooth dexterity. When she saw me, she hurriedly picked up the four-foot rattlesnake who had been sunning himself while his box was being cleaned and poured him into his cage. The snake raised his head but made no attempt to strike or even to rattle. I was impressed but not astonished. In captivity, rattlers often grow sluggish and can be handled with comparative impunity.

Grace came forward, drying her hands on her apron. "Oh dear, I meant to get dressed up for you," she said, trying to smooth down her thatch of brown hair. "But I haven't anybody here to help me with the snakes except Mother—and she's eighty-four years old. Don't trip over an alligator," she added as I came forward. I noticed for the first time in the high grass a dozen or so alligators and crocodiles. They ranged from a three-foot Chinese croc to a big Florida 'gator more than twelve feet long. I threaded my way among them without mishap, although several opened their huge jaws to hiss at me.

"They don't mean anything by that, any more than a dog barking," Grace explained fondly. "They're very tame and most of them know their names. Now come in and meet my little family of snakes."

We entered the barn. The walls were lined with cages of all sizes and shapes containing snakes. Grace stopped at each cage, casually lifting the occupant and pointing out his fine points while she stroked and examined him. Grace unquestionably had one of the world's finest collections of reptiles. I watched her handle diamondback rattlesnakes from Texas, vipers from Italy, fer-de-lance from the West Indies, a little Egyptian cobra, and the deadly karait from India.

Then I saw Grace perform a feat I would have believed impossible.

We had stopped in front of a large, glass-fronted cage containing apparently nothing but newspaper. "These little fellows arrived only a short time ago, so they're very wild," explained Grace indulgently. She quietly lifted the paper. Instantly a forest of heads sprang up in the cage. Grace moved the paper slightly. At the movement, the heads seemed to spread and flatten. Then I saw that they were not heads but hoods. I was looking at the world's most deadly creature—the Indian cobra.

Man-eating tigers are said to kill 600 natives a year, but cobras kill 25,000 people a year in India alone. Hunters have been mauled by wounded elephants and lived to tell about it, but no one survives a body bite from a big cobra. I have caught rattlesnakes with a forked stick and my bare hands, but I'm not ashamed to say I jumped back from that cage as though the devil were inside—as indeed he was.

Grace advanced her hand toward the nearest cobra. The snake swayed like a reed in the wind, feinting for the strike. Grace raised her hand above the snake's head, the reptile twisting around to watch her. As the woman slowly lowered her hand, the snake gave that most terrible of all animal noises—the unearthly hiss of a deadly snake. I have seen children laugh with excitement at the roar of a lion, but I have never seen anyone who did not cringe at that cold, uncanny sound. Grace deliberately tried to touch the rigid, quivering hood. The cobra struck at her hand. It missed. Quietly, Grace presented her open palm. The cobra hesitated a split second, his reared body quivering like a plucked banjo string. Then it struck.

I felt sick as I saw its head hit Grace's hand, but the cobra did not bite. It struck with its mouth closed. As rapidly as an expert boxer drumming on a punching bag, the snake struck three times against Grace's palm, always for some incredible reason with its mouth shut. Then Grace slid her open hand over its head and stroked its hood. The snake hissed again and struggled violently under her touch. Grace continued to caress it. Suddenly the snake went limp and its hood began to close. Grace slipped her other hand under the snake's body and lifted it out of the cage. She held the reptile in her arms as though it were a baby. The cobra raised its head to look Grace in the face; its dancing tongue was less than a foot from her mouth. Grace braced her hand against the curve of its body and talked calmly to it until it folded its hood. It curled up in her arms quietly until I made a slight movement; then it instantly reared up again, threatening me.

I had never seen anything to match this performance. Later, Grace opened the cobra's mouth to show me that the fangs were still intact. The yellow venom was slowly oozing over their tips.

If Grace Wiley had wished to make a mystery out of her amazing ability I am certain she could have made a fortune by posing as a woman with supernatural power. There isn't a zoologist alive who could have debunked her. But Grace was a perfectly honest person who was happy to explain in detail exactly how she could handle these terrible creatures. I spent several weeks with her studying her technique and now that I understand it I'm even more impressed than I was before.

When a cobra attacks, it rears straight upward. If you put your elbow on a table, cup your hand to represent the open hood, and sway your forearm back and forth, you have a good idea of the fighting stance of a cobra. Your index finger represents the tiny, mouselike head that does the business. Your range is limited to the length of your forearm. Here is a large part of the secret in handling cobras. With a little practice you can tell a cobra's range to the inch. Also, the blow of a cobra is comparatively slow. A person with steady nerves can jerk away in time to avoid being bitten.

Another important thing to understand in handling a cobra is its method of striking. Its fangs are short and do not fold back. Instead of stabbing, it must actually bite. It grabs its victims and then deliberately chews while the venom runs down into the wound it is making.

When Grace approached a wild cobra, she moved her hand back and forth just outside the snake's range. The cobra would then strike angrily until it became tired. Then it was reluctant to strike again. Grace's next move was to raise her hand over the snake's hood and bring it down slowly. Because of its method of rearing, a cobra cannot strike directly upward, and Grace could actually touch the top of the snake's head. The snake became puzzled and frustrated. It felt that it was fighting an invulnerable opponent who, after all, didn't seem to mean it any harm.

Then came the final touch. Grace would put her open palm toward the snake. At last the cobra was able to hit her. But it had to bite and it could not get a grip on the flat surface of the palm. If it could get a finger or a loose fold of skin it could fasten his teeth in it and start chewing. But its strike is sufficiently slow that Grace could meet each blow with the flat of her palm. At last Grace would be able to get her hand over the snake's head and stroke its hood. This seemed to relax the reptile and from then on Grace could handle it with some degree of confidence.

I don't mean to suggest that this is a cut-and-dried procedure. Grace knew snakes perfectly and could tell by tiny, subtle indications what the reptile would probably do next. She had been bitten many times—she would never tell me just how many—but never by a cobra. You're only bitten once by a cobra.

"Now I'll show you what I know you're waiting to see," said Grace as she put the snake away. "My mated pair of king cobras." Dropping her voice reverently, she added, "I call the big male 'The King of Kings.'" She led the way to a large enclosure and for the first time in my life I was looking into the eyes of that dread reptile, the king cobra or hamadryad.

The common cobra is rarely more than five feet long. Even so, it has enough venom in its poison glands to kill fifty men. Grace's king cobras were more than fifteen feet long. The two hamadryads contained enough venom, if injected drop by drop, to kill nearly a thousand human beings. That wasn't all. The hamadryad is the only snake known to attack without any provocation. These fearful creatures have been reported to trail a man through a jungle for the express purpose of biting him. They are so aggressive that they have closed roads in India by driving away all traffic. This is probably because the hamadryads, unlike other snakes, guard their eggs and young, and if a pair sets up housekeeping in a district, every other living thing must get out, including elephants. When a king cobra rears up, it stands higher than the head of a kneeling man. They are unquestionably the most dangerous animal in the world today.

When Grace first got these monsters, she was unable to handle them as she would ordinary cobras; so she had to devise an entirely new method of working with them. When the kings first arrived, they were completely unapproachable. They reared up more than four feet, snorting and hissing, their lower jaws open to expose the poison fangs. "A very threatening look, indeed," Grace called it. She put them in a large cage with a sliding partition. Unlike other snakes, hamadryads are knowing enough to notice that when their keeper opens the door in the side of the cage to put in fresh water, he must expose his hand for a fraction of a second. These cobras soon learned to lie against the side of the cage and wait for Grace to open the door. She outwitted them by waiting until both of the hamadryads were on one side of the cage and then sliding in the partition before changing water pans.

She did not dare to go near them with her bare hands; she used a padded stick to stroke them. Yet she was able to touch them four days after their arrival. "I petted the kings on their tails when their heads were far away," she told me. "Later in the day I had a little visit with them and told them how perfectly lovely they were—that I liked them and was sure we were going to be good friends."

A few weeks later, the King of Kings began shedding his skin. Snakes are irritable and nervous while shedding, and the hamadryad had trouble sloughing off the thin membrane covering his eyes. Grace wrote in her diary: "I stroked its head and then pulled off the eyelids with eyebrow forceps. It flinched a little but was unafraid. It put out its tongue in such a knowing manner! I mounted the eyelids and they looked just like pearls. What a pity that there have been nothing but unfriendly, aggressive accounts about this sweet snake. Really, the intelligence of these creatures is unbelievable."

The King of Kings was so heavy that Grace was unable to lift him by herself. Jule offered to help her carry the snake outside for a picture. While Jule and Grace were staggering out the door with the monster reptile between them, the king suddenly reared and rapped Jule several times on her forehead with its closed mouth. "It's trying to tell you something!" exclaimed Grace. It was indeed. I saw that the Chinese crocodile had rushed out from under a table and had grabbed the hamadryad by the tail. Jule relaxed her grip and the king dropped its head and gave a single hiss. The croc promptly let go and the ladies bore the cobra out into the sunlight. I was the only person who seemed upset by the incident.

Out of curiosity, I asked Grace if she ever used music in taming her snakes. She laughed and told me what I already knew: all snakes are deaf. Grace assured me that the Hindu fakir uses his flute only to attract a crowd and by swaying his own body back and forth the fakir keeps the snake swaying as the cobra is feinting to strike. The man times his music to correspond to the snake's movements and it appears to dance to the tune. The fakir naturally keeps well outside the cobra's striking range. Years later when I was in India, I discovered that this is exactly what happens. I never saw any Oriental snake-charmer even approximate Grace's marvelous power over reptiles.

Grace's main source of income was to exhibit her snakes to tourists, although she was occasionally able to rent a snake to a movie studio (she always went along to make sure the reptile wasn't frightened or injured), and sometimes she bought ailing snakes from dealers, cured them, and resold them for a small profit to zoos. While I was with her, a dusty car stopped and discharged a plump couple with three noisy children who had seen her modest sign *Grace Wiley—Reptiles*. Grace explained that she would show them her collection, handle the poisonous snakes, call over the tame alligators, and let the children play with Rocky, an eighteen-foot Indian Rock python which she had raised from a baby. The charge was twenty-five cents. "That's too much," the woman said to her husband, and they went back to the car. Grace sighed. "No one seems interested in my snakes. No one really cares about them. And they're so wonderful."

One day Grace telephoned me to say that she had gotten a new shipment of snakes, including some Indian cobras from Siam. "One of them has markings that form a complete $G$ on the back of his hood," she told me. "Isn't it curious that the snake and I have the same initial! I call him My Snake." We laughed about this, and then Jule and I went out to Cypress to take a last set of pictures of Grace and her snakes for an article I was doing about this remarkable woman.

We took several pictures and then I asked Grace to let me get a picture of the cobra with the $G$ on the hood. "I didn't look very well in those other pictures," said Grace anxiously. "I'll comb my hair and put on another blouse." She was back in a few minutes. Jule and I had set up our cameras in the yard behind the barn. I wanted a shot of the cobra with spread hood, and Grace brought it out cradled in her arms. Before allowing me to take the picture, she removed her glasses as she felt that she looked better without them. The cobra refused to spread and Grace put it down on the

ground and extended her flat palm toward it to make it rear—
something I had often seen her do before, but never without her
glasses.

I was watching through the finder of my camera. I saw the cobra
spread and strike as I clicked the shutter. As the image disappeared
from the ground glass of my Graflex, I looked up and saw that the
snake had seized Grace by the middle finger. She said in her usual
quiet voice, "Oh, it's bitten me."

I dropped the camera and ran toward her, feeling an almost
paralysing sense of shock, for I knew that Grace Wiley was a dead
woman. At the same time I thought, "Good Lord, it's just like the
book," for the cobra was behaving exactly as textbooks on cobras
say they behave. He was deliberately chewing on the wound to
make the venom run out of his glands. It was a terrible sight.

Quietly and expertly, Grace took hold of the snake and gently
forced its mouth open. I knew that her only chance for life was to
put a tourniquet around the finger instantly and slash open the
would to allow the venom to run out. Seconds counted. I reached
out my hand to take the snake above the hood so she could immediately start squeezing out the venom, but Grace motioned me
away. She stood up, still holding the cobra, and walked into the
barn. Carefully, she put the snake into his cage and closed the
door.

This must have taken a couple of minutes and I knew that the
venom was spreading through her system each moment. "Jule,"
said Grace, "call Wesley Dickinson. He's a herpetologist and a
friend of mine. He'll know what to do." Calmly and distinctly she
gave Jule the telephone number and Jule ran to the phone. Then
Grace turned to me. Suddenly she said, "He didn't really bite me,
did he?" It was the only emotion I saw her show. I could only say,
"Grace, where's your snake-bite kit?" We both knew that nothing
except immediate amputation of her arm could save her, but anything was worth a chance.

She pointed to a cabinet. There was a tremendous collection of
the surgical aids used for snake bite but I don't believe any of the
stuff had been touched for twenty years. I pulled out a rubber
tourniquet and tried to twist it around her finger. The old rubber
snapped in my hands. Grace didn't seem to notice. I pulled out
my handkerchief and tried that. It was too thick to go around her
finger and I twisted it around her wrist. "I'll faint in a few minutes,"
said Grace. "I want to show you where everything is before I lose
consciousness."

Cobra venom, unlike rattlesnake venom, affects the nervous

system. In a few minutes the victim becomes paralysed and the heart stops beating. I knew Grace was thinking of this. She said, "You must give me strychnine injections to keep my heart going when I begin to pass out. I'll show you where the strychnine is kept. You may have to give me caffeine also."

She walked to the other end of the room and I ran alongside trying to keep the tourniquet in place. She got out the tiny glass vials of strychnine and caffeine and also a hypodermic syringe with several needles. I saw some razor blades with the outfit and picked one up, intending to make a deep incision to let out as much of the venom as possible. Grace shook her head. "That won't do any good," she told me. Cobra venom travels along the nerves, so making the wound bleed wouldn't be very effective, but it was all I could think of to do.

Jule came back with a Mr. Tanner, Grace's cousin who lived next door. Tanner immediately got out his jack-knife, intending to cut open the wound, but Grace stopped him. "Wait until Wesley comes," she said. Tanner told me afterward that he was convinced that if he had amputated the finger Grace might have lived. This is doubtful. Probably nothing except amputation of her arm would have saved her then, and we had nothing but a jack-knife. She probably would have died of shock and loss of blood.

Grace lay on the floor to keep as quiet as possible and slow the absorption of the venom. "You'd better give me the strychnine now, dear," she told Jule. Jule snapped off the tip of one of the glass vials but the cylinder broke in her hands. She opened another tube and tried to fill the syringe; the needle was rusted shut. Jule selected another needle, tested it, and filled the syringe. "I'm afraid it will hurt," she told Grace. "Now don't worry, dear," said Grace comfortingly. "I know you'll do it very well."

After the injection, Grace asked Jule to put a newspaper under her head to keep her hair from getting dirty. A few minutes later, the ambulance arrived, with Wesley Dickinson following in his own car. Wesley had telephoned the hospital and arranged for blood transfusions and an iron lung. As Grace was lifted into the ambulance, she called back to Tanner, "Remember to cut up the meat for my frogs very fine and take good care of my snakes." That was the last we ever saw of her.

Grace died in the hospital half an hour later. She lived about ninety minutes after being bitten. In the hospital, Wesley directed the doctors to drain the blood out of her arm and pump in fresh blood. When her heart began to fail she was put into the lung. She had become unconscious. Then her heart stopped. Stimulants were given. The slow beating began again but grew steadily weaker. Each time stimulants were given, the heart responded less strongly and finally stopped forever.

We waited with Mr. and Mrs. Tanner at the snake barn, calling the hospital at intervals. When we heard that Grace was dead, Mrs. Tanner burst into tears. "Grace was such a beautiful young girl—and so talented," she moaned. "There wasn't anything she couldn't do. Why did she ever want to mess around with those awful snakes?"

"I guess that's something none of us will ever understand," said her husband sadly.

Grace was born in Kansas in 1884. She studied entomology at the University of Kansas and during field trips to collect insects it was a great joke among Grace's fellow students that she was terrified of even harmless garter snakes. Later, however, after her marriage failed, Grace turned with a passionate interest to the creatures she had so long feared. In 1923 she became curator of the Museum of Natural History at the Minneapolis Public Library but quarreled with the directors, who felt that her reckless handling of poisonous snakes endangered not only her own life but that of others. She went to the Brookfield Zoo in Chicago; here the same difficulty arose. Finally Grace moved to California where she could work with reptiles as she wished.

An attempt was made by several of Grace's friends to keep her collection together for a Grace Wiley Memorial Reptile House, but this failed. The snakes were auctioned off and the snake that had killed Grace was purchased by a roadside zoo in Arizona. Huge signboards bearing an artist's conception of the incident were erected for miles along the highways.

So passed one of the most remarkable people I have ever known.

# FOCUSSING

1. Working with a partner, discuss how the life of a 70-year-old is similar to and different from the life of a 20-year-old. List as many impressions as you can of old age, elderly people, and growing old. Compare your list with the lists of other classmates and discuss any similarities or differences. Place your list in your Work in Progress file.

2. Collect pictures and advertisements that feature elderly people. With your partner, decide whether these pictures confirm your impressions of old age or give you new ideas. After the discussion, make a collage on growing old using the pictures that you gathered.

3. Working in a group of three or four, identify some older characters portrayed on television or film. Discuss the role and personality of each of these characters, and enter the information in the following chart (a sample entry has been provided):

| Movie/ T.V. Show | Name of Character | Role | Personality |
|---|---|---|---|
| *Back to the Future* | Doc | scientist, inventor | scatterbrained, excitable, caring |

When your group has completed its chart, you may want to enter it into a word processor and print out a copy for each member.

4. Think of a good experience you had with an older person, a grandparent, for example. Share your memory with a partner and listen to your partner's story. Write a poem that briefly describes your affection for the older person.

**or**

Write a journal entry about an elderly person in your life. Include a physical description and two important things that you learned from her or him.

# DR. HEIDEGGER'S EXPERIMENT

*by Ev Miller, based on the story by*
*Nathaniel Hawthorne*

## CHARACTERS

DR. HEIDEGGER,
*a scientist*

MR. MEDBOURNE,
*a merchant who has
lost all his money*

COLONEL KILLIGREW,
*a man who eats and
drinks too much*

MR. GASCOIGNE,
*a ruined politician*

WIDOW WYCHERLY,
*a former beauty*

*NOTE: During this play, four of the elderly characters grow young, then old again. Since they are always on stage, they cannot change their makeup or put on wigs. But old age can be represented by cracked voices and bent-over postures.*

*SCENE: Dr. Heidegger's study. It is an old-fashioned room that is filled with bookcases and books. At the centre is a table. On it are four wine glasses and a silver pitcher. As the curtain rises, Dr. Heidegger answers the door, and two old men enter.*

**HEIDEGGER:** Mr. Medbourne! Colonel Killigrew! It's good to see both of you again. Did you come over here together?

**MEDBOURNE:** I should say not! We met out in front. If I had known that Killigrew had been invited, I would not be here.

**KILLIGREW:** I feel the same way about Medbourne.

**HEIDEGGER:** Gentlemen, it's been at least 20 years since we've seen each other. Can't we be civilized?

**MEDBOURNE:** Well. . . .

**KILLIGREW:** I can if he can.

**HEIDEGGER:** Good. Make yourselves at home. How are you, Colonel?

**KILLIGREW:** Awful. My gout is killing me.

**MEDBOURNE:** Perhaps you shouldn't have drunk so much when you were young.

**KILLIGREW:** I thought you said you were going to try to get along.

**HEIDEGGER:** That's right, no more fighting. How have you been, Medbourne!

**MEDBOURNE:** Not so good. I invested all my money—and lost it. Now, in my old age, I must beg from relatives.

**KILLIGREW:** You were always too greedy for money.

**MEDBOURNE:** That's a lie!

**HEIDEGGER:** Gentlemen, please! *(There is a knock on the door.)* Ah, my other guests have arrived.

**KILLIGREW:** I hope they are better company than this oaf.

**MEDBOURNE:** Are you calling me an oaf?

**KILLIGREW:** I'm certainly not calling the doctor an oaf.

**HEIDEGGER:** These guests are old friends of yours.
(*He opens the door. Mr. Gascoigne and Widow Wycherly enter.*)

**HEIDEGGER:** Mr. Gascoigne, thank you for bringing Madame Wycherly over.

**GASCOIGNE:** It was my pleasure. It's not every day that I have the company of such a lovely woman.

**WYCHERLY** (*pleased*): You were always one for words, Wilbert.

**KILLIGREW:** Clara! What a wonderful surprise!

**WYCHERLY:** John! Is it really you? It's been so long.

**KILLIGREW:** It's been much too long. You are as lovely as ever.

**WYCHERLY:** I am a wrinkled old woman, and you know it!

**KILLIGREW:** I still regret the fact that you did not marry me 50 years ago.

**HEIDEGGER:** Madame, you remember Mr. Medbourne, don't you?

Dr. Heidegger

**WYCHERLY:** Why, of course. How are you, Charles?

**MEDBOURNE:** I feel much better now that I've seen you, Clara.

**WYCHERLY:** What a lovely thing to say.

**MEDBOURNE:** Gascoigne, how are you?

**GASCOIGNE:** I am in perfect health for a man my age. I plan to run for office again.

**MEDBOURNE:** Really? I didn't know that a man could run for public office after being convicted of corruption.

**GASCOIGNE** (*angry*): I was innocent of those charges! And I resent your bringing this up in front of Clara.

**MEDBOURNE:** I'm sure Clara knows all about it.

**GASCOIGNE:** Well, what about you? Your shady dealings were investigated by the law more than once.

**MEDBOURNE:** I was never charged!

**KILLIGREW:** That's because you paid off the officials.

**MEDBOURNE:** Stay out of this, you fat old fool!

**GASCOIGNE:** He may be fat. But at least he didn't steal money from every widow in the county.

**KILLIGREW:** I am not fat!

**HEIDEGGER:** Gentlemen, please stop quarreling.

**KILLIGREW** (*still angry*): Dr. Heidegger, I don't understand this little party of yours. Medbourne, Gascoigne, and I are not exactly good friends. Don't you remember that all three of us wanted to marry Madame Wycherly when we were young?

**HEIDEGGER:** I am aware of that. But I do have a reason for inviting all of you here. I hope you will help me perform an experiment. Please sit down and make yourselves comfortable.

*(He picks up a large black book. He opens it and takes a faded rose from between the pages.)*

**MEDBOURNE:** What is that?

**HEIDEGGER:** It is a rose that bloomed 55 years ago.

**WYCHERLY:** Why have you saved it all these years?

**HEIDEGGER:** It was given to me by Sylvia Ward. As you know she died before our wedding. I kept the rose in her memory. Now, do you believe that it could ever bloom again?

**WYCHERLY:** Nonsense!

**KILLIGREW:** Of course not!

**GASCOIGNE:** Do you take us for fools?

**HEIDEGGER:** Watch.

*(He drops the rose into the pitcher on the table. After a long moment, he reaches in and takes out a fresh, red rose.)*

**WYCHERLY:** It is a miracle!

**GASCOIGNE:** It's a trick!

*(Killigrew looks into the pitcher.)*

**KILLIGREW:** How did you do that?

**HEIDEGGER:** Have you ever heard of the Fountain of Youth?

**MEDBOURNE:** What?

**HEIDEGGER:** Ponce de Leon, the Spanish explorer, searched for it several centuries ago.

**MEDBOURNE:** I've heard that tale, but I believe it is a fantasy.

**HEIDEGGER:** No, it is not.

**WYCHERLY:** Did Ponce de Leon actually find the Fountain of Youth?

**HEIDEGGER:** No, because he didn't search in the right place. The Fountain of Youth is in the southern part of Florida.

**KILLIGREW:** You are joking.

**HEIDEGGER:** No, I am not. The fountain is surrounded by several huge magnolia trees. They have been kept alive for thousands of years by the wonderful water.

**GASCOIGNE:** How did you get it, Doctor?

**HEIDEGGER:** A friend of mine knew of my interest in such matters. He sent me what's in this pitcher.

**MEDBOURNE:** I don't believe it.

**HEIDEGGER:** It is true.

**KILLIGREW:** What would be the effect of this water on the human body?

**HEIDEGGER:** You can judge that for yourself. All of you are welcome to drink as much as you need to restore your youth.

**GASCOIGNE** *(suspicious)*: Why haven't you used it yourself?

**HEIDEGGER** *(laughs)*: I've had enough trouble growing old. I am in no hurry to grow young again. I'd rather just

Mr. Medbourne

watch the experiment.

**KILLIGREW:** That's fine with me. Just give me some of that water.

**GASCOIGNE:** Do you really believe this story, Killigrew?

**KILLIGREW:** Can it hurt to try the water? I don't think Dr. Heidegger would try to poison us.

**HEIDEGGER:** I assure you that the water is not poisonous.

**GASCOIGNE:** Well. . . .

**WYCHERLY:** If it will convince you, Wilbert, I will drink first.

**KILLIGREW:** I will join her.

(*They move toward the table.*)

Colonel Killigrew

**HEIDEGGER:** Wait. Before you drink, maybe you should decide upon some rules for passing through the perils of youth again. After all, you each have a lifetime of experience to direct you.

**MEDBOURNE:** What kind of rules?

**HEIDEGGER:** Rules of behaviour.

**MEDBOURNE:** Are you suggesting that we might make the same mistakes twice?

**HEIDEGGER:** Perhaps.

**WYCHERLY:** We have learned lessons from our past mistakes. I know *I* have. I've often thought that if only I could live those times over again, I would change them completely.

**HEIDEGGER:** Would you really?

**WYCHERLY:** I *know* I would.

**KILLIGREW:** I would, too.

**HEIDEGGER:** Very well. Drink, then.

(*He pours the water into the four glasses. Each guest picks up a glass.*)

**KILLIGREW:** To our youth!

**MEDBOURNE:** To a new life!

**GASCOIGNE:** To vigour!

**WYCHERLY:** To beauty!

(*They drink the water. As the following conversation takes place, their voices become more youthful. They stand straighter.*)

**WYCHERLY:** I can feel it! I'm beginning to feel younger!

**KILLIGREW:** My gout has gone! I no longer feel the pain!

**GASCOIGNE:** I must admit that I do feel a bit strange.

**MEDBOURNE:** Strange? You are simply feeling younger.

**WYCHERLY:** But I want to feel younger than this. I want to be a girl again.

**KILLIGREW:** And I want to be the handsome young man I was 50 years ago.

**WYCHERLY:** Give us more, Doctor. We are still too old!

**MEDBOURNE:** Yes! Quick! Give us more!

Mr. Gascoigne

HEIDEGGER: Be patient. You took a long time growing old. Surely you can be content to grow young in half an hour.
(*He fills their glasses, and they drink the water quickly. Now they begin to act like people in their 20's.*)

MEDBOURNE: It's been years since I've felt so positive about life.

GASCOIGNE: I feel like climbing a mountain.

WYCHERLY: I have begun to feel pretty again.

KILLIGREW: My dear, you are charming!

WYCHERLY (*blushing*): Why, thank you. Does anyone have a mirror?

HEIDEGGER (*pointing*): There is one on the wall over there.

WYCHERLY (*looking in the mirror*): It's true!

KILLIGREW: I feel like singing the songs I knew as a youth.

MEDBOURNE: I suppose that means tavern songs. Didn't you spend most of your youth drinking in taverns?

KILLIGREW: Of course not!

MEDBOURNE: Then sing another kind of song.

KILLIGREW: Well, I . . . can't think of any others.

MEDBOURNE: Ha! I knew it!

GASCOIGNE: Forget it. There are more important things than singing.

KILLIGREW: Like what?

GASCOIGNE: Like politics. There is nothing greater than a man who serves his country.

MEDBOURNE: Spoken like a true thief.

GASCOIGNE: I resent that. I served my country well. Poverty has made you a rude man, Medbourne.

MEDBOURNE: I won't be poor for long. I am young again, and I already have a deal in mind.

GASCOIGNE: A deal! Have you ever done an honest day's work?

MEDBOURNE: Look who's talking!

KILLIGREW: You are both too serious about life. Life is filled with good wine and good times. Why waste it on boring matters?

MEDBOURNE: Killigrew, you are a fool!

KILLIGREW: And you are a miser!

WYCHERLY (*turning away from the mirror*): Gentlemen, please don't quarrel. We are lucky to be young again. But, Dr. Heidegger, please give me another glass of that water. I am not yet young enough.

HEIDEGGER: There is plenty of water left.
(*He fills their glasses. Then he returns to his chair, holding the rose. After his guests drink again, they begin to act like teenagers.*)

WYCHERLY (*posing before the mirror*): Look how young I am!

KILLIGREW: But we look foolish in these old clothes.

MEDBOURNE: Only old codgers wear clothes like these. And there is only one old codger in this room.
(*The others laugh as he points at Dr. Heidegger.*)

WYCHERLY: Thank goodness we're not old like that!

GASCOIGNE (*pretending to walk with a cane*): Thank goodness we don't have to walk like this!

MEDBOURNE: The old look so foolish.

WYCHERLY: I must get a new dress.

KILLIGREW: We'll all get new clothes. Then we'll have a party.

WYCHERLY: Yes! I love to dance. (*She dances over to Dr. Heidegger.*) Doctor, you dear, *old* soul, get up and dance with me.
(*The others laugh.*)

HEIDEGGER: No, thank you. My dancing days are over.

WYCHERLY (*like a spoiled child*): Dance with me!

HEIDEGGER: I'm sure that one of these young men would be glad to have a such a pretty partner.

KILLIGREW: Dance with me, Clara!

GASCOIGNE: No! She is my partner!

MEDBOURNE: Wait! She promised to marry me many years ago.

KILLIGREW: She promised me!
(*Gascoigne grabs one of her hands. Medbourne grabs her other hand. Killigrew grabs her by the waist. They pull her in different directions.*)

WYCHERLY (*pleased by all the attention*): Gentlemen! Please don't fight over me!

MEDBOURNE (*pushing Killigrew*): Stay away from her, you fool!

KILLIGREW (*shoving Medbourne into Gascoigne*): Don't push me around!

GASCOIGNE (*getting into the fight*): She doesn't belong to either of you!
(*They fall against the table as they fight. The table turns over, and the water spills from the pitcher.*)

HEIDEGGER: Gentlemen! Madame Wycherly! Please stop fighting!
(*They all stand still. Then they look confused as old age begins to return.*)

HEIDEGGER: Look. (*He holds up a faded rose.*) My poor Sylvia's rose has faded again.

WYCHERLY (*aging as she speaks*): It has grown old.

KILLIGREW: Does the water's magic wear off?

HEIDEGGER: Yes. (*He touches the rose to his lips.*) Still, I love this rose whether fresh or faded.

MEDBOURNE: Are we old again so soon?

Widow Wycherly

**KILLIGREW:** Ow! My gout!

**HEIDEGGER:** Yes, you are old again.

**GASCOIGNE:** Give us more water.

**HEIDEGGER:** I cannot. It's all over the floor.

**WYCHERLY:** You mean you have no more?

**HEIDEGGER:** That's right. But I am not sorry. If the Fountain of Youth were at my doorstep, I would not drink from it. That is the lesson you have taught me.

**KILLIGREW:** But we must have more of it!

**HEIDEGGER:** There is no more.

**GASCOIGNE:** But you said the Fountain of Youth was . . . where?

**MEDBOURNE:** He said the southern part of Florida.

**WYCHERLY:** We can find it.

**KILLIGREW:** We'll travel there together. Dr. Heidegger, will you come with us?

**HEIDEGGER:** Haven't you learned a lesson from all this?

**MEDBOURNE:** There is only one lesson to be learned. Being young is far, far better than being old.

**WYCHERLY:** I must be beautiful again. I cannot stand being old and ugly.

**HEIDEGGER:** Madame Wycherly, being old does not necessarily mean being ugly.

**GASCOIGNE** (*leading the others toward the door*): There is no time to lose. We will find the Fountain of Youth, and we will stay near it. We will drink from it morning, noon, and night. We will be young forever!

**HEIDEGGER** (*holding up the faded rose*): Good luck to you, my dear, *old* friends.
(*The curtain falls.*)

**THE END**

# CLOSE UP

1. Working with a partner, fill in the following chart on the characters in the play:

| Character | Physical Appearance | | Character Flaw | |
|---|---|---|---|---|
| | Before Drinking | After Drinking | Before Drinking | After Drinking |
| Medbourne | | | | |
| Killigrew | | | | |
| Gascoigne | | | | |
| Wycherly | | | | |

2. Pretend that you are Dr. Heidegger. Write a letter to your friend who sent you the water from the fountain of youth. Tell him what happened to you and your four friends and what it taught you.

3. Make a drawing of all the stage props required in the play. Label them and write a brief point-form description of each.

4. Dr. Heidegger must make a report to a scientific institution on whether this potion should be mass-produced and sold in drugstores. Pretend that you are Dr. Heidegger. Jot down
   (i) a description of the potion;
   (ii) your evaluation of its benefits and dangers; and
   (iii) your final recommendation about whether or not it should be sold.

# WIDE ANGLE

1. In your journal, write an entry beginning "If I could drink from the Fountain of Youth, I would go back to the time when . . . "

2. Starting at the point in the play where Killigrew says "I feel like singing the song I knew as a youth," rewrite the ending of the play. (You and your partners might want to imagine that the characters don't behave so foolishly, or that they drink so much water they become young children.) Dividing the roles among partners, read your ending for another group, then listen to their version.

3. In a small group, brainstorm an argument either for or against this statement: "The characters in *Dr. Heidegger's Experiment* have sex-stereotyped roles." Hold a debate with a group that has taken the opposite stand. Three classmates will act as judges, summarize the arguments, and decide which is the most convincing. You may wish to refer to the definitions you prepared for Focussing #1 of Free to Be. The column of character flaws in the chart in Close Up #1 above may also be helpful.

# TOMMY WESTON

*by Myfanwy Phillips*

'LL BE 91 next birthday and I've only been sick one day in my life. You know why? I don't take drugs, I don't take pills, I don't take aspirins and I keep away from doctors especially. "I was a professional soccer player for five years and then I painted the lettering on signs for all the movies and burlesque shows in Toronto. I did that, winter and summer, including Christmas Day, for forty-two years.

"My wife's been dead two years. If she had lived twenty-six more days we'd have been married sixty-six years. The real difference is missing her, mostly. She was good, even though I was never home. When I'd come in at night she'd say, 'Take your shoes off.' And I'd yell back, 'What's the matter with you?' Now, I take them off because it's me that's got to clean up if there is any mud on them.

"I never did anything at all. I never even cleaned the windows. Now I do it all. I cook for myself—my favourite dish is bacon and eggs. I can cook that good! The thing I hate is making the bed. Sometimes I don't make it. I just crawl back in!

"I live with Tiny and he lives with me. He's 98 so he's beating me. That's no dog, boy. He won't eat dog food, he eats what I eat. Sometimes he'll eat dessert and sometimes he won't. He likes ice cream, does he ever! I talk to him every night and he talks to me and if anyone ever touched him I'd get a good one in! If somebody invites me over for dinner and not my dog, I don't go.

"I do everything anyone else does. Well, I won't say *everything*! I don't feel any different now from when I was young. The only thing I haven't got is my teeth. There's all that lawn out there to be cut and I do that. I don't know a weed from a flower, but I dig the yard, right or wrong, and every spring I put in new flowers. I shovel my driveway and sometimes Johnson's next door, too. Don't you think that's what I should do? Do things like everyone else? Sometimes I go up to the cemetery to see my own grave. My name is right there and they're just waiting to put the year on. But I'm not going to sit here and die.

"I see that I'm getting old but I think to myself, What the hell! You make life as you make it yourself. There are a lot of things that shouldn't be worried about. I'm not going to waste any time at all and if anybody tells me different I'll say, 'How the hell old are you?' And I can tell them I'm 90 and still around, doing all right. I'm having a good time. I wake up every morning and thank God I'm still breathing. There's just one thing though—sometimes when I look in the mirror I want to go and get my gun because I think someone has broken into my house. It sure doesn't look like me."

# CLOSE UP

1.  a) You are the reporter who interviewed Tommy Weston. Using his answers as a guide, write down the questions that you asked him during the interview.
    b) List the qualities that you saw in Tommy Weston as you interviewed him. Compare your list with a partner's and discuss any differences.

# WIDE ANGLE

1.  Using the list of questions from Close Up #1, interview an older person in your family or community. Tape the interview and play it for others who also read about Tommy Weston. Write a statement about what you learned from doing the interview. You can copy the statement into the Personal Assessment column when you record this activity on your Personal Record Sheet (see p. 184).
2.  Write down the interview you taped in Wide Angle #1. When you and a partner have proofread it, type it and send it to your community newsletter. (You may want to transcribe your interview directly into a word processor, polish it on screen, and print out a finished copy.) Enclose a covering letter telling who you are and why your interview should be published.

# THE SECLUDED LOT

## by Elizabeth Morison Townshend

"**I**'D LIKE TO inquire about a lot," the old man said, the effort of decision evident in his voice. "At my age you never know. . . ."

"It's a good investment," Mr. Jerome replied. Through years of experience he knew these rather delicate matters must be handled with a businesslike approach. "Lots have gone up a good third in value over the past few years. That is, if you ever wanted to resell."

"No, I won't want to resell."

Mr. Jerome looked at the old man thoughtfully. The old-timer was difficult to bracket. *Don't be fooled by the frayed cuffs*, he told himself, *there's probably more life-savings under his mattress than most people have in the bank.*

"This section was just opened up last year," he said, pointing to the large map on the wall. It might have been any map in any real estate office, except for the heading. The dreaded title was blazoned forth:

### REST HAVEN CEMETERY

"I'd prefer an older location." The old man looked down at his unpolished shoes, embarrassed. "I mean, where trees and shrubs have had a chance to grow."

"We've still a few left in the older sections—at various price ranges. The Avenue lots are more expensive, of course."

"Too much traffic," the old man said.

"There's one or two on Ridge Road and Cypress Hill—exclusive areas, many old families up there."

"I'd like a good view," the old man explained. "But more important, privacy."

"That will run the price up," Mr. Jerome warned. He was not quite sure how much price mattered.

"Haven't you something a little out of the way, sort of hard to find? I don't want relatives interfering—nosing about, you know."

Mr. Jerome studied the map thoughtfully. The blacked-in marks indicated which plots had been sold and occupied. With the exception of the new areas, there were few white vacancies left.

"There might be room for just one more off Willow Walk here," he said. "Needs a bit of clearing, though, and a proper entrance. It would be very private."

"Just the one?"

"Yes."

"Then I think I'd like to see it—if you have the time."

Mr. Jerome looked at his watch: "Yes, I will have the time."

"The size?"

"A little bigger than standard: forty inches by nine feet—sets off the headstone just right."

They entered a black limousine and drove slowly through the cemetery. The shade trees stretched their branches over the consecrated ground. A warbler began its plaintive melody. Others joined the chant, until a veritable choir filled the air. Through the open window came the fragrant smells of spring. Here were splashes of brilliant pink azaleas, extravagant dogwoods, forsythia with weeping golden blossoms. They passed prim beds of narcissi and tulips, clumps of bleeding-heart, drifts of pansies and forget-me-nots among the low-growing evergreens.

"Spring is kind of a promise," the old man was saying, obviously moved.

All winter Mr. Jerome, the head gardener and the men at the greenhouse had planned and anticipated just this impression. Now it all seemed so spontaneous and natural—worth hiring the extra clippers and cutters, seeders and transplanters. Yes, Mr. Jerome was pleased.

Where Willow Walk circled downhill again, the limousine came to a halt. Mr. Jerome guided the old man between chiselled, high-polish marbles, between tall and rectangular shafts of granite.

"That's Carrara marble," Mr. Jerome informed him. "This is Vermont. Nice colour, that rose—specially imported Aberdeen granite—about the most durable there is." Carefully circling a slightly raised mound, Mr. Jerome continued: "Now don't let them fool you on synthetics—that new cement and marble chip mix—it won't hold up at all."

Parting the branches of a heavy thicket, Mr. Jerome led the way. Against a natural crag was just room for a bigger than standard lot. Covered with a tangle of unruly vines and underbrush, it was obviously an afterthought.

"Well, here we are," Mr. Jerome said brightly. It was in far worse condition than he remembered and quite inaccessible. Besides, a bramble had caught on the sleeve of his good suit and left a slight tear.

"Of course, it needs a little fixing."

"No, I like it the way it is—wild and secret and uncared for—hidden by that thicket of branches."

For some time, the old man stood there, gazing off into the distance. "Am I allowed . . . " he hesitated, correcting

himself. "Is the purchaser allowed to visit it at any time?"

"Come as often as you like," Mr. Jerome adjusted his black tie. "'Perpetual care, you know, is included in the purchase price."

"I don't want perpetual care." The old gentleman was indignant. "As if you could make promises for the next generation and the next. I mean, with atomic and hydrogen bombs and goodness knows what else."

"Then in that case, we could give you a special price."

In Mr. Jerome's language this meant the highest possible figure at which the customer would buy. Shrewdly, he estimated the demand, the desire and upped the figure ten per cent.

"It's higher than I thought," the old man said sadly. "But it's just what I wanted."

"Then why not take it?" Mr. Jerome was an expert in these matters. "After all, it's for eternity."

"And eternity," the old man added, "is kind of a long time."

"Then it's settled." Mr. Jerome hastened to close the deal. "The contract can be worded to accord with your wishes."

"My last wishes," the old man said.

Mr. Jerome was glad to be back in the safety of his mahogany office again. Carefully he crossed out the *Per-*

*petual Care* clause and instructed his secretary, Miss Jones, to type in the old man's name on the blank lines between the small print—*Mortimer Blake*.

The old man adjusted his glasses, but the print was obviously too fine for him to read.

"No loans or mortgages may be raised on a burial lot, you understand—nor can they be seized for debt." Mr. Jerome recited the routine clauses with a let's-be-done-with-it indifference.

Waiting, embarrassed, the old man glanced at the file clerk—sorting a large stack of documents and correspondence. This particular one had her puzzled. Undecided, she slipped it into a box marked "Pending", and the old man wondered what, under the circumstances, *pending* might mean.

"Please sign here." Mr. Jerome pushed the document towards him. The old man signed in a shaky hand.

"Good afternoon, Rest Haven." Miss Jones used just the right intonation over the telephone. "Services tomorrow at eleven in the chapel."

The telephone rang again. "It's about the advertisement in the *Herald*, sir."

Mr. Jerome picked up the receiver. "The same ad—just a gentle reminder," he said, "and the usual space."

Slowly old Mr. Blake counted out his money. Yes, he had brought the entire sum in cash. Between phone calls, Mr. Jerome made out a receipt and handed him his copy. "Good morning, Rest Haven," the efficient Miss Jones was saying. Then her voice took on that tone of practised solemnity: "One minute, please . . . "

Fumbling with his hat, the old man started for the door.

During the ensuing year old man Blake made periodic visits to his lot. All the workmen in the cemetery knew him by name. But in this separate little world, where personal feelings were respected, nobody thought it odd that he went quite regularly to commune with nature and the life everlasting.

As a cortège neared Willow Walk, Mr. Jerome could see the old man in the distance, parting the bushes and disappearing from view. After the Committal Service—when everything possible had been done for the Departed and the Bereaved had gone their sorrowful ways—something prompted Mr. Jerome to intrude on the old man's privacy— perhaps a word or two of comfort, which he knew so well how to administer.

On the other side of the thicket he was surprised to find Mr. Blake stooping over a high, square, white box, intent on fixing something. A bee circled slowly overhead, then dove for its target.

"Ouch!" yelled Mr. Jerome. "That cursed bee stung me."

"I'm sorry," the old man said, "but that sting cost the bee its life."

Then it was that Mr. Jerome began to understand. The full implications left him aghast. There was no precedent for this in all cemetery history.

"How dare you operate a beehive in this cemetery?"

"It's on my property. I purchased it, did I not?"

"No business such as this is allowed within this sanctuary."

"I'm not soliciting business. The bees are just going about their normal and natural pursuits. Besides, Rose Haven Nectar brings a special price.

"You sell the honey?" Jerome was shocked.

"Maybe it was just beginner's luck," old man Blake replied modestly, "But those twenty-dollar Beginner's Beekeeping Outfits certainly work wonders. Like the advertisement said, I had over a hundred pounds of surplus honey the first year."

"This is preposterous!" Mr. Jerome exploded, his highly-trained sensitivities deeply offended.

"Experienced beekeepers figure three to five acres of heavy flowering plants for each colony of bees," the old man went on. "Of course, in my small rooming house it was out of the question. Then I saw this beautiful acreage and acquired property of my own."

"It's dreadful—unheard of," Jerome spluttered.

"You don't need much capital," the old man continued with enthusiasm. "Only queen-size cells with eggs inside and some royal jelly. The worker bees do the rest."

"All this time, a veritable factory." Mr. Jerome was beside himself. "And right under my very nose."

"With good beekeeping management, the colonies should increase to thirty in a few years."

"Oh, no!" Jerome's well-modulated voice rose to a shout: "Look here, I won't have it. You must stop this at once!"

"Why should you want me to stop?"

"For obvious reasons: we can't have the mourners stung . . ."

"Mr. Jerome, I have done you a great service. Your flowers have never been so magnificent or plentiful."

"That's true," he was forced to admit.

"Why? Because of my bees. They pollinate your flowers. Now, if you could spare me a few moments."

At that particular second Mr. Jerome was fully occupied, easing another attacker gently off the lapel of his serge suit. All his spare time would be devoted to a solution of Mr.

Blake's special problem. *It must be illegal*, he thought, with every intention of rushing back to the office to examine the small print.

The old man straightened and looked at him proudly.

"Mr. Jerome, I have reached an important decision: I should like to buy another lot."

# CLOSE UP

1. Through most of the story, Mr. Blake seems rather meek and mild. At the end of the story, however, we get a surprise: he's strong and independent. Make notes on Mr. Blake's character, finding details that make us think he is weak, then details that show he is strong. With the help of two partners, draft a list for each of the two sets of details.

# WIDE ANGLE

1. Working with a partner, decide how the story would continue after Mr. Blake says, "Mr. Jerome, I have reached an important decision: I should like to buy another lot." Make point-form notes of what both men would say. Role-play the conversation for other groups.

2. Write a magazine advertisement for Mr. Blake's Rose Haven Nectar. Your advertisement should include a drawing (or a picture) and a short paragraph that will convince people that Rose Haven Nectar is delicious honey. It should also feature a slogan, an easy to remember phrase that catches people's attention. If you are using a computer, there are programs, such as The Newsroom®, that are useful tools when you are creating an advertisement.

3. At one time, society tended to regard elderly people as weak, dependent, and finished with living. Like Mr. Blake, however, many people begin new and challenging ventures when they are old. Colonel Sanders started the Kentucky Fried Chicken chain in his sixties, and Grandma Moses began painting her wonderful pictures very late in her life. Ask your librarian to help you find out about one Canadian woman and one Canadian man who became successful in their later years. Make a display to show their accomplishments. Include a photograph of each person and a brief description of his or her successful venture.

# AN OLD MAN'S LARK
## *by Donald Jones*

From the fine nursing home
unnoticed one afternoon
with saved-up spending money
from his children far away

he bolted across the lawn,
caught a streetcar downtown,
had two cheeseburgers, a malt,
and watched a double feature.

His money all gone, he spent
the summer night on a park bench,
was found there the next morning
by his helpers young and hurt.

# OLD WOMAN
### by Dionne Brand

She sleeps
in a shed
with newspapers
for her pillow.
She walks
almost barefooted,
her knees are knots
that ache.
She used to work,
her fingers
too stiff now
to thread needles.
She begs a coin
her hand outstretched
"move along old woman"
they say.
She is
too old
to live
like this
I think.

# CLOSE UP

1. In "An Old Man's Lark" the poet points out that sometimes society tends to overprotect elderly people forgetting that some elderly people are strong and energetic. Note the details that emphasize the old man's youthfulness.
2. The woman in the poem "Old Woman" has a difficult life. Describe three of her difficulties, writing one sentence for each.

# WIDE ANGLE

1. The old woman meets the old man on the day of his escapade. With a partner, role-play the conversation between the two old people, in which they express their feelings about the way they are living.
2. Many people are forced to retire from work when they reach 65 years of age. Some retirees are bored because they no longer have jobs, and some retirees don't have enough money to live comfortably. Imagine that you are a politician who is trying to find out what happens to people after they retire. In a small group, find one or two newspaper or magazine articles on the subject and read them together. Brainstorm a plan to help elderly people remain active in society. Write down your plan in the form of a pamphlet you could give to people during your election campaign.
3. Write a story that begins with the following line: "One day, the old woman was shuffling along the street when suddenly she saw a wonderful sight."

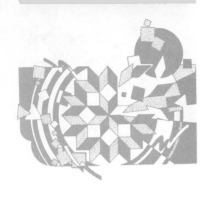

# KALEIDOSCOPE

1. View a film in which elderly people play an important role. (*The Sunshine Boys, Harold and Maude*, and *Cocoon* are good examples.) After viewing it, read a number of movie reviews. Using the reviews as a guide, write a review of the movie for either a teen magazine or the community newspaper.

2. Ask some elderly people if you can take slides of them for an audio-visual presentation titled "Older People in Our Community." Take as many slides as possible and write a narrative to accompany them. Tape your narrative to play as the slides are being shown.

3. Work in a group of three. You are a team of architects hired to design a home for senior citizens. List the features, both necessary and luxurious, that you would include in an ideal home. Draw the plan for the building and the surrounding landscape. If your class has a computer-assisted drawing program, you may want to use it to make your plan. Give your home an appropriate name.

4. Refer to the list of impressions about old age that you drew up for Focussing #1. Now that you have read the selections and done the activities in this cluster, think about whether your impressions are the same or different. Revise your list if necessary and proofread it before you re-file it.

# CROWFOOT

*by Ethel Brant Monture*

T WAS IN THE YEAR 1821 that a second son came to the lodge of Many Names, head chief of the Moccasins band of the Blackfoot tribe, and a chief of their Confederacy.

The baby's first months belonged to his mother. She had prepared and decorated the cradle as befitted the son of a chief and she it was who carried it proudly. When she rode her horse she sometimes hung the board to her saddle horn but most of the time the baby saw the world from her back where he was tucked inside her shawl behind her shoulder.

It seemed that as soon as the boy found his feet his father began his training. By the time the little boy was four the back of a horse was as familiar as the ground to him, for with the Blackfoot riding was as normal as breathing. His father put a bow in his hand and he practised shooting it constantly. As he grew older he went on miniature hunts for small game with other boys and with them he learned to herd the horses.

Nemorkan was the first name chosen for this son in his early boyhood, a name which he bore through his training by the wise old chief who supervised the boys. Every means that would produce a hardy, vigorous youth was employed. Diving into icy streams and then racing for two or three hours to a new campsite toughened them for long expeditions. In that day the life of the Blackfoot Confederacy was interwoven with many well-organized military and religious societies. The first of these was a society of two. A young boy would choose another of his age and these two would share their life's experiences. Nemorkan's inseparable companion seemed to be his half-brother, Three Bulls. (This name was common to many Indians on the plains because the buffalo was their symbol of courage. The name Three Bulls implied that the bearer had the bravery and courage of three bulls.) And by this time Nemorkan had another name, a growing-up name. He was Kayastah or "Ghost Bear".

Kayastah had grown and learned his lessons so well that at thirteen his father allowed him to go on his first battle expedition. His older brother, already accomplished in the war games, had won a notable victory when he defeated a great enemy in the Crow nation and for this he was given his warrior's name of Crowfoot.

Some time after this victory Crowfoot was honoured by his father's band. He was sent as one of fourteen ambassadors on a peace mission to the Snake Indians in Montana, a large band belonging to the Shoshoneans. These carriers of good will were waylaid and all slain by an overwhelming force of the very people to whom they were sent to make peace. Angered by the wanton act that had destroyed his eldest son, Chief Many Names assembled the largest war party in Blackfoot history, about ten thousand warriors. He himself was the leader, for he must be the avenger of his eldest son. After twenty days' travelling in the middle of winter they came to the Snake territory. Scouts found the enemy, eight hundred lodges of them, in a strong position. The fight lasted for thirty-six hours, but the fury of the Blackfoot attack was at last victorious. Kayastah, now the chief's eldest son, bore the battle flag in the front ranks and was severely wounded. After the battle his father publicly appointed him his brother's successor in recognition of his bravery. He honoured his son further by giving him his brother's good name. So Kayastah became Crowfoot and this was to be his name for the rest of his life.

Young Crowfoot began to attend and listen in the councils. He became convinced that to speak well for one's people was even better than to be a great warrior, for the Blackfoot were a socially sophisticated people, wealthy in lands, lodges and herds of horses. A tangible sign of their prosperity was the summer encampment where the great circles of lodges could be seen painted with totemic designs of family honours. A good lodge needed twenty buffalo skins for a cover and the many lodges with good new covers were evidence of good hunters on swift horses.

Crowfoot, Three Bulls and their mother survived four dreadful smallpox epidemics, which took more than a fourth of their people. There is no record of these losses but it is said that Many Names, his father, died in the last one. It had seemed that Crowfoot had a charmed life in the battles also, for he took part in nineteen of them. He was wounded six times but the only mark of these wounds was a lameness that remained to the end of his days.

In appearance Crowfoot was tall, of slender but sinewy build. He had a fine face with high forehead, good profile and keen, alert eyes. His whole person suggested repose and strength. When he rode his horse in midsummer he held an umbrella over his head. For ordinary occasions he wore deerskin clothing, as did the other men, but for ceremonial wear he had a magnificent robe of buffalo skins worked to a wonderful whiteness and softness, as rich as ermine. It was ornamented with beadwork in a gorgeous pattern. A glowing sun was the central motif on the front, surrounded by totemic designs. A great treasure was his white chimney-pot hat trimmed with a band of eagle feathers. He carried an eagle feather fan on great occasions and at all times he wore handsomely trimmed moccasins. The women of his household had quick and clever hands.

Many of the men were his equals in war deeds and accomplishments for war was a Blackfoot tradition, but long before his father died Crowfoot was the acknowledged young chief, leading the councils by the power of his eloquence. Like all Indians his people had a profound respect for wise speech, and he was proving himself to be one of the nobility, that is, of the orators. Crowfoot had a fine herd of horses and he shared them freely with those in need. The door of his tipi was always open, especially to the young men. As an astute politician, he knew this hospitality added to his prestige. He never abused his power. His father had lived to see him become a chief of his tribe; later he was chosen a chief of the Confederacy.

The North West Mounted Police came on the scene in December 1874. The chiefs of the Confederacy welcomed the band of red-coated men with their good guns, which gave the laws teeth to grip and hold the outlaws and took them out of their country. Fort Macleod, built for them near the international border, had a stout little jail from which the traders found it impossible to bribe their way out. Fort Macleod was named for James Farquhar Macleod who had come to Canada from the Highlands of Scotland. He had long been a professional soldier and eventually became a commissioner of the Mounted Police.

Colonel Macleod went with Crowfoot to meet the other chiefs of the Confederacy in whose territory he was. He later wrote that he was "received with stately ceremony", and found the chiefs "intelligent men who conducted the interviews as dignified gentlemen". The chiefs told Colonel Macleod they were grateful to the Mounted Police for getting the wild traders with their arsenals and bad whisky, both of which killed their young men, out of their land. Colonel Macleod cultivated the friendship of the chiefs for a reason. He had a mission which he intimated first to the Council when he told them that great men of the country were to come for they wanted to make a treaty with them. The word "treaty" had no meaning to them.

Crowfoot was learning from the white men ideas that seemed strange to his people. The young men looked askance at a ruling he made after a successful horse raid on the Crees. It was understood by everyone that horses taken in a raid were likely to be stolen back. That was an old rule. It was not possessing the horses so much as the danger of taking them that made the game exciting. Such raiding was not directed toward conquest of enemy territory or extermination of a tribe. Creeping into a guarded camp and coming away with the chosen horses without blood being shed was a *coup* to gloat over at society gatherings. Yet they all knew it was a recognized act of aggression. If some were killed on either side— well, one must die sometime!

When Crowfoot ordered that the horses taken from the Crees by his own band, the Moccasins, were to be returned to their owners, he was obeyed. He could not give this order to other bands for he did not have the right, but he advised other chiefs to do it also. Some even took his advice, for they respected him, but now they did not understand him. He had gone ahead of them. Crowfoot was pioneering in social relationships.

In December 1876, Sitting Bull with some thousands of his Sioux people and many horses crossed the border from the south and made camp near Wood Mountain. He told the North West Mounted Police who went to find the reason for the intrusion, that he and his people were driven out of their country and they were only looking for peace for they had not slept sound for years. Crowfoot and his people were in camp in the Cypress Hills, east of Medicine Hat, and Sitting Bull went there to pay a visit. Crowfoot made him welcome in his tipi, for they were old friends, and he made a feast in his guest's honour. Sitting Bull had long admired Crowfoot's wisdom and his good government of the Confederacy. He said he would like Crowfoot to give his (Sitting Bull's) young son his own name. "We will be friends to the end of our days. My children will be your children and yours will be mine." He gave Crowfoot many horses as gifts.

The heralded proposal from the "great men" in the Canadian government was that the Blackfoot Confederacy cede to the government their ancient territory for Canadian settlers. The Indians met the representatives of the government at the Milk River in southern Alberta to discuss this proposal. A story remembered from that time tells of the man who spread a sheaf of dollar bills on the ground, and said, "This is what the white man trades with. This is his buffalo robe. As you trade with skins we trade with these pieces of paper." Crowfoot took up a handful of clay and dropped it on the fire and cooked it. Then he said to the visitor, "Now, put your money on the fire. See if it will last as long as the clay." The man replied, "No, my money will burn because it is made of paper." Crowfoot said, "Your money is not as good as our land. The wind will blow it away. The fire will burn it. Water will rot it. Nothing will destroy our land."

A trader, son of an Indian mother and a white man, warned, "All you Indians, all the chiefs have not tried to send these mounties back east. They are going to give pieces of blue-backed paper. That is a dollar but it means there will be no more buffalo." But this was a story they could laugh at, for every tribe had piles of buffalo skins for the trading.

On September 18, 1877 the "great men" came. The Honourable David Laird, Lieutenant-Governor of the North West Territories and Indian Superintendent, was one of them. He was a Canadian from Prince Edward Island. The other was Commissioner James Macleod of the North West Mounted Police. Commissioner Macleod had sympathy for the Blackfoot, but he also had a stern duty before him. With the Honourable David Laird he was to lead the Blackfoot to "cede, release, surrender and yield up" to the government of Canada fifty thousand square miles of their prairie kingdom. For this land and in "extinguishment of all past claims" each man, woman and child was to be paid at once twelve dollars. Later there would be other benefits like cattle, medals, implements and a yearly payment forever of a few more dollars for each member of the tribe, with the chiefs in power getting the most.

The meeting place for the council was at Blackfoot Crossing, a favourite home camp of the people and a place of unusual beauty. On this September day the river glimmered in the sunshine and the cottonwoods and willows shone with golden leaves. The coulees were all aglow with the bronze and russet browns of the wild rose and buffalo berry bushes. The Confederacy made camp, a settlement of a thousand lodges. The Indians were in their finest clothing and each cooking fire sent a smoke signal high in the clear sky. A large tent had been erected to serve for a council chamber at one end of the encampment. The bell-shaped tents of the Mounted Police shone white at the other. The commissioners arrived in great style, escorted by officers of the police in their red coats and spiked helmets. After all were assembled in the large tent the council was opened with a fanfare from the police band.

Neither Crowfoot nor his brother Three Bulls would accept any small gifts from the commissioners until the people had heard the terms of the treaty read. James Bird, the son of a Hudson's Bay Company employee who had taken an Indian wife, was the interpreter for them. They were very quiet and they asked time for conferring. They still had no real knowledge of the small acreage that ceding would confine them to, but the Confederacy trusted Crowfoot completely. If they had not, a rebellion might have flared up, and this would have had disastrous results. Crowfoot was under tremendous pressure.

He went to stay alone in his tipi and the commissioners waited impatiently. At last he gave the word that he would sign on the morning of the fifth day, September 22nd. Having made the decision, overwhelmed with worry and sorrow, he moved his tipi out of the camp circle to a lonely place.

When the morning of the fifth day came a cannon was fired from the hill as a signal that the council was to begin. The cannon boomed again as Crowfoot made his mark on the long parchment of the treaty, the bagpipes wailed gaily and the Union Jack was hoisted. The other chiefs of the Confederacy made their marks, Three Bulls signing for the Blackfoot.

In 1878 at the time appointed for the first treaty payment, the Indians were shocked when they received less than had been agreed upon, and Colonel Macleod had no good explanation to give them. Some of the Indians met the situation by using another of their names and collecting twice, but this was frowned on by the chiefs. The promised cattle had not come either.

Meanwhile, American troops had tirelessly patrolled the border, on watch for Sitting Bull and his Sioux. When the herds came down from Canadian pastures the troops were ordered to prevent the buffalo returning to Canada. A gigantic round-up and slaughter was carried out by the hundreds of skilled hunters and skinners assembled for the purpose. To be sure that no small herds strayed off and escaped killing, the Canadian pastures were fired. Sitting Bull and his Sioux must be brought to their knees.

Edgar Dewdney, an Englishman, Indian Agent in the North West Territories, reported to his superintendent, "in 1879 a series of prairie fires were set at different points simultaneously as if by prearrangement. The country north of the border was burned over from Wood Mountain on the east to the Rockies in the west and almost as far north as Qu'Appelle." A note in the report of the Hudson's Bay commissioners stated, "The general impression is the fires were started by the Americans to keep the buffalo south of our border." With irony unhappily typical of their history, the Indians of the plains have been blamed for the sudden total extinction of the northern buffalo herd by their improvidence and wanton wastefulness.

Though the trickery behind the extermination of the buffalo

could be concealed, the effects could not. The Indians of the plains were immediately rendered utterly destitute. Never before had large numbers of them, whole communities, known hunger from actual scarcity of food. Now they could not find enough meat for the children, for even the small game like deer had been destroyed by the fires. They were reduced to eating gophers and other rodents, and in desperation a few even ate horsemeat. Some of the old people starved to death. Then in the midst of desolation, the herds of horses suffered an epidemic of mange.

From the time they reached the treaty site the Confederacy began a new way of life. The farm teacher from Pincher Creek had built a house to live in and there were a few huts the old people had made. There was a small herd of cattle and land had been broken for root crops. The government's plan had begun to operate. These people, who had long been the only planners of their lives, were bending to an unknown yoke that would often chafe. Their opinions were not asked, nor were their views on methods and values consulted. Ordered about like children or morons, their only defence was apathy.

The new food was distasteful to them. Whereas the old buffalo diet had made them a strong, hardy people, the fat pork or bacon of inferior quality from Ontario farms was horrible to them, for no one knew how to cook it. No one had an appetite for the potatoes and turnips from the farm manager's plot. The tipis all had many sick and dying people.

At this time Crowfoot, having devoted the sixty years of his whole life to achieving Blackfoot ideals, was honoured by his people for his wisdom and goodness. The other chiefs acknowledged him chief of chiefs. So even now, though he had signed the white man's treaty, there was no rebellion against him, for he had earned their trust.

In 1883 the Canadian Pacific Railway, in process of building, came into the Blackfoot country. Crowfoot was ill with a throat ailment and his people were worried. The railway had begun to lay tracks on Confederacy lands without asking permission. Crowfoot objected, "This is no part of the treaty." His people moved tipis to the land and camped there, saying "No" to the surveyors. Commissioner Macleod was sent for, but they held their ground. The Commissioner sent telegrams to the government at Ottawa and a compromise was made. "If the railway is allowed through your land up the Cluny Hill to Gleichen we will give in return the same amount of land on the south side of the river as we take." The Blackfoot Council saw this was fair and the railway went forward. Because of this fair dealing, Indians never hampered the Canadian Pacific in its operations. As a representative of the Confederacy, Crowfoot was given another medal by the railway company, good for transportation over their line.

Another plains people, the Métis, were also suffering from the destruction of the buffalo herds. The Métis were the descendants of French adventurers, voyageurs and other early travellers who had married "daughters of the land" or Indian wives. Of these the largest number had lived for years as a group in the Red River country in Manitoba.

When Canada purchased territorial sovereignty from the Hudson's Bay Company, the Métis and other settlers there, to their consternation, were not notified of the purchase. Surveyors suddenly appeared on their land. Led by one of their own men, Louis Riel, the Métis either rose in rebellion or, discouraged by this callous treatment, moved farther north and made new homes in Saskatchewan north of the wide area burned to kill off the buffalo herds. Crowfoot and Riel had discussed the Métis and the Cree people who were neighbours and sympathetic to the Métis. Crowfoot told him the Confederacy had now a treaty of peace with the Crees, their one-time foes. In the talk of rebellion and war, Crowfoot made it clear to Louis Riel that the Blackfoot Confederacy would take no part. "We are at peace," he said. The Métis implored Riel to return to Saskatchewan to lead them in their second rebellion, but the Confederacy refused to join them, even though the young men would have welcomed the excitement of a battle, bottled up as they were on their reserve territory.

Attempts were made to reconcile the Indian to the lot imposed on him, attempts that were often well meant but usually inadequate because they were confused, ignorant and fundamentally lacking in respect.

The Canadian government and the Canadian Pacific Railway invited Crowfoot and his brother Three Bulls, North Axe of the Piegans and Red Crow of the Bloods to go on a trip to the east. This trip was to be a "lesson in civilization" for them. Later some of the Cree chiefs were added to the group. But when the time came, Crowfoot's beloved son had just died. He was in great mourning, even ill. By the custom of his people he could not take part in any public affair before the funeral rites and the period of mourning were over. He had many other troubles, for recent deaths in his family had greatly impoverished him; yet reluctantly he agreed to go. They went as far east as Montreal, where the Canadian Pacific Railway was their host. They were well entertained and given more medals. When they came back to Ottawa, the government and that city honoured them. The Mayor made a flowery speech, attempting geniality by the use of a few eastern Indian terms like "manitou" and "wampum" which had no meaning to plains Indians.

But by this time Crowfoot was really very ill and sad and had no heart for festivities, so that he went directly home from Ottawa. Crowfoot never again fully recovered his health. The lingering character of his illness would indicate that it was tuberculosis, or consumption as it was called then. His people cared for him like a beloved father, and he talked much to them of the new life they must follow. He begged them to cultivate the friendship of good people as far as they were able.

But for all his bravery in attempting to meet new conditions and adapt to a new way of life, for all his intelligence and sensitivity to the drift of the times and the circumstances, it could not be concealed from his people that a great chief, a great hunter, brave warrior, eloquent spokesman, intelligent diplomat, good man— was hunter, warrior, effective spokesman no longer. In his approaching death the decline and death of the old Indian ways were all too intimately represented. All his wisdom, all his strength and gentleness, all his peace-loving efforts to solve their problems had not established the old Confederacy in the new confederation called Canada. Not with anything like the old dignity. Not like themselves.

In the fall of 1889 he told them he would die in the spring. Two days before he died he sank into a coma. Even the medicine men thought it was death, but they waited and in the evening he revived. He took a small portion of food and enjoyed a pipe. All his relatives had gathered about and he asked them not to mourn for him. On Friday afternoon when he died his people obeyed his wish. But according to their custom, his favourite horse was shot for his use in "the land of the sand hills beyond the sunset".

In his last hours he said, "What is life? It is the flash of a firefly in the night. It is the breath of a buffalo in the wintertime. It is the little shadow which runs across the grass and loses itself in the sunset."

So passed one of the good people who have walked the earth.

# FOCUSSING

The word *hero* refers both to females and males. Any person who performs a heroic deed is a hero.

1.  a) Brainstorm, in a group of three or four, ideas that you associate with the word *hero*. The following categories might help you.
    - the names of heroes from today and from history
    - fictional heroes from movies, television, books, comic books, and rock music lyrics
    - the qualities of heroes

    Using a computer, create a data base on heroes. Enter the ideas your group has brainstormed into the data file. After reviewing your data base, define the word *hero* in your own words.

2.  Write a journal entry on one of the following topics:
    - My Personal Heroes
    - Why People Need to Have Heroes
    - The Differences between Famous People and Heroes

3.  Using pictures from magazines, make a poster of at least five people who have done something heroic. Under each picture briefly explain why you think the people qualify as heroes.

# NELLIE McCLUNG
### by Terry Angus and Shirley White

I N 1880 at the age of seven, Nellie Mooney came to Manitoba with her father and mother to meet her brothers who had come west earlier. Nellie's mother had persuaded the family to leave their log house at Chatsworth in Grey County, Ontario, and settle in the West, because she saw no future for her sons on the farm in Ontario. She felt they would become hired hands at best. Little did Mrs. Mooney suspect that the child who would really flourish would be one of her daughters, Nellie.

The family travelled by ship to Owen Sound, and by train from Duluth, Minnesota, to St. Boniface, Manitoba. Then came the toughest part of the westward journey: 288 km by oxen over almost impassable roads to a location near the junction of the Assiniboine and Souris Rivers, now known as the Wawanesa District in Manitoba. During their first bitterly cold winter on the prairies the Mooney family had grave doubts about their move. As wolves howled at night and the wind whistled through their one-room log cabin, thatched only with prairie grass, the family of eight thought more than once of returning to Ontario. Persevering, however, over the years, they slowly began to prosper. Winters did not last forever and the summers brought excellent crops. Young Nellie Mooney, too, seemed to thrive on this difficult beginning. She possessed a hardy spirit, and at the age of 15 she passed an examination that qualified her to be a teacher. She took her first job teaching at Manitou, Manitoba, one year later. Her career had started.

It was in Manitou that she met her future husband, Wesley McClung, a druggist, whom she married in 1896. "His mother, God bless her, educated him," she explained years later, "so Wes was not the sort of man who thought his wife should always be standing behind him ready to spring to attention."

Nellie became interested in women's rights and a group called the WCTU, The Women's Christian Temperance Union, after many discussions with her mother-in-law. Her first efforts to gain signatures on a petition for women's rights ended the way her first touch with politics ended—with people laughing at her.

Unwilling to allow failure to deter her, however, Nellie McClung turned to writing. Her mother-in-law encouraged her to submit a short story to a magazine contest by doing her housework for her. She received favourable comments for her story from the magazine (but not the prize) and as a result she expanded her story into her first book, *Sowing Seeds in Danny*. The book became a runaway bestseller in 1908 and sold well over 100,000 copies. Suddenly Nellie McClung had become a name to watch.

Although Nellie already had a family of four sons and a daughter, she turned back to some of her earlier concerns. At the turn of the century, women had no right to vote and they also lost control of any money they had when they married. To Nellie McClung and many other women this seemed a grave injustice. Nellie plunged into the suffrage struggle by making countless speeches. "The great army of women workers are ill-paid, badly housed, and their work is not honoured or paid for," she complained.

She became an eloquent speaker and slowly the women of Manitoba began to unite in her cause.

Perhaps Nellie McClung's most famous public appearance took place in the Walker Theatre in Winnipeg on January 28, 1914. On that night Nellie staged a mock parliament to poke fun at the Manitoba provincial government's attitude toward women's rights. Nellie reversed the real-life situation on stage and had men begging for the right to vote while she, as premier, refused

their questions for the same silly reasons that the government had recently given women. The put-on was brilliant and the show was not only financially successful, it also made the cause of women's rights known and acceptable to many. Nellie McClung used laughter as her lever and the Walker Theatre was filled with converts. In 1916, in Manitoba, the women's suffrage bill was passed in the legislature.

Nellie McClung and her family moved further west to Edmonton in 1912, and she immediately set about to improve the rights of women in Alberta. Elected to the legislature in 1921, she helped women win the right to sit in the Senate, which they hadn't been able to do previously because the word "persons" in the British North America Act of 1867 had been interpreted to mean only "men".

Nellie continued to write novels of pioneer life on the Prairies. These captured the attention and sympathy of many readers. Her writing also took the form of serious social criticism and her arguments often contained specific attacks on the nature of Canadian society. She spoke harshly about everything from land speculators to charity systems, and suggested full employment and economic security as two of the worthiest goals Canadian society could have. She believed the greatest injustice that had been done to the human race was the economic dependence of women. She believed this had to be rectified.

After her defeat for re-election in 1926, she devoted her time to her family, her writing and travelling. In 1938 she was appointed to the Canadian delegation of the League of Nations. This achievement was only overshadowed by the outbreak of war in 1939 and the inability of the League of Nations to prevent it.

Saddened by the 2 world wars which had occurred in her lifetime, Nellie still managed to keep a buoyant outlook, even in her 70s. A fitting memorial to Mrs. McClung has been erected on the farm where she was born. It seems to summarize well the life of one of Canada's most important suffragists, a reformer far ahead of her time. The plaque donated by the Canadian government, affixed to the stone memorial, bears the inscription:

Nellie Mooney McClung—lecturer, teacher and writer—ardent advocate of women's rights in Canada—author of *Sowing Seeds in Danny* and other works— born at Chatsworth, 20th October, 1873— died in Victoria, B.C., 1st September, 1951.

# CLOSE UP

1. Talk with a partner about what you would include in an obituary for Nellie McClung. Write the obituary, dated September 2, 1951, the day after her death in Victoria, B.C. Remember to include the details that made her a hero.
2. Imagine that you are Nellie McClung and write a point-form outline for the speech you are preparing for your first appearance in the Alberta legislature. The speech will be a statement of your beliefs. Work with a partner and include at least five beliefs each.

# WIDE ANGLE

1. Pretend that you are working for the suffragists in 1900 and you have been asked to prepare a one-page flyer for distribution at meetings and rallies. Work with a partner to create the hand-out. If your class has a computer graphics program or a newspaper program, use it to design and print your flyer.

   **or**

   Working in a group of three or four, make up five suffragist slogans. Print them on poster paper, illustrate or decorate them, and make a suffragist bulletin board. If your school has a graphics department, you could paint your poster there. You might also like to make suffragist buttons using your slogans.
2. In a group of three or four, discuss the changes you would like to make

   a) in your school;   c) in your city or country; or
   b) in your family;   d) in the world.

   After listing the changes you would make, read through the article to discover how Nellie McClung was able to influence society. Write out a plan of action to bring about your own changes.
3. With the help of your librarian or history teacher, read another piece of writing on Nellie McClung. In a group of three or four, choose a scene from Nellie's life that is suitable for dramatization. Write a script and act it out for the rest of the class. Some suggestions are

   * a dialogue between Nellie and her husband, Wes, about Nellie's activities;
   * a meeting of the suffragists; and
   * Nellie making her first appearance in the League of Nations.

# MARTHA LOUISE BLACK

*by Terry Angus and Shirley White*

THE SKY was red; tongues of flame shot through the black clouds of smoke. Five-year-old Martha Louise Munger rubbed her stinging eyes and stared in horror at the bedlam which surrounded her. Adults with blackened and bloodstained faces dragged screaming children from the house. People hurried by with wheelbarrows full of family possessions. The roar of the fire, the cries of children, the screaming of stampeding horses—all became imprinted on the little girl's memory. She would never forget that night in October of 1871 when the great Chicago fire drove her family and thousands of others out of their homes to the sandy shore of Lake Michigan.

Yet it was appropriate that tiny Martha Louise Munger should undergo such an experience at an early age. Born in Chicago in 1866 to a wealthy businessman and his wife, Martha was the only one of the Munger's first five children to survive infancy. Her life would be a series of adventures often no less exciting and frightening than her first vivid childhood memory. Over twenty-five years later, a palmist told her: "You are leaving this country. You will travel far. You will face danger, privation, and sorrow. Although you are going to a foreign land, you will be among English-speaking people. . . . You will have another child, a girl, or an unusually devoted son." What the palmist did not tell Martha was that this prediction would come true within a year. Married, the mother of two, Martha had little reason to think that her life in the suburbs of Chicago would change so drastically.

The news that flashed around the world that year was that gold by the bucketful had been found in the Klondike. Gold fever hit Martha's husband, Will Purdy, as it did countless others. Intrigued, Martha put the children in her parents' care, and she, Will and her brother, George departed for Seattle—the first stop in a long and dangerous trek to Dawson City in the Yukon.

In Seattle, Will Purdy abruptly changed his mind. He decided not to go, and he asked Martha to return home. But Martha Louise was eager to finish the voyage, so she and Will went their separate ways, never to see each other again.

The ship sailed and Martha and her brother survived the overloaded passage to Skagway. On July 12, 1898, they joined others to walk the dreaded 68 kilometres over the Chilkoot Pass. As Martha trudged along, she noticed scores of dead horses that had slipped and fallen down the perpendicular ice-covered rock. Snow slides and rock slides had resulted in countless stone markers and grave sites where tragedy had occurred. Afraid to look down, Martha edged her way along the narrowing path. Suddenly her foot slipped and she fell into a crevice in the rock. Her leg was cut and throbbed with pain. She wept as the others passed her on the trail. Finally her brother screamed at her impatiently, "For God's sake, Polly, buck up!" Martha moved on. The last three kilometres of the descending trail were a nightmare. The trail wound through a scrub pine forest which tripped them and tore their boots to pieces. Tired and faint, Martha stared at her cut and bleeding hands and begged the others to leave her on the trail to rest for the night. George half-carried her to the end. As they arrived at Lake Bennet, Martha felt an exhausted thrill of satisfaction—she had made it over the Chilkoot Pass!

A three-week layover at Lake Bennet was needed to construct a pine dory. During the twelve days they sailed, Martha and her fellow travellers trolled for salmon and trout to eat. Camping at night, they shot squirrels for meat and picked raspberries, strawberries, blueberries, and cranberries. Finally they arrived at Dawson City, a sprawl of tents, shanties, and log cabins housing about twenty thousand men and a handful of

women, most of them searching for gold.

But finding gold was not Martha's main concern when she discovered that she was expecting a baby. She couldn't walk out the Chilkoot Trail in her condition—she would have to have her baby in Dawson. Her daily diet consisted of cornmeal mush, prunes, and clear tea. Food prices were so high (milk was sixteen dollars a gallon, butter three dollars a pound) she could afford little else. Worse still, it would cost $1000 to deliver the baby in a hospital, so Martha decided that she would have to have the baby at home. Alone, in a tiny cabin on January 31, 1899, Martha gave birth to a son. When George and the working men returned from work that evening, they were astounded to find a baby wrapped in red flannel.

The years passed. A degree of stability returned to Martha's life. She went to Chicago and returned with her two older children. Financed by her father, Martha established and managed two sawmills on the Klondike River a short distance from Dawson. She received a divorce, settled her children in school and proved herself a shrewd businesswoman. In the spring of 1902 she encountered a full scale walk-out of all her men. They were led by a foreman who was " . . . sick of being ordered around by a skirt." She had survived worse, and she rode it through with the help of the Mounties. Later, consulting legal counsel concerning mill business, she met George Black, a clever, good-looking lawyer who was keenly interested in politics. They were married after a two-year courtship.

Martha and George Black settled down to bringing up their three boys and enjoying the Yukon. Martha won a two hundred dollar prize for assembling a collection of 464 varieties of native wild flowers. Her exhibit was sent to the World's Fair in Seattle to demonstrate that the Yukon was not a barren wilderness. Her interest in artistic botany, as she called it, led to an appointment as a Fellow of the Royal Geographical Society, and she began mounting displays for the Canadian Pacific Railway.

When World War I broke out, George organized a Yukon Infantry Company. The Company left Dawson in October of 1916. Aboard ship were 3500 men and one woman—Martha Louise Black. Martha had petitioned generals and the prime minister to allow her on board with the men.

After the war, Martha and George returned to the Yukon. George Black was elected to Parliament and won four successive elections. When he was appointed Speaker of the House in 1930, George and Martha became the official hosts for the House of Commons. In 1935 Martha took over from her critically ill husband. Embarking on a new career at the age of seventy, she became the second woman elected to Parliament.

When Martha Louise Black died at the age of 91 in Whitehorse, the *Whitehorse Star* reported: "A blithe spirit has left the Yukon. Martha Louise Black was the unrivalled queen of all that host of men and women who sought the northern magic. . . . She, above all, caught and reflected the true spirit of the Yukon and some of it died with her."

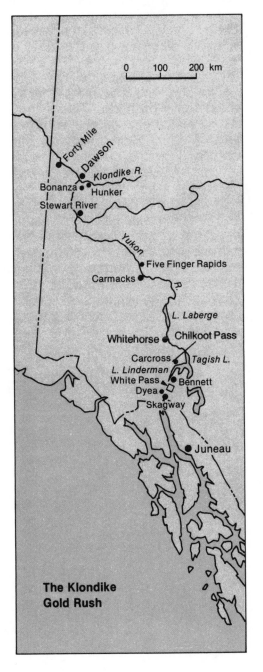

The Klondike Gold Rush

# CLOSE UP

1. "Martha Louise Black was an extremely courageous woman who faced many dangers." Make point-form notes to support the above statement. Using your notes, write a paragraph that could be used as an introduction to a book or article about Martha Louise Black.

2. a) Pretend that you are a newspaper journalist sent from the *Whitehorse Star* to interview Martha Louise on her ninetieth birthday. With a partner, make up at least five questions you would ask her. Have another pair of students answer your questions.

   b) You are the artist at the *Whitehorse Star*, and the writer of the article on Martha Louise has asked you to do an illustration for the story. Draw a picture of your favourite scene from Martha Louise's life, write a caption for the picture, and then write two or three sentences explaining why you chose the scene.

# WIDE ANGLE

1. There were other heroes during the Klondike gold rush. Ask your history teacher or librarian to help you find a story about one of them. Share your story with a small group. Ask your listeners to jot down questions as you tell the story. Answer their questions.

2. Make a *Superwoman of the Klondike* comic strip based on Martha Louise's life story. Pick out her most heroic actions. Use a computer cartoon-writing program if one is available. When your comic is complete, you may wish to share it with some elementary school students.

# THE WELCOMIN'
## *by David Poulsen*

I SUPPOSE I must've been standin' there about an hour and a half when I saw the train just sort of lumbering down the track towards us. It was a cold day, too, so actually I guess it was the steam I saw first.

January's always the coldest month in southern Saskatchewan and that particular January, the one that got 1943 off and rolling, was a beaut.

Still, I bet half of Swift Current was right there on that platform waitin' for that train to arrive, and me with 'em.

Even the town band was out and all dressed up in their uniforms. They'd already played a couple of tunes, kinda to give the whole thing a little atmosphere, you know, like a celebration. It probably helped to keep 'em from freezin' to death too, in those uniforms. There wasn't a whole lot to 'em. I imagine they mostly got used in the summer . . . for parades and stuff like that.

I mean it WAS a celebration. What else do you call it when two war heroes are bein' welcomed home?

I'd had a lot of time to think about the whole thing—I mean wars and heroes and all that—while I'd been standin' there on the platform. I'd thought a lot about how I remembered Ray Harmon and Orrie Franchuk, too, before they left for the war, especially when I saw "Hammer" Hammermeister on the platform.

I couldn't believe it if you wanna know the truth . . . Hammer Hammermeister in Swift Current to welcome back his two worst enemies.

It was seein' him standin' there shiverin' like the rest of us that really started me thinkin' . . . you know, rememberin'.

I guess when you start rememberin' things about somebody special in your life, you just naturally go back to a time that really stands out. You know, like when you're thinkin' about your Dad, you automatically remember the time he brought home a puppy and had it hid in a box so you couldn't see it and he walks in all casual and says "Hey, anybody know where I should put this box of books? Oh, guess right here'll be O.K." he says, and then sets the box down and there's a puppy in there, not books at all and you wanna kiss 'im but you can't 'cause he's a man and when you're nine years old, there's some things you just can't do.

Well, that's about the way it was for me with Ray Harmon and Orrie Franchuk. The special time I remember about them was just about two years before that day on the platform. It was the most important hockey game of my life, maybe the most important hockey game in the whole history of Swift Current . . .

The Beavers were playin' the Elrose Flyers, and as much as it's possible for a ten-year-old kid to hate is how much I hated the Flyers, especially Hammer Hammermeister.

You wouldn't've believed that game. I mean, you gotta realize that the winner was headin' off to Ottawa to play their team for the National Championship.

All season long, Elrose and us had been really close. They beat us twice, we beat them once and we tied 'em once.

And now here it was *the* game and we were losing 2-1

in the third period. We got our goal while Hammermeister was in the penalty box. He was usually good for two or three penalties and maybe a fight every game.

He had one of their goals as well. I mean, Hammermeister was a great player, there was no denyin' that, but he was so dirty and, on top of that, he was from Elrose so there was no way you could keep from hatin' the guy.

Well, there we were with seven minutes left in the game and me screamin' my lungs out in the bleachers. My Dad, who didn't usually get too excited about stuff, was kind of sittin' up tall and watchin' everything real close and even Mom had quit talkin' to Iris Oldfield in the row behind us and was payin' attention to the game.

And then, sure enough, there was Hammer Hammermeister livin' up to his name and practically runnin' one of our guys through the boards. Only the ref caught him and he was gone for another two minutes.

I knew this was it. We had to get one during this penalty or forget it. I guess our guys knew it too because Ray Harmon made a great play to get around one of their defencemen and then slid a pass across in front to his winger and just like that it's 2-2!

Boy, did I give it to Hammermeister as he was comin' out of the penalty box, but I doubt if he heard me 'cause the noise in that place was unbelievable.

Then came the most exciting five minutes of my life. With about two minutes to go Ray Harmon stole the puck from one of their defencemen, faked the goalie right out of his socks and bingo it's 3-2 for the Beavers.

But the thing wasn't over—not by a long shot. Now, you

wouldn't think a team, leadin' by one goal with less than a minute left in the game would allow a breakaway would you?

Sure enough, though, 30 seconds to go and suddenly, who's got the puck and headin' in on goal but Hammer Hammermeister. Orrie Franchuk was our goalie and he had been playin' great all through the game and I remember prayin' real quick that he had one more save in him. I remember how I promised God that I'd never say damn again, at least until I was twenty-one, if he'd let Orrie make that save. It's funny how your mind works at a time like that.

Anyway, Hammermeister let go a shot and one thing I'll

say about Hammer Hammermeister, he had about the hardest shot I've ever seen. I don't know how Orrie could've even seen the shot, maybe he didn't but somehow he got his glove over there and sure enough, the puck was in that glove. I couldn't believe it, no kidding, I just couldn't. I think it was bedtime that night before my heart sort of got back to beatin' normal. I guess that was about the best day I've ever had so far in my life.

And now here's Hammer Hammermeister, standin' on that platform, waitin' for Ray and Orrie to get off the train.

It was funny. I tried to picture Orrie and Ray over there fightin' the Germans, it was a place called Dieppe, somewhere or other in France, and every time I'd picture a German in my mind he'd look like Hammer Hammermeister.

The train was gettin' closer. People were startin' to kind of push forward, so I did too 'cause I wanted to make real sure I could see those guys.

I could see Ray Harmon's Mom and Dad, smilin' away and movin' up to the edge of the track. I have to admit I was gettin' pretty excited myself. Maybe not quite as much as when the Beavers beat the Flyers—but almost.

The train finally stopped and the band started playin' like crazy. Only thing is, they played for about ten minutes and nobody got off the train. Nothin' happened. Finally the band quit playin' and people sort of stood around for a few minutes.

Then just about the time everybody was gettin' ready to give up and go home, Ray Harmon came into the doorway of the train. Except it wasn't Ray Harmon, you know what I mean?

The guy that was in the doorway of that car was leanin' on crutches 'cause one of his legs was gone and his right arm was all bandaged up. That seemed strange to me 'cause the battle had been months before and I figured a guy would've healed up in that time.

But the worst part was his face. I mean, I remember that face with the biggest grin on it you ever saw after that goal against the Flyers. Comin' off that train, it was a face that didn't look like it had ever grinned, and maybe never would again. I don't know if I'm explainin' it exactly right. It was like he was dead, only his body was still alive.

They brought him down off the train and his Mom and Dad and two guys that looked sort of like doctors led him through the crowd. They came right by me and I swear Ray Harmon looked right at me, but he never said nothin' or let on he knew me or anythin'. I figured at the time maybe he hadn't seen me after all.

It sure seemed awful quiet on that station platform. The

band guys were just standin' there holdin' their instruments and nobody seemed to feel like celebratin' anymore.

Then another guy was standin' in the door of the train and he was hangin' on to Orrie Franchuk. Orrie had this bandage across his eyes and I heard a couple of women say "Oh my God," and one guy behind me said, "Why didn't they let us know it was like this?"

Of course it was later that we found out the truth about Dieppe. It was a lot different than what we had all been readin' and hearin' from those war correspondents. Orrie and Ray were with the South Saskatchewan Regiment that attacked a place called Pourville. I guess Orrie only got about 50 yards up the beach and behind a sea wall and then he got pinned down by machine gun fire for about four hours. Never moved. Never fired a shot. He lost his eyes when he finally made a dash back to the water and a bullet ricocheted off the landing-boat thing he was tryin' to get into and hit him.

Ray Harmon was quite a ways from Orrie and he got off the beach and up to this bridge. A lot of guys never made it across that bridge and Ray was one of the ones who didn't.

I guess he'd laid there wounded and holdin' onto the bottom half of his leg tryin' to keep it from fallin' off for about two hours before the Medics were able to get to him. . . .

Seein' those two guys like that, I don't know, it sort of got to me.

You know, the craziest thing about that day at the train station though . . . after they led Orrie through the crowd I turned around and Hammer Hammermeister was standin' there cryin'. I'm not talkin' about a little tear in the corner of his eye, the man was practically bawlin'. I mean I was too but you can expect that from a kid. But Hammer Hammermeister, with tears rollin' down his face?

I don't remember them havin' any more welcomin's for war heroes. But maybe that was just as well. It didn't turn out to be much of a celebration anyway.

# CLOSE UP

1. In a group of three or four discuss the following:
   a) what the narrator expected to happen when the train arrived;
   b) what Ray Harmon and Orrie Franchuk had been through and how they felt about it; and
   c) why a "tough" guy like Hammer Hammermeister was crying.

2. We see Orrie and Ray in two roles—as hockey heroes and war heroes. Draw two illustrations—one showing Orrie as a hockey hero, and the other showing Ray as a war hero. Read the story carefully to get the details necessary for your illustrations.

3. You are a reporter for a radio station in Swift Current, and you were present at the railway station for the welcomin'. Write and record a short radio commentary on the topic "The Price of Being a Hero." Play it for a group that read the story.

or

You are the editor of the newspaper in Swift Current. Write a short editorial for the paper, entitled "Welcoming Home Two Heroes." Whichever activity you choose, ask a partner to comment on your work, using the Checklist for Re-seeing and Revising (p. 182), and to help you revise so it is ready to be broadcast or published.

# WIDE ANGLE

1. One of the most terrible battles Canadians were involved in during World War II was the battle at Dieppe. Ask your history teacher or librarian for information on that battle. If your library has an "on-line" data base, you can do a computer search for the information. Make note of some of the heroic acts and tell the class about them.

2. With a partner, interview a veteran of World War II who lives in your community. First, prepare a list of questions. One question should ask for an example of heroism. If possible, tape your interview and play it for the class.

3. Imagine that you are either Ray Harmon or Orrie Franchuk and write a monologue in which you describe one of your experiences and express your feelings about being a war hero. In a small group, read your monologues for each other. Try to read it with the emotions Ray or Orrie would feel.

4. Write a poem using one of these titles (or one of your own):
   "No More Welcomin's"     "The Price I Paid"
   "The Truth About War"     "War Is Not a Game"
   "The Hero of Swift Current" "Going Off to War"
   If you (or one of your friends) play a musical instrument, put your lyrics to music and present your song to the class.

# TERRY FOX

*by Meguido and Melanie Zola*

STACK, CLICK, clunk, tumble! Blocks all over the living-room floor. This is not a fun game anymore. The blocks keep falling when they're supposed to stay.

But two-year-old Terry Fox wrinkles his brow and goes at it again. Stack, click, clunk. A tower takes shape.

These are the beginnings of a hero.

Born July 28, 1958, in Winnipeg, Manitoba, Terrance Stanley Fox, known to everyone as Terry, moves with his family to British Columbia in 1966. They settle in Port Coquitlam, a suburb of Vancouver.

THE FOX family is a close and loving one. Terry's father, Rolly, works for the Canadian National Railways. His mother, Betty, manages a card shop. Terry has an older brother, Fred, a younger brother, Darrell, and a younger sister, Judith.

All of them are strong-willed, but Terry in particular loves nothing better than a challenge. Once he starts something, he just will not give up until he sees it through. In play fights with his dad and two brothers, Terry is the one who doesn't quit until he comes out on top.

Terry's determined ways stay with him through his school years. He is not an outstanding student, but he works hard at his studies and finishes high school with almost straight A's.

That's Terry Fox: if he decides to do something, he'll do it.

TAKE TERRY'S ambition to play basketball. He lets nothing get in the way of it.

The coach in grade eight tells him he's too short and would do better at wrestling. Terry isn't put off so easily.

He goes into all types of training for basketball. He even does cross-country running, much as he hates it. And every chance he gets, he practises basketball shots with his friend Doug Alward.

Chosen nineteenth on a team of nineteen players, Terry finally makes the Mary Hill Cobras basketball team. He plays only one minute in the entire season, but he still does not give up. He keeps practising to improve his game, and by grade twelve, he is a starting guard on the Port Coquitlam High School Ravens basketball team. On his last day of school, Terry shares the Athlete of the Year award with Doug Alward.

Terry's mom says it best: "Terry is average in everything but determination."

AVERAGE. Just an ordinary guy. That's what Terry Fox calls himself, too.

After high school, Terry goes to Simon Fraser University to study kinesiology, the science of body movement. He plans to become a physical education teacher.

Early in 1977, while he is in his first year, Terry is bothered by a pain in his right leg. At first he ignores it. He is on the basketball team and is determined to finish the season. One morning, however, it is suddenly so bad he can't stand up. His worried father takes him to the hospital.

Terry is diagnosed as having osteogenic sarcoma, a bone cancer. The doctors feel that they must act quickly to stop the cancer from spreading. Three days later Terry's leg is amputated above the knee.

"I cried and cried," says Terry.

That Terry decides to fight back is remarkable.

As Prime Minister Pierre Trudeau later says of him: "Learning to walk again would have been admirable enough. Trying to run a short distance would have marked him as a man of courage . . ."

HOW TERRY fights back is more remarkable yet. For Terry Fox, the "ordinary guy," is planning something extraordinary.

Terry has read an article given him by Terry Fleming, who had been his basketball coach. It tells of a one-legged athlete, Dick Traum, who ran in the New York City Marathon.

"I can do that," thinks Terry. In fact he is soon dreaming of doing even more. He will run right across Canada to raise money for cancer research. "It will be my own, personal Marathon of Hope."

This idea stays with Terry as he goes through the long months of special treatment and sees the courage of other cancer victims.

As he is to write later, in a letter asking companies to sponsor his cross-Canada run:

"There were the faces with the brave smiles, and the ones who had given up smiling. There were the feelings of hopeful denial, and the feelings of despair . . . I could not leave, knowing these faces and feelings would still exist, even though I would be set free from mine.

Somewhere the hurting must stop . . ."

THREE WEEKS after his leg is amputated, Terry has his first artificial leg, or prosthesis, and he is trying to walk. Three weeks after that, he is out playing pitch-and-putt golf.

Over the next two and a half years, Terry builds up his strength and prepares for his marathon.

His training includes even basketball—the wheelchair kind. Terry joins the Vancouver Cablecars team and discovers he has to learn a lot all over. His hands blister at first from the wheelchair, but they soon toughen up. The hardest part is getting over the urge to jump to his feet to go after the ball. For a while, he even has to strap himself into his chair.

But Terry learns fast. Within two months he is picked to go with the team to the National Wheelchair Games in Edmonton. The Cablecars win the basketball trophy.

TERRY STARTS actually running in the early morning darkness of February 1979.

He begins with 500 metres. Then it's 1000. Within his first week he is running up to 1500. But it's hard to find the right way to run with his artificial leg. It was not designed for running with and it keeps causing blisters and bleeding.

Terry's determination keeps him training. On August 30, 1979, he enters the Prince George Marathon in northern British Columbia. He finishes ten minutes after the last two-legged runner, but he has run the full course.

The athletes are moved by Terry's toughness and stamina. "That's courage!" says the winner.

Terry beams at his mother when he gets back home: "You should have been there, Mom. It was the best thing I've ever done."

But the best is yet to come.

Terry announces to his good friend, Doug Alward: "I'm going to run across Canada—will you come?"

Doug doesn't bat an eye. He knows Terry has been up to something with all this training. Doug just says, "Yes, when?" And they set spring as a target date.

Next, Terry has to tell his family: "Mom, I'm going to run across Canada—a marathon, on my own—to raise money for cancer research. Will you tell Dad for me?"

Betty Fox gasps, "Terry, that's crazy!" She tries to talk him out of it.

But Betty and Rolly Fox know all about their determined son—and soon the whole family is helping Terry lay the difficult groundwork for his marathon. They hold garage sales and dances to raise money for living expenses along the way.

Next Terry sends out his letter asking some major corporations to sponsor his run. Terry's plea, "Somewhere the hurting must stop," touches deeply. Among others, Ford, Imperial Oil, and Adidas respond to Terry's letter. They provide a van, gas money, and running shoes. The Canadian Cancer Society agrees to promote the run.

THE MARATHON of Hope begins April 12, 1980, on a cold, rainy morning in St. John's, Newfoundland.

Terry dips his artifical leg in the grey Atlantic. He begins his run: two hops on his good leg, a stride on his artificial leg, lifting his shoulders and torso for leverage.

It's not easy. Terry plans to average forty kilometres a day and be back home in November. The first day, he manages less than twenty because of the cold and fog.

The second day a blizzard strikes.

Terry's artificial leg still causes blisters and bleeding. Then its valve system fails.

One day Terry gets dizzy because the strain on his heart is so great.

"That really scared me," he will admit later. But his reaction is typical: he rests a few minutes in the van, does fifteen push-ups on the road and starts running again. People take one look at this young, one-legged runner, and their hearts warm. They ask Terry and Doug into their homes for meals. Motel owners give them free rooms. Children donate their allowances, and one group writes a song to welcome Terry to their school.

Terry jokes with the children. "I bet some of you feel sorry for me," he tells them. "Well, don't. Having an artificial leg has its advantages. I've broken my right knee several times, and it didn't hurt a bit."

Donations begin to come in. Port aux Basques, Newfoundland, donates $10,000 from its 10,000 citizens. One dollar from each Canadian now becomes part of Terry's dream.

There are still disappointments. Sometimes Terry reaches a town only to find that no one is waiting—and that means no money for cancer research. It can be very discouraging, especially since every step is so painful for Terry.

In spite of pain and disappointments, Terry writes: "I told myself . . . I would keep going no matter what happened. If I died, I would die happy because I was doing what I wanted to do. How many people could say that?"

JUST THE running would be hard enough on Terry. But often he can't even rest and relax when the long day's run is over. People want to meet him. He has to face press conferences and make speeches at receptions and fund-raising dinners.

The pressure sometimes makes Terry crabby and demanding. Putting up with Terry's moods is not always easy for Doug. At one point, while they are in Nova Scotia, the two friends are barely speaking to each other. Terry feels desperately lonely.

When Betty and Rolly Fox learn of the situation, they fly to Halifax for a week to be with him. Their presence and their common-sense advice help clear the air. They encourage the boys to talk out their problems, and soon everything is going smoothly again.

AT THE END of May, Terry's younger

brother, Darrell, joins them. Darrell is easygoing and cheerful, always ready with a joke. Having him along really gives Terry's spirits a lift, especially on tough days.

And there are still tough days. As the Marathon of Hope moves on through Prince Edward Island, New Brunswick and Quebec, there are days when Terry has to run against a howling wind or through pouring rain, days when he nearly gets hit by cars and days when they collect almost no money.

But there are good days, too. Several times Terry manages to run almost fifty kilometres. On June 6, he writes in his diary: "Today I had tremendous support. Everybody honked and waved. People all over looked out of their homes and stores and cheered me on."

Another day: "Later in the town there was tremendous support and it quickened my pace right up . . . I flew!"

Having people support him means everything to Terry.

AND THEN, Ontario! The people of Ontario rise to the occasion magnificently. They are with Terry Fox all the way. So is the media. Bill Vigars of the Ontario division of the Cancer Society has made sure Terry's run is well publicized. He's planned appearances for Terry at football and baseball games in Ottawa and Toronto. And Terry is to meet two of his hockey heroes, Darryl Sittler and Bobby Orr.

Hawkesbury, the first town inside the Ontario border sets the tone for the rest of the province. Cheering crowds welcome Terry with balloons and a brass band. There is a police escort, with lights flashing. The escort will stay with Terry all through Ontario.

In Ottawa, Canada's capital, Terry meets Governor-General Edward Schreyer, Prime Minister Pierre Trudeau and other dignitaries. When Terry makes the official kick-off at a Canadian Football League exhibition game, the crowd of 16,000 gives him a standing ovation.

Terry has become a celebrity. Even at dawn, which is when Terry starts his run, or in the rain, people line the highways to see him pass. In shopping malls he is nearly mobbed. Everyone wants to shake his hand, get his autograph.

On July 11, Terry takes Toronto by storm. His whole family has flown in for the occasion. Fred, Judy, and Darrell are with him as he runs down University Avenue. The crowd, eight or ten deep on either side, roars its approval. Cancer Society volunteers run along with huge green garbage bags to collect all the cash thrown their way. Everyone wants to support Terry's Marathon of Hope.

Also running with Terry is Darryl Sittler, former captain of the Toronto Maple Leaf hockey team. But while Sittler's face is laughing and relaxed, Terry's grimace of determination reflects the difficulty of every step he takes.

A CROWD of 10,000 greets Terry's entry into Nathan Phillips Square in front of the Toronto City Hall. He is introduced as "the toast of Toronto and the hero of all Canada." It is truly a moment of triumph for Terry and his cause.

Yet this is but another moment that Terry Fox takes in his stride. He says to the crowd, "Those claps, take them for yourself. If you've given a dollar, you are part of the Marathon of Hope. That ovation was for you, wherever you are in Canada."

Each day's run through the heavily populated centres of southern Ontario becomes a parade. Donations pour in. The crowds, the support, are wonderful, but exhausting. The heat is stifling, and everyone tries to persuade Terry to settle for thirty kilometres a day instead of pushing for forty. But Terry won't slow down.

THE PRESSURE eases when Terry heads north. There are still crowds and receptions to face, but the weather is cooler and the towns are farther apart.

Terry has his twenty-second birthday in Gravenhurst, Ontario. He runs thirty-two kilometres before he is whisked off to a birthday celebration. There are birthday telegrams from everywhere. One from British Columbia has 1000 signatures.

About this time a newspaperman reports having seen blood running down Terry's artificial leg.

With Terry so much in the news, there is an immediate uproar about it. Terry is said to have "terrible problems." Some people are saying he has run far enough and should quit.

Terry says the blood is nothing new to him, and the pain is mild compared to what cancer victims suffer. He runs forty-two kilometres to prove there's no reason for worry.

Or is there? Perhaps Terry Fox is not faring as well as he says.

Darrell notices that running is much more of an effort for Terry. His temper is short. He needs his private time.

THERE ARE still many victories for Terry. People have been telling him for weeks how difficult it will be to make it up the steep Montreal River Hill near Wawa, Ontario. When the time comes, Terry runs the three kilometres uphill without his usual break. "Is that it?" he grins victoriously at the top.

Another time, Terry is joined on the road by ten-year-old Greg Scott. Greg, like Terry, has lost a leg to cancer. Terry pounds out ten kilometres while Greg keeps up on his bicycle. Terry is inspired! Greg has brought him fresh assurance that the Marathon of Hope is worth every step.

Terry has now run two-thirds of the way across Canada. He feels an even deeper commitment to the Marathon of Hope and to the people of Canada than when he started: he won't let them down now.

And yet, despite the good times, things aren't quite right for Terry.

NEARING THUNDER Bay, Ontario, Terry feels a sharp pain in his chest.

He is about thirty kilometres out of the city: crowds are lining the road. Terry is not about to disappoint them. He runs.

A camera crew is filming him. The crowd is cheering. Someone yells, "You can make it all the way, Terry!"

But Terry knows that his run is over—at least for now. When he reaches the van he hoists himself in and asks to be taken to the hospital.

A doctor examines Terry, takes X-rays and calls in a specialist. Terry guesses the truth before they tell him: it is cancer again, this time in his lungs.

Terry's parents come at once from Vancouver to take him home.

At a press conference before he leaves Thunder Bay, Terry says:

"I'll fight. I promise I won't give up . . . The thing about cancer [is that] I'm not the only one. It happens all the time to other people. . . . This just intensifies what I did. It gives it more meaning. It'll inspire more people . . . I'd like to see everybody go kind of wild, inspired with the fund-raising."

"INSPIRED fund-raising" is exactly what happens. A nation-wide telecast is organized—a tribute to Terry Fox.

Terry watches from his hospital bed. He can't believe his eyes! Celebrities like John Denver, Anne Murray, Elton John, Glen Campbell, Gordon Lightfoot and Nana

Mouskouri sing for him. Ballerina Karen Kain dances. The Stratford Festival's Opera Company performs.

Pledges jam the television network's phone lines. (One little boy calls in to donate his parents' house but he doesn't know the address.) By the end of the evening, over $10 million has been pledged to the Terry Fox Fund.

Donations and pledges from individuals, corporations, and· even governments continue flooding in. Some $25 million is raised. And it all began with one letter from Terry Fox:

> "Somewhere the hurting must stop . . . and I was determined to take myself to the limit for those causes . . . The people in cancer clinics all over the world need people who believe in miracles. I'm not a dreamer, and I'm not saying that this will initiate any kind of definite answer or cure to cancer, but I believe in miracles. I have to."

SURELY THE Marathon of Hope's monetary legacy alone has been a miracle.

Yet Terry has given the world much more than can be counted in dollars and cents.

Terry Fox is the ordinary guy who has responded to his troubles by reaching out to help others. In doing this, he becomes a symbol of hope and courage to millions throughout the world.

And so Canada heaps honours upon Terry. His university, his province, the Canadian Press. The Canadian Cancer Society and others bestow upon Terry Fox their highest awards.

He becomes the youngest-ever Companion in the Order of Canada, the nation's highest civilian award. September 13 is designated Terry Fox Marathon of Hope Day. Every year on this day Canadians will run, jog, or walk ten kilometres in aid of cancer research. His achievements are to be commemorated with a special stamp. The list goes on.

Letters and messages pour in for Terry from all over the world. Some are from prominent people like Pope John Paul II and the President of the United States. Most—thousands upon thousands—are from ordinary people whose hearts Terry has touched.

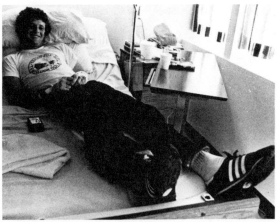

The legacy of Terry Fox's marathon of Hope grows. But, sadly, his own personal marathon comes to a close.

Certainly, Terry fights hard. His courage and determination win him many battles against the disease. But the outcome of the war itself is not in doubt. It is only a matter of time. . . .

Terry's family is with him at his death on Sunday, June 28, 1981.

Schools, municipalities, businesses fly their flags at half-staff across the country. On every federal government building the flags are lowered too—the first time such an honour has been given to an ordinary member of the public.

Canada mourns her "ordinary guy," Terry Fox.

But along with the sadness there is a sense of celebration, of victory. Celebration of a hero who fights magnificently to the end for himself and for others. Celebration for a life that is a triumph over death.

Terry Fox has done what he promised to do. He has taken himself to the limit for his cause. And he may gladly say, along with the Apostle Paul: "I have fought a good fight. I have finished my course. I have kept the faith."

# CLOSE UP

1.  Work with a partner to make a chart showing the accomplishments of "Terry the Ordinary Guy" and "Terry the Hero."

| Accomplishments of | |
| --- | --- |
| Terry the Ordinary Guy | Terry the Hero |
| | |

2.  Terry had to overcome many problems in his life. Work with a partner to draft a tribute to Terry Fox, to be given at a school assembly just before the next Terry Fox Run, in September. Your tribute should include the problems Terry overcame and the qualities he had that made his victories possible.

# WIDE ANGLE

1.  Write a letter to the Canadian Cancer Society explaining why you think they should continue to promote the Terry Fox Run. Ask a partner to help you revise and edit your letter.
    **or**
    Write an article for your school newspaper telling your fellow students about Terry Fox's accomplishments and asking them to participate in the Terry Fox Run.
    **or**
    Write and deliver a p.a. announcement about the Terry Fox Run that could be used at Run time.
2.  Look in your school or public library's vertical file or microfiche file to find one newspaper report from the beginning of Terry's run, and one from the end. With two partners, read the two articles and note the differences between them. (You may notice a difference in the reporters' attitudes toward Terry, for example.)

# KALEIDOSCOPE

1. Complete the following chart when you have read the selections in this cluster.

| Name | Heroic Actions | Long-Term Achievements |
|---|---|---|
| Crowfoot<br>Martha Louise<br>Nellie<br>Orrie and Ray<br>Terry | | |

2. On a map of Canada, mark the home and/or the travels of each of the heroes featured in the cluster. You may wish to indicate each hero in a different colour. If part of a hero's story takes place outside of Canada, expand your map accordingly.

3. Find a short biography of one of your personal heroes. (Look in your school or public library.) Make a chronological summary of his or her life similar to this summary of Nellie McClung's life:

**Nellie McClung**
1873—born on a farm in Chatsworth, Ont.
1880—family moved west to Manitoba.
1889—taught grades 1-8 in one-room school.
1894—became active in WCTU.
1896—married Wes McClung. They had 5 children.
1908—wrote 1st novel, about temperance.
1911—McClungs moved to Winnipeg, Nellie joined Canadian Women's Press Club, campaigned for laws to improve conditions for women factory workers.
1912—helped found the Political Equality League. Worked for votes for women in Manitoba until Wes McClung was transferred to Alberta in 1914.
1916—women granted the vote in some provinces.
1921—elected as Liberal member of Alberta Legislature. Supported such measures as old age pensions, mothers' allowances, better conditions in factories, a minimum wage, prohibition, birth control, easier divorce, public health nurses, no matter which party introduced them.
1924—referendum ends prohibition in Alberta.
1926—defeated in election by 60 votes, probably because of prohibition stand.

> **1927**—joined Emily Murphy and 3 other Alberta women in court case to establish that women were "persons" and could be appointed to the Senate.
> **1936**—appointed to first board of governors of CBC.
> **1939**—on Canadian delegation to League of Nations.
> **1951**—dies at Victoria, B.C.

4. Imagine that you have been hired by a television network to create a hero for a new program. Decide what sort of program it will be (e.g., cartoon, situation comedy, space adventure). Write a point-form profile of your hero's personality and his or her heroic qualities. Draw a picture of your hero.

5. For each subject you are studying this year, find out about one person who has done something special in that field. Your teachers will help you with your research. Pool your information with other students and together produce a pamphlet in which ten exceptional people are described in brief paragraphs. Be sure to include pictures or illustrations, and to cover a variety of subject areas.

6. Working in a group of six, prepare a hero magazine that you will present to Grade 2 children in a neighbourhood school. You may wish to use large sheets of bristolboard for each section. Some ideas you could explore are listed below.
   - a hero crossword puzzle
   - a collage
   - a story about a hero
   - an illustration of a hero in action
   - a cartoon strip
   - a poem about a heroic act or person
   - an advertisement for what a hero eats, drinks, wears, drives, etc.
   - a newspaper account of a hero saving someone
   - a caricature (an exaggerated imitation) of a hero you admired when you were younger (e.g., Mr. T., He-Man, Wonder Woman)
   - hero stickers or buttons
   - jokes about heroes

# STUDENT HANDBOOK

## USING LANGUAGE TO LEARN

PEOPLE SPEAK AND WRITE not only to be understood, but also to understand. Every time you come across a new concept, you naturally try to fit it into what you already know, and by talking through an idea or jotting down what you think about it, you get closer to understanding it. When you express your ideas, either in a conversation or in some kind of writing, you get a chance to "check out" your own thinking.

Talking with others about what you're learning will help you with all your subjects. It is just as important to talk to partners about how to plan a geography assignment, solve a problem in math, devise a good menu in food shop, or construct something in wood shop, as it is to discuss the meaning of the poem or story you're reading in English class.

Learning is the process through which we try to understand new ideas. In "Polar Night," Close Up #3 (p. 346) asks you to join with two partners to consider some of the passages in the story. Through your discussion you will come to an awareness of what you really think about what you've read. Also, your response will be influenced by the viewpoints others have expressed. At the learning stage you are still letting ideas roam around in your head, and you are not yet ready to make a final, polished statement.

Communication is the process of telling people what we understand or showing people what we have imagined. Wide Angle #2 for *The Monkey's Paw* (p. 317) asks you to think up a new ending to the play, write a draft script, and share your script with your classmates. The next Wide Angle activity asks the audience to communicate their opinions of the rewritten play to you and your partners in a drama review. The review will help you to re-see your script. You will have an opportunity to hear about what was strong and weak in your presentation, and you can revise your draft as you choose. After you re-see and revise your work with the help of others, you can then go on to proofread it. (Again, your partners will give you a hand.) Proofreading is the last stage of work before you produce a polished version of your writing. Later in this handbook you will learn in more detail about re-seeing, revising, and proofreading. You will also see how to go about developing an idea through the rough draft stage into a polished piece of writing.

When you share ideas, feelings, opinions, and beliefs with others, whether in conversation or through your writing, you extend your view to see things you might not have seen by yourself. After you and your partners communicate your thoughts to each other and compare them, you will usually be ready to make a clear statement about what you have learned.

## READALOUD

FOR CENTURIES, people have loved to have stories told to them. Children are always happy to listen to a fairy tale or adventure story. Teenagers like to scare each other by telling ghost stories around a fire. Many people buy cassettes of novels and plays to entertain them when they are driving or relaxing at home.

The Readaloud selection at the beginning of each cluster is a chance for you to sit back and listen to a story, a story that will introduce you to the topic of the cluster. There are no activities to complete. All you have to do is listen carefully and think about what you are hearing as your teacher or a classmate reads the story out loud. You may have questions and opinions about it that you want to discuss later, during the Focussing activities. Most of all, enjoy the story!

## KEEPING A JOURNAL

SOMETIMES YOU are not sure what you are thinking until you find a way to express your ideas in your own words. Keeping a journal allows you a chance to explore new understandings and to connect them with what you already know. A journal is a place where you can write freely without worrying about whether your writing is good enough to show other people. Mainly, you are recording your own reflections and, through that process, perhaps coming to conclusions, or starting points for new awareness. You can always use the notes you have in your journal as the seed of some writing for a special audience, such as your classmates, your teacher, or some person or group outside school.

You may wish to use your journal (or your private disc, if you are using a computer) to record

- events or experiences that are important to you in some way;
- interesting conversations or discussions you have had;
- a list of times and dates when you saw or went out with someone you care about, along with comments about what you did;
- information about something you want to remember;
- your emotions—maybe some occurrence has you feeling

excited, angry, happy, sad, frightened, or curious;

- a thought or comment about an issue you have encountered while speaking with someone, reading a book or magazine, listening to the radio, or watching television, videos, or a movie;
- a list of things you want to accomplish, or goals you have set for yourself;
- advice that has been given to you about a specific problem you are facing;
- a prediction about some aspect of your life (you can check it later to see whether or not it came true);
- a note about something you heard, read, or saw that impressed you;
- a record of a historic or special event that you could share with someone who missed the event.

A journal can help you figure out what you're feeling and thinking. It can also make learning about new concepts easier and improve your ability to express yourself in writing. Here are some suggestions for using your journal to grasp new ideas that are presented in your classes:

- When you are working in a small group, build a bridge between what you did in the group the day before and what you hope to do today. Jot down what you remember from yesterday's work and then share your observations with others in the group. This activity may suggest some directions the group needs to explore, especially if people disagree on what happened the day before.
- At the end of a day, write down something important that you thought about or learned in your classes. If you want a more detailed record, you can do the same thing after each class. Some days you'll have more comments in this category than on other days.
- When you're working in a small group and the discussion isn't going very far, call "time out" and give group members five minutes to write down what they think the discussion should focus on. That will give quieter people in the group an opportunity to express themselves, and it will help everyone to reconsider what they want to say.
- If you're trying to figure out something and you find you're stuck, use your journal to write down everything you know about the problem and then look things over carefully. Sometimes you already have a solution—you just need a chance to see your thoughts on paper.
- Use your journal to write down questions you want to ask your group or your teacher or someone else who has information you need.
- Keep a record of what you've done in a class or a series

of classes so you can show others (and yourself) what you've accomplished.

## CONFERENCING

Conferencing is a way of re-seeing, with other people's assistance, what you have written. When you sit down with a partner or your teacher to have a conference, you have an opportunity to talk about your ideas to someone who wants to listen.

What does conferencing involve? Your partner will ask you questions about your work, and in answering them, you will come to understand your work better. You can have a conference with your partner to see how your ideas are forming as you begin to write, and you can also have a conference to discuss the various stages of your work as it moves from first draft to a final, polished effort.

No two conferences will be exactly alike, but in every case you will be working cooperatively with one or more partners to explore and shape your ideas.

**Thinking It Through** lists some questions that you and your partner may want to ask during a conference.

## THINKING IT THROUGH

### WHY AM I WRITING OR SAYING THIS?
Am I trying to
   organize facts;
   convince someone about something;
   record my feelings;
   share an idea;
   give directions;
   comfort or congratulate someone;
   describe an experience, an event, a person, a place, an
      object;
   tell a story;
   make a complaint;
   explain a situation;
   or any or all of the above?

### WHO IS MY INTENDED AUDIENCE?
Am I writing or speaking to
   myself;
   a friend;
   a relative;
   someone I dislike;
   a younger person;
   someone who will respond with information or comments;
   a group of people with a common interest;
   an unknown audience?

## WHAT AM I WRITING OR TALKING ABOUT?
What am I trying to say?
What information do I already have?
What information, if any, do I still need?

## HOW AM I ORGANIZING MY IDEAS?
What form will I use for what I have to say? Will I use
  a letter;
  a descriptive paragraph;
  a poem;
  a diary or memoir;
  a journal entry;
  an explanation accompanied by an illustration;
  a chart;
  a brief note;
  a script;
  a biographical sketch;
  a formal argument proving a thesis;
  an audio-visual presentation;
  an oral report?

As you revise, edit, and proofread your writing, you may find spelling, punctuation, and/or grammatical errors. When you have a conference with your partners or your teachers, they too may find parts of your work that need rewording. Whenever you correct problems, you can record the process on a Personal Usage Sheet. First state the problem you had, and then record your corrected version. An example of a completed Personal Usage Sheet is provided below. (Your teacher will provide you with blank Personal Usage Sheets or tell you how to use a word processor to create a Personal Usage Data File.)

# PERSONAL USAGE SHEET

NAME *Michael Mallett*

| DATE | MY WRITING PARTNERS | TITLE OF MY WRITTEN WORK | CORRECT USAGE OF WORD OR WORDS |
|---|---|---|---|
| September 18 | Pauline and Claude | "On the Sidewalk Bleeding" (new ending) | *Problem* <br> The use of "there," "their," and "they're." <br> *Corrections* <br> "There, in the alley," said the drunk, pointing. <br> They could do no more than sit in their chairs and wait. <br> "It's the Royals," Laura said. "They're coming to see you, Andy." |
| September 29 | Pauline and Claude | "Nellie at Home" | *Problem* <br> The use of quotation marks for written speech. <br> *Correction* <br> "Congratulations, Nellie!" he said. "I can't tell you how proud and happy I am." |
| October 12 | Delroy | "Collecting on a Bet" | *Problem* <br> Running two sentences together. <br> *Correction* <br> Ellen turned the corner. Simon saw her and tried to hide. <br> or <br> When Ellen turned the corner, Simon saw her and tried to hide. <br> or <br> Ellen turned the corner; Simon saw her and tried to hide. |
| October 30 | Yvette | "The Graveyard Ghost" | *Problem* <br> Mixing past and present tense. <br> *Correction* <br> We huddled together at the edge of the cemetery and slowly began to creep toward the tombstone. |

## BEING PARTNERS

Many of the activities in this book call for you to work with partners. Often you'll discuss your ideas with them before you start working on an activity. Your partners will help you revise, edit, and proofread your work. Sometimes, you and your partners will create something together and present it to the class. The following suggestions may help to make the process of working with partners both more pleasant and more productive.

**DISCUSS** **Talking together** will help you to sort out your thinking, test your ideas, come up with new ideas, and check whether you have expressed yourself effectively. To get a fresh view of your work, you can ask your partners to read it aloud to you.

**NOTE** While you are thinking, planning, discussing, writing, revising, and proofreading, **jot down notes** and reminders to yourself and to your partners. You may forget what you have thought or said, but if you've written notes, you'll always have a record to check.

**LISTEN** **Listen to one another** attentively. Try to understand what your partners are saying so you can learn from them or help them if they have problems.

**ENCOURAGE** **Encouragement** is vital; everyone likes to be praised. If you are impressed by something that your partners have done, say so. The purpose of encouragement is to identify strong points and help the person build upon them. Encouragement should be specific. "Hey, that's great!" isn't as helpful as, "I really like the word *exuberant*. It captures the mood you want perfectly."

**COMMENT** Part of the writing partner's task is **to offer helpful criticism**. Your critique should help your partners to make their writing clearer and more effective. You won't do them any good if you offend them or tell them something vague. Which would you rather hear: "That's really dumb!" or "You don't need that sentence. You said the same thing two sentences earlier."?

**CONSULT** If you have problems with your writing, **ask for help** from your teacher and classmates. Someone else's perspective may help you to see things in a new light.

## CHECKING ON YOUR OWN

You won't always be able to work with partners. Although sharing your work with other people is probably the best way to edit and proofread, there are ways to re-see your writing on your own. You can make your writing "talk" by putting yourself in the position of your audience. Try to imagine that you have never seen or heard your work before, then use the following strategies:

1. Read the whole piece aloud several times to get the general effect and to hear how it sounds. Sometimes you can hear things that you cannot see.
2. Read the piece aloud, sentence by sentence or line by line to see if it makes sense when you hear it. This strategy will help you to isolate specific problems.
3. Tape your writing as you read it aloud. Play back the tape and try to identify any missing links between your ideas, or any awkwardness in the way you have expressed yourself.

## THE WRITING FOLDER

The writing folder is a way of organizing your work and keeping a record of what you've done. It could be an accordian-pleated file folder, a three-ring binder divided into sections, or some similar system that holds the following components:

**FILES**
1. Work in Progress File
2. Private Writing File
3. Polished Writing File

**CHECKLISTS**
1. Checklist for Re-seeing and Revising
2. Checklist for Proofreading
3. Checklist for Making Positive Comments
4. Personal Record Sheet
5. Personal Usage Sheet (discussed above)

Any number of the components can be used with a piece of writing. Copies of the Checklists, the Personal Usage Sheet, and the Personal Record Sheet will be given to you by your teacher.

## Work in Progress File
**CONTAINS ROUGH DRAFTS**
- work to be polished
- work to remain as it is
- work to be set aside for awhile
- work to be used later in new compositions
- Checklist for Re-seeing and Revising
- Checklist for Proofreading

## Private Writing File
**CONTAINS PERSONAL WRITING THAT IS NOT FOR OTHERS TO LOOK AT**
- writing about personal reflections and insights
- work that is private for now but may be shared later

## Polished Writing File
**CONTAINS WORK THAT IS FINISHED**
- work that has been revised
- work that has been looked at and edited by a partner
- work that has been proofread
- polished work that you may choose to give to the teacher for evaluation
- Checklist for Making Positive Comments
- Personal Record Sheet

### ABOUT THE CHECKLIST FOR RE-SEEING AND REVISING
The checklist below provides some questions that you and your partners can consider when you look over your rough drafts. The questions will help you to re-see your writing in terms of
- the purpose of the piece;
- the audience you are writing for;
- the format you have chosen;
- the words and the sentence structure you have used.

After you and your partners have discussed a particular piece of your writing with this checklist in mind, you may choose to change your piece in keeping with your writing partners' suggestions, and then go on to proofread it with the help of the Checklist for Proofreading. In some cases, your discussion may lead you to begin your piece again in a new direction.

## Checklist for Re-seeing and Revising

Have I said what I wanted to say in the way I wanted to say it?

- ☐ Did I discuss my ideas with partners before I began to write?
- ☐ Did I begin my piece of writing in a way that gets the reader's attention?
- ☐ Do the details I have written about come in the best order?
- ☐ Are some of my points repetitive or unnecessary?
- ☐ Have I used the same words too often?
- ☐ Have I used vivid and interesting words to describe actions, objects and people?
- ☐ Do I have a strong and appropriate ending?
- ☐ Do my partners clearly understand what I am trying to say?
- ☐ Are my paragraphs too long? Are they long enough to make my point?
- ☐ Did I keep my audience in mind as I was choosing my words?

When you revise or edit, you are reworking your rough draft to make your writing as clear and as interesting as possible.

### ABOUT THE CHECKLIST FOR PROOFREADING

The checklist below is designed to help you catch problems in punctuation, spelling, and sentence structure. Proofreading is the final clean-up of a piece of writing before you put it in the Polished Writing File.

## Checklist for Proofreading

Have I checked my writing for surface errors?

- ☐ Did I double-check the spelling of all words I was unsure about?
- ☐ Did I leave wide margins so that my work is uncrowded and easy to read?
- ☐ Did I indent each new paragraph?
- ☐ Did the punctuation I used make my meaning clear?
- ☐ Did I capitalize names and titles and the first word of each sentence?
- ☐ Did I use a variety of sentence types?
- ☐ Did I use complete sentences where necessary?

When you proofread, you try to find and correct mistakes in surface details, such as punctuation, grammar, usage, spelling, and handwriting.

**ABOUT THE CHECKLIST FOR MAKING POSITIVE COMMENTS**

You will be looking at your partners' work and telling them your opinions in order to help them re-see, revise, and proofread their writing.

We all benefit from knowing what we've done well. As a last step before your partners put their work in their Polished Writing Files, write down two or three things that you really liked about their pieces of writing. Then sign your comments and attach them to the final copies. That way, your partners will have a tribute to what they have accomplished, and there will be a record of your contributions to your partners' work.

The Checklist for Making Positive Comments lists some questions that you can ask yourself when you are preparing to write a final statement on your partners' work.

## Checklist for Making Positive Comments

**What are the things that my partners have done particularly well in their writing?**

- [ ] Has the writer used any words or phrases that I find especially effective?
- [ ] Has the writer expressed any ideas to which I can easily relate?
- [ ] Has the writer given me any new insights about the world around me?
- [ ] Has the writing stirred strong feelings in me?
- [ ] Has the writer reminded me of an experience I have had?
- [ ] Has the writer explained something to me that I didn't know before?
- [ ] Has the writer used a particularly striking title?
- [ ] Has the writer sparked my imagination?

**ABOUT THE PERSONAL RECORD SHEET**

You can use the Personal Record Sheet to get a clear overview of what you have accomplished over a period of weeks. Here is one page of a Personal Record Sheet. (You may wish to use a word processor to set up a Personal Record Data File that can be stored on disc and printed out at the end of the year.)

# PERSONAL RECORD SHEET

Name _Michael Mallett_

| ASSIGNMENT | DATE BEGUN | DATE COMPLETED | MATERIALS OR RESOURCES USED | PARTNERS | PERSONAL ASSESSMENT OF THE VALUE OF THE ACTIVITY |
|---|---|---|---|---|---|
| A script for a continuation of A *Special Gift* | Oct. 1 | Oct. 20 | Script, A *Special Gift* | David and Ching Yen | 1. I realized how hard it is to be yourself when other people make fun of you.<br>2. I learned how a script-writer shows the difference between the characters' speeches and the stage directions. |
| A survey about friendship | Nov. 15 | Dec. 3 | Computer | Caitlin | 1. I learned how to summarize the results of a survey and enter the data into the computer.<br>2. Caitlin taught me how to use the computer to make charts and print out copies. |

# APPLYING THE COMPUTER

## About Word Processors

A word processor is a computer program especially for people who write. If you had in front of you many pens, pencils, and sheets of paper, a pair of scissors, a bottle of glue, an eraser, a filing cabinet, a typewriter, and a photocopier, you might be able to do all of the things a word processor can do. Word processors take the drudgery out of writing. You can make notes, expand them into an outline, rearrange sentences and move whole paragraphs, all without having to recopy your work each time you make a change.

A good word processor has the following features:
- it allows you to type both capital letters and small letters;
- it has a "word-wrap" feature so that words are not split inappropriately at the end of a line;
- it displays clear, well-spaced letters as well as many lines of text on the screen;
- it allows you to move words, lines, and paragraphs very easily;

- the editing commands are uncomplicated, easy to enter, and easy to remember. They are either on the screen all the time or are readily available in a "help" menu;
- a warning system is available to protect you from accidentally erasing your work from the computer's memory.

Using a word processor makes writing and editing fun, but it is still up to you to do the thinking that is behind every piece of good writing. You are the one who must decide which ideas you are going to put into the computer and how they should be arranged and developed.

It may not be possible for you to use a word processor for all of your written work. Take into consideration both your typing skills and the time that is available to you on the computer before you decide how you want to use the word processor.

## Using the Word Processor

Anything you write—letters, reviews, memoirs, stories, scripts—can be written on a word processor. It can also help you to make lists, charts, and reports neatly. You can use it as an aid to thinking by saving your ideas in point-form or in an outline in the computer.

The word processor eliminates the need for you to recopy work as you proceed through the stages in the writing process. During the re-seeing and revising process it will make it easy for you to change and expand your outlines and drafts into completed pieces of writing. After you proofread, you can make your adjustments on screen and then print out a final copy (or many copies) that doesn't have mistakes or messy corrections.

## Other Computer Applications

1. Idea generators and essay organizers are computer programs that provide extra pre-writing inspiration.
2. Newspaper programs, such as The Newsroom®, can help you write, illustrate, and print newsletters, newspapers, flyers, pamphlets, bulletins and advertisements.
3. A modem is a device that lets computers exchange information over the telephone. If you have a modem you can link up with students in other classes, schools, and communities to exchange ideas, send "electronic" mail, or establish an inter-school bulletin board.
4. If your classroom computer is on-line with another computer, you can get information from its datafiles and display it on your computer's screen. "On-line" information retrieval services and databanks can help you find information that might take days or weeks to locate searching through library shelves and card files.
5. There are new computer programs that allow you to

write interactive stories that are read on screen. The program, according to your instructions, allows your reader to make choices that influence the course of the story. Other programs allow you to write a story and to illustrate it using a graphics tablet.

New applications for the computer are being developed all the time. There are now programs that can help you to write poetry, study an author's writing style, and correct your grammar. You can use a computer to play word-games and to create puzzles.

Computers are very sophisticated communication devices. The suggestions above show you and your partners some of the ways to express your thoughts and feelings using a computer. Remember, computers are like any other tool for communication: the more creative you are with them the more fun you'll have and the more useful they'll be. Don't be afraid to use your imagination when you sit down at the computer keyboard with your partners.

# FORMATS

Here are explanations of the formats for writing and speaking that are asked for in the activities. Ask your classmates or teacher for help if there are terms in this glossary (or elsewhere in *Your Voice and Mine 1*) that you don't understand.

## Ballad

A ballad is a poem that tells a story in several short verses. In many ballads a chorus is repeated after every verse. Often ballads are put to music and sung. Here is one verse and the chorus from "The Ballad of the Bluenose" by David Martins:

In the town of Lunenburg down Nova Scotia way,
In 1921 on a windy day,
A sailing ship was born—the Bluenose was her name,
You'll never see her kind again.

**CHORUS**

Bluenose! The ocean knows her name,
Sailors know how proud a ship was she.
Bluenose! Leaning in the wind,
Racing ev'ry wave on the sea.

## Brainstorm

Brainstorming is a way of collecting many ideas in a short time. You can brainstorm with one partner or several. To brainstorm, find a comfortable place to talk and write notes. Decide how much time you are going to spend brainstorming. Group members, one at a time, should tell their ideas about the topic or question at hand. One person, chosen before the brainstorming starts, should jot down all the ideas. Don't make comments until all the ideas are recorded and/or the time for brainstorming is over. After brainstorming you can talk about the ideas and choose which ones you want to take further.

## Bulletin Board

A bulletin board is an eye-catching way of displaying information, whether the information be pictures or words. To attract attention to the bulletin board, try some of the following suggestions:

- fix the material you want to display to a colourful background, which you can then pin to the bulletin board;
- write in large, clear letters that can be easily read;
- divide the bulletin board into sections with bold headings that indicate what each section contains;
- experiment with attaching three-dimensional displays to your bulletin board.

## Caption

A caption is a sentence or two that explains what is happening in a drawing or photograph. It tells the who, what, where, when, and why of the scene. A picture of a girl seated at a computer might have this caption: "After school, Carmella sits at the library computer to do research for her assignment." Captions that accompany cartoons have a different purpose; they are meant to amuse the reader. See the cartoon on p. 43 for an example of a humorous caption.

## Cinquain Poem

A cinquain poem is a five-line poem that doesn't rhyme. It has the following format:

| | |
|---|---|
| line 1 | states the topic |
| line 2 | describes the topic |
| line 3 | expresses action |
| line 4 | shows feelings |
| line 5 | gives a strong reaction to the topic |

Here is a cinquain:

> lightning
> sudden, brilliant
> flaring, blinding, scorching
> makes my heart race
> amazing.

## Collage

A collage is a pictorial design made from photographs and scraps of cloth, paper, string, and the like, all of which are arranged on a background and glued. The photographs often are clipped from newspapers and magazines. A collage can be used to make a statement about a topic or idea.

## Dialogue

A dialogue is a conversation between two people. When you write a dialogue you must be careful to follow certain rules of punctuation so the reader knows which character is speaking the lines. Here are the opening lines of dialogue from "The Most Dangerous Game":

"Off there to the right—somewhere—is a large island," said Whitney. "It's rather a mystery—"

"What island is it?" Rainsford asked.

"The old charts call it 'Ship Trap Island,' " Whitney replied.

## Diary

A diary is a person's private record of his or her feelings and experiences. Here is a sample diary entry:

*June 10, 1985*

Arvinder woke me up early to tell me that lightning had struck the oak tree on our front lawn. I didn't even know there had been a storm! I went to the window and I couldn't believe what I saw. The oak used to be twenty-five metres tall, but it wasn't half that size any more. The top of the tree had fallen over into the driveway. There were wood chips and branches everywhere, as if the tree had exploded. Part of the tree trunk was black from the heat of the lightning. Finally I noticed my bike, or what was left of it. It was crushed underneath the fallen treetop. Arvinder thought it looked funny, all bent up, but I didn't see anything to laugh about.

## Editorial

An editorial is an article written by the editor of a magazine or newspaper. In it, the editor expresses her or his personal views on a current issue (an election, for example, or a world event) and presents an argument to support those views. Most newspapers have an editorial page, which consists of editorials and letters to the editor.

## Headline

A headline is the title appearing at the top of a newspaper article. Headlines usually are set in large type to catch the reader's attention.

# Match-up Game

A match-up game involves two lists. Each item in the first list corresponds to one (and only one) item in the second list. The two lists aren't in any particular order, and the player of the game doesn't know which items belong together. From each item in the first list, the player draws a line to its partner in the second list. When all the items have been matched up, the player checks to see how many of her or his guesses were right. Here is a simple match-up game:

Gander — Ontario
Windsor — Saskatchewan
Saskatoon — Newfoundland

# Memoir

A memoir is a written or taped record of a significant time in a person's past. The excerpt from *My Grandfather's Cape Breton* (pp. 330-333) is an example of a memoir.

# Monologue

A monologue is a long speech made by a character in a play, a story, or a poem. Some characters speak their monologues for other characters to hear; some characters speak their monologues only for themselves, which gives the reader a chance to learn what that character is really thinking.

# Narrative Poem

A narrative poem is a poem that tells a story.

# Obituary

An obituary is a newspaper article summarizing the life of a person who has recently died.

# Review

A review describes a book, film, record, television show, concert, or some other performance or work of art. The reviewer gives personal opinions of the strengths and weaknesses of what he or she saw or heard. Here is a brief movie review as an example:

## Pale Rider

It is such a pleasure to have Clint Eastwood back again in the saddle that one overlooks *Pale Rider's* shortcomings and is content that the most ancient of movie genres has returned in fine form, starring the one American actor who can still personify *the* Western hero. Directed by Eastwood, *Pale Rider* plays straight and simple to mythology; the good guys against the bad guys, the triumph of good over evil. And Eastwood—a raw-boned, larger-than-life hero whose wonderfully aged and wrinkled face at once suggests hatred and rage and fear, all of it banked and softened by the wisdom of experience—has never been better.

## Role-Play

To role-play is to pretend that you are another person. If you were role-playing Crowfoot, for example (see pp. 140-148), you would try to think, act, speak, and react exactly the way he would.

## Script

A script is the format for writing a play, whether it is to be presented on stage, on radio or television, or as a movie. The characters' names are followed by what they say (their dialogue). In addition to the dialogue, there are stage directions, which describe what the stage should look like, what special effects should be used, and how the actors should speak and move.

## Stanza

A stanza is a unit of lines in a poem, much like a paragraph in a story. Another word for stanza is *verse*.

## Storyboard

A storyboard is a series of drawings or pictures that looks like a comic strip without words. It is used to plan the scenes in a movie or a television show.

## Word-search Game

A word-search game is a puzzle in which words are hidden in rows and columns of letters. The words may be oriented vertically, horizontally, or diagonally. Here is a small word-search game, with the hidden words circled.

# TO CHEAT DEATH

# STRANDED IN THE DESERT

*by Arthur Roth*

**M**ARGARET Starr was puzzled. She looked out over the steering wheel at the rough sandy track in front of her. Beside her in the front seat, eight-year-old Madge, her daughter, was squabbling with her brother, Andy, age eleven.

"Hush, you two. I'm trying to think." She slowed the car to a stop. The signpost, where she had turned off the main highway an hour earlier, had read JUNIPER 47. She had noted her mileage at the time and the speedometer now showed an added twenty-nine miles. That was better than halfway to Juniper, but the dirt road was getting narrower and hard to follow. What worried Mrs. Starr even more was the fact that she had not seen another car since leaving the highway. She was beginning to regret her idea of taking the road to Juniper. At the time it had seemed a shortcut that would save thirty miles or so, and she had been bored driving through the monotonous desert landscape. She now suspected that the road to Juniper was no longer used by normal traffic.

Mrs. Starr's husband, Andrew Senior, was an air force sergeant stationed in Louisiana. Several weeks earlier he had been ordered to California to take a special month-long technical course. It was summer, the children were home from school, and Mrs. Starr had decided to surprise her husband by driving out to California to visit him for a few days.

She looked at the twin ruts that stretched in front of her. She hated to turn around and go back to the main highway, but she hated even more following such a narrow dirt road. Supposing she got a flat tire? Finally she made up her mind.

"Aw, Mom, we didn't even see a rattlesnake," Andy complained. Andy had been trying all day to spot a rattlesnake somewhere on the desert floor.

Mrs. Starr backed the car off the road and started to turn around. She drove forward into a harmless-looking clump of dead brush, trying to make enough room to turn. Suddenly she felt a sharp thud. She stopped the car and backed up.

Looking through the windshield, Mrs. Starr could make out a long, pointed branch that had been hidden inside the bush. She didn't know it, but the pointed end of the branch had poked a hole in the car's radiator. Pulling on the wheel, she turned the car around and headed back to the main highway.

They hadn't gone more than a couple of miles when Andy began to shout, "Smoke, Mom! The car's smoking!"

Mrs. Starr noticed a burning smell, and then a plume of smoke or steam came shooting out from underneath one side of the hood.

"Now what's wrong?" she said. She slowed the car and pulled off to one side of the road.

"We're burning up," Madge said.

"No, we're not, dummy," Andy said. "We're boiling over." In a minute he was out of the car and pointing to the plumes of steam jetting out from the car's grill. "Here it is."

Mrs. Starr looked down at the front of the car and shook her head. She didn't know much about automobiles, but she knew the engine wouldn't run very long on boiling water.

She opened the hood and looked inside. The whole top of the engine was wet with steam. Near the bottom of the radiator, water was shooting through the hole made by the branch. She wondered if she could stop the leak, but then realized even that wouldn't do much good. Most of the water had already been lost.

"Mommy, I'm hot," Madge said.

"I know, honey," Mrs. Starr said. "I can't believe this heat." She slammed the hood down and looked at her watch. Three-fifteen. It must be over one hundred degrees, she thought. They would have to find shelter of some kind or they would burn up in the heat. "Okay, you kids, back in the car, both of you."

It wasn't long until heat began to build up inside the metal vehicle. Half an hour later Mrs. Starr felt the first stirrings of fear.

"Andy, did you finish your root beer?" she asked.

"Yup."

"Where's the bottle?"

"Here." Andy held it up.

Mrs. Starr looked ahead through the windshield. Waves of heat were shimmering over the ground, starting with wavy ripples that flattened out in the distance to form a solid, shining surface; it looked like a large lake or inland sea. How long could they last without water? she wondered. Two days? Four days? Supposing she walked to Juniper? That was eighteen miles. Or she could walk back to the main highway—that was twenty-nine miles. Juniper was a lot closer. But what if Juniper were a ghost town? What if the road ahead just petered out into endless desert? Anyway, how could she leave the children?

"I'm hot," Madge whimpered again.

"I know." Mrs. Starr took a Kleenex out of a box and wiped her brow and cheeks. The heat in the car was impossible, but at least they were out of the direct rays of the sun. Perhaps they should all lie down outside in the shade of the car. . . ?

Taking the keys, she said, "All right, everybody out. We're going camping."

She opened the trunk and pulled out an old blanket she and her husband kept there for picnics. Using rocks, she anchored one end of the blanket to the top of the car and the other end to the ground, making half a tent. Next she dragged a suitcase full of clothes out of the trunk and spread them out on the sand. Then she and the children lay in the makeshift shelter. It was still hot, but not as bad as inside the car. There was even a hint of a breeze now and again.

"Are we going to stay here all day?" Madge asked.

"I hope not, honey," Mrs. Starr said. "Someone will be along soon, I'm sure."

"Keep an eye out for rattlesnakes," Andy said.

"Andy, you stop scaring Madge," Mrs. Starr ordered. "There are no rattlesnakes around here and you know it."

"There are so, there are desert rattlers," Andy said. "Sidewinders."

"Just stop talking about them, all right?"

How long would it take to walk twenty-nine miles? she wondered. She had never walked that far in her life. She knew she couldn't do it during the daylight hours—the heat was too much. But she could walk at night. It might take her two nights and in the daytime she would have to shelter in the shade of a bush or rock. But how would the children survive? Andy might be strong enough to walk out with her, but not Madge.

Gradually the sun sank behind the range of faraway hills. Not long after dark the temperature dropped to an almost comfortable level. By ten o'clock, both children were asleep. Mrs. Starr woke up several times that night, thinking she heard an animal nearby, but each time it proved to be a false alarm. When dawn came she decided she would stay all day with the children in the hope that a car would come along. Or perhaps they could signal an airplane passing overhead. Yesterday afternoon she had noticed one, but it was flying too high for the pilot to see anyone on the ground.

In the morning Mrs. Starr made the children eat a tuna fish sandwich left over from yesterday's lunch. Then she had Andy take everything out of the trunk and glove compartment. He laid the items on the ground in front of her. From the trunk came a twenty-foot length of heavy rope for towing, a flashlight, a lug wrench for removing a wheel, a jack, a box of tools for emergency repairs, and a couple of oily rags. From the glove compartment Andy took several maps, a plastic bottle of white glue, a box of Kleenex, and a pencil. Then from the backseat Andy dragged a plastic bucket full of such toys as an empty water pistol, a colouring book, a box of crayons that belonged to Madge, and several comic books. There was also a pair of toy binoculars that Andy had been using to look for rattlesnakes.

Mrs. Starr now set about making a distress signal. With Andy's help, she wrestled the spare tire out of the trunk and propped it against a low bush. If she could set the tire on fire with gasoline, the column of smoke should be seen for miles around, and possibly by a passing airplane. But gasoline was dangerous, she knew, just as likely to explode as to catch fire. And that tire was full of air that would also explode with the heat. Then she thought of the rearview mirror. With a screwdriver from the tool box she and Andy took the mirror off the car. If a plane flew over, Andy could flash the mirror to attract the pilot's attention. Andy, who was a Boy Scout, knew the signal for an SOS—three longs, three shorts, three longs. He would pass his hand over the face of the mirror quickly for a short and not so quickly for a long. Andy was delighted to be put in charge of signaling aircraft, and every once in a while he would practise making his SOS signals.

Mrs. Starr now tackled the problem of getting water. She knew there was still some left in the bottom of the radiator. Andy managed to open the drain valve with a pair of pliers and catch the remaining liquid in his plastic bucket. But Mrs. Starr was bitterly disappointed when she looked at the orange-coloured antifreeze. She tasted it and spat out. No one could possibly drink it. However, she didn't throw it away. Instead, she dampened a rag with the fluid and wiped her children's faces with it. It helped to cool them off, and every hour or so she would give Andy and Madge another face bath with the antifreeze.

All day she thought about how to make a good signal fire. There was oil in the engine. Perhaps she could use it to set fire to the spare tire. Again Andy proved to be a big help. He crawled under the engine, found the drain plug, and let enough oil run out to thoroughly soak some rags and clothing. He replaced the plug and came wriggling out from under the car. With a torn-up comic book and the oily rags, Mrs. Starr prepared a fire.

Early that afternoon a plane flew over. Mrs. Starr swiftly set fire to the comic book pages. Meanwhile Andy was flashing his mirror at the sky. The oily rags caught fire and soon a plume of smoke began to rise. However, the pilot showed no sign that he had noticed the flashing mirror or column of smoke. After the plane flew over, Mrs. Starr threw sand over the fire to put it out. Then she got everything ready for a new fire to signal the next plane that might appear.

She now decided to try digging for water. Somewhere she had heard or read that you could often find water just a few feet underground. She dug for an hour or so in the loose soil, using her hands and the claw end of a hammer from the tool box. Andy and Madge helped her, but all they found was dry sand. However, Mrs. Starr noticed that the ground was quite a bit cooler a foot or so down. This gave her an idea, and she scooped out shallow pits for Andy and Madge. She made both of them lie in the holes, with only their faces showing, then completely covered their bodies with sand. She was now quite worried about their appearance. Madge's lips were cracked and swollen, and her throat hurt when she swallowed. Andy said his stomach hurt, and he complained of cramps in his legs. Mrs. Starr smeared her children's faces with cold cream from a small jar she had in her purse. She used lipstick to keep their lips from drying out and cracking. For the rest of the day the children lay under the blanket tent with their mother. Mrs. Starr was also beginning to feel the lack of water. Her tongue felt like a balloon and at the corners of her mouth were deep cracks that opened painfully with the slightest movement of her lips.

By the end of the second day Mrs. Starr was beginning to think she had made a big mistake in not hiking out right away. She could probably have reached the main highway by now. It seemed that very few cars used the road they were on—a week might go by before another vehicle came along. She also realized that being spotted by a plane was not very likely. No one was looking for them, and planes flew over too high to be able to see people on the ground. Perhaps she would try to walk the eighteen miles to Juniper that night; she should be able to reach it before morning.

That evening, just at sunset, she had a serious talk with her children.

"Andy, you're the oldest, so I'm leaving you in charge," she said. "You have to take care of things until I get back."

"But I'm scared. What if an animal comes?"

"You have the flashlight. You can scare an animal with it. Just shine the light in its face. But don't worry, there aren't any big animals in the desert. And I'll be back by tomorrow morning. You keep yourself and Madge covered with sand and stay under the blanket."

Earlier, Mrs. Starr read the labels on the box of crayons and the bottle of glue. She knew crayons were always nonpoisonous because children might put them in their mouths. There might be some food value in the crayons, she decided, so she made Andy and Madge eat several apiece. Then she told them to drink the glue. The label said it was made from dairy products, so it, too, might provide some nutrients or moisture. Finally she hugged and kissed both children, left the makeshift tent, and started walking to Juniper.

By midnight, she knew that she would have to turn back. Although a half-moon shed plenty of light, the old road was difficult to follow and twice she lost it. The second time she strayed, she grew frightened she would not be able to find her way back. She might never see her children again. It would have been better if she had tried hiking back to the main road. At least she would have her car tracks to follow.

She rested for several minutes, then started back. On the way she ran across a stunted tree. She broke several branches off its trunk and dragged them behind her. It was almost dawn when she reached Andy and Madge. Sitting down under the blanket, she peeled the bark away in long strips. She and the children licked the stripped branches and chewed the bark so as to get every last drop of moisture available. It seemed to help a little, but Mrs. Starr knew her children wouldn't last much longer if she didn't get help soon. Both of them were weak and Madge cried a lot— harsh, choking sobs because her body was too dried out to produce any tears. The skin on both children's faces had begun to shrivel and wrinkle.

All that day Mrs. Starr rested. At sunset she told the children she was leaving them for a little while to look for water. Either because they trusted her or were too weak to complain, they said nothing. She kissed them both, alarmed at how hot and flushed their cheeks felt. Then she smeared their faces with the last of the cold cream and lipstick. As she walked away from the car, this time in the direction of the main highway, she wondered if she would ever see them again.

Although she found the hiking much more tiring than the night before, she forced herself to keep going, stopping for short rests every half-hour or so. After every rest she found it harder to struggle to her feet and continue her grim march. Her loafers were starting to come apart and the flapping sole on one of them caused her to stumble and fall several times. On one of these falls she cut both knees and blood streamed down her legs. Finally light began to glow in the eastern sky. She had no idea how far she had walked. She could remember no landmarks from her drive in and therefore had no way of judging how many miles she had covered. Once she spotted a lizard and tried to catch it, but it vanished into a crack in a rock with a wriggle of its tail.

As the sun rose higher and higher, she realized she would soon have to stop walking. She would drop in her tracks if she tried to keep going in the glaring heat. She kept looking for a large rock, one that cast enough shade to shelter her. Finally she spotted one in the distance. And it was close to the road, too, in case a car came along. She would have to build a sign in the middle of the road in case she went to sleep or passed out. She would make a stone marker of some sort, pile three or four rocks high enough so any car coming along would have to stop. Then what? Could she leave her loafers in the road, pointing in the right direction? Then she noticed something odd about the rock—there seemed to be a constant whirlpool of dust behind it. Suddenly she realized it was a moving vehicle trailing a plume of dust!

She ran forward, waving both arms, afraid the driver would turn around before he reached her. Then, for the fifth or sixth time, she tripped and went sprawling.

The two young rock hounds were out prospecting in their jeep when they discovered Mrs. Starr lying in the middle of the road. Because her face was so black and shriveled, they thought she had been in a fire. They also thought she was dead. Then one of the men detected a pulse. He lifted Mrs. Starr's head and let some water from a canteen trickle into her mouth. After a minute or two she came to and drank more water. After a few more minutes and another long drink of water, she recovered enough to direct the young men to where Andy and Madge were waiting.

Mrs. Starr and her children were taken to a nearby hospital where, after several days of treatment, they recovered their health.

Mrs. Starr had never thought of herself as a particularly brave or clever woman. Yet experts said that she had done all the right things to save the lives of her children. Most people, they said, would not have thought of burying the children to help keep them cool, or chewing the bark of branches, or eating the crayons and drinking the glue—all those imaginative things that, added up, helped Mrs. Starr and her children to cheat death in the desert.

# FOCUSSING

1. Scan newspapers for one week and clip stories about people who survive terrible ordeals. Make a collage of the stories for the class. The following is an example of a story you might cut out:

> **Boy survives freeze**
> Milwaukee, Wisc. (AP)—A 2- and-a-half year old boy who came back from the dead with ice in his blood is certain to end up in medical textbooks, doctors say.
>
> A search of medical literature has found no case of anyone surviving with a body temperature colder than the boy's 16° C.
>
> But yesterday, Michael Troche was surviving—alert and eager for his two favourite things, "gum and popcorn," said his mother, Judy Troche.
>
> Two weeks ago, the boy was so severely frozen after wandering away from his home in a temperature of −29°C that ice had formed beneath his skin and he appeared "clinically dead." Doctors said he had been outside for as long as 3-and-a-half hours before he was found.

2. In a group of three or four, brainstorm ten qualities that people must have in order to survive difficult situations. (You might find the newspaper stories from Focussing #1 helpful.) Make a list of these qualities and put it in your Work in Progress file for later use with other activities.

3. Ask many different people for their ideas about the word *survival*. Use a tape recorder for this "person in the street" interview. You might ask someone new to Canada, a war veteran, another teenager, a single parent, or a police officer. Compare your interview with those of your classmates.

4. "You're not dead until you're forgotten." With a partner, list the ways that people can survive after death, e.g., Nellie McClung through her writing and her political achievements. Combine your lists with those of other groups to make one list that could be posted in your classroom. You could use a word processor for writing and "merging" your lists.

# THE MOST DANGEROUS GAME

*by Richard Connell*

"**O**FF THERE to the right—somewhere—is a large island," said Whitney. "It's rather a mystery—"

"What island is it?" Rainsford asked.

"The old charts call it 'Ship Trap Island,' " Whitney replied. "A suggestive name, isn't it? Sailors have a curious dread of the place. I don't know why. Some superstition—"

"Can't see it," remarked Rainsford, trying to peer through the dank tropical night that was palpable as it pressed its thick warm blackness in upon the yacht.

"You've good eyes," said Whitney, with a laugh, "and I've seen you pick off a moose moving in the brown fall bush at four hundred yards, but even you can't see four miles or so through a moonless Caribbean night."

"Nor four yards," admitted Rainsford. "Ugh! It's like moist black velvet."

"It will be light enough in Rio," promised Whitney. "We should make it in a few days. I hope the jaguar guns have come from Purdey's. We should have some good hunting up the Amazon. Great sport, hunting."

"The best sport in the world," agreed Rainsford.

"For the hunter," amended Whitney. "Not for the jaguar."

"Don't talk rot, Whitney," said Rainsford. "You're a big-game hunter, not a philosopher. Who cares how a jaguar feels?"

"Perhaps the jaguar does," observed Whitney.

"Bah! They've no understanding."

"Even so, I rather think they understand one thing—fear. The fear of pain and the fear of death."

"Nonsense," laughed Rainsford. "This hot weather is making you soft, Whitney. Be a realist. The world is made up of two classes—the hunters and the hunted. Luckily, you and I are hunters. Do you think we've passed that island yet?"

"I can't tell in the dark. I hope so."

"Why?" asked Rainsford.

"The place has a reputation—a bad one."

"Cannibals?" suggested Rainsford.

"Hardly. Even cannibals wouldn't live in such a God-forsaken place. But it's gotten into sailor lore, somehow. Didn't you notice that the crew's nerves seemed a bit jumpy today?"

"They were a bit strange, now you mention it. Even Captain Nielsen—"

"Yes, even that tough-minded old Swede, who'd go up to the devil himself and ask him for a light. Those fishy blue eyes held a look I never saw there before. All I could get out of him was: 'This place has an evil name among seafaring men, sir.' Then he said to me, very gravely: 'Don't you feel anything?'—as if the air about us was actually poisonous. Now, you mustn't laugh when I tell you this—I did feel something like a sudden chill.

"There was no breeze. The sea was as flat as a plate-glass window. We were drawing near the island then. What I felt was a—a mental chill; a sort of sudden dread."

"Pure imagination," said Rainsford. "One superstitious sailor can taint the whole ship's company with his fear."

"Maybe. But sometimes I think sailors have an extra sense that tells them when they are in danger. Sometimes I think evil is a tangible thing—with wave lengths, just as sound and light have. An evil place can, so to speak, broadcast vibrations of evil. Anyhow, I'm glad we're getting out of this zone. Well, I think I'll turn in now, Rainsford."

"I'm not sleepy," said Rainsford. "I'm going to smoke another pipe up on the afterdeck."

"Good night, then, Rainsford. See you at breakfast."

"Right. Good night, Whitney."

There was no sound in the night as Rainsford sat there, but the muffled throb of the engine that drove the yacht swiftly through the darkness, and the swish and ripple of the wash of the propeller.

Rainsford, reclining in a steamer chair, indolently puffed on his favourite brier. The sensuous drowsiness of the night was on him. "It's so dark," he thought, "that I could sleep without closing my eyes; the night would be my eyelids—"

An abrupt sound startled him. Off to the right he heard it, and his ears, expert in such matters, could not be mistaken. Again he heard the sound, and again. Somewhere, off in the blackness, someone had fired a gun three times.

Rainsford sprang up and moved quickly to the rail, mystified. He strained his eyes in the direction from which the reports had come, but it was like trying to see through a blanket. He leaped upon the rail and balanced himself there, to get greater elevation; his pipe, striking a rope, was knocked from his mouth. He lunged for it; a short, hoarse cry came from his lips as he realized he had reached too far and had lost his balance. The cry was pinched off short as the blood-warm waters of the Caribbean Sea closed over his head.

He struggled up to the surface and tried to cry out, but the wash from the speeding yacht slapped him in the face, and the salt water in his open mouth made him gag and strangle. Desperately he struck out with strong strokes after the receding lights of the yacht, but he stopped before he had swum fifty feet. A certain coolheadedness had come to him; it was not the first time he had been in a tight place. There was a chance that his cries could be heard by some-one abroad the yacht, but that chance was slender, and grew more slender as the yacht raced on. He wrestled himself out of his clothes, and shouted with all his power. The lights of the yacht became faint and ever-vanishing fireflies; then they were blotted out entirely by the night.

Rainsford remembered the shots. They had come from the right, and doggedly he swam in that direction, swim-ming with slow, deliberate strokes, conserving his strength. For a seemingly endless time he fought the sea. He began to count his strokes; he could do possibly a hundred more and then—

Rainsford heard a sound. It came out of the darkness, a high, screaming sound, the sound of an animal in an ex-tremity of anguish and terror.

He did not recognize the animal that made the sound; he did not try to; with fresh vitality he swam toward the sound. He heard it again; then it was cut short by another noise, crisp, staccato.

"Pistol shot," muttered Rainsford, swimming on.

Ten minutes of determined effort brought another sound to his ears—the most welcome he had ever heard—the muttering and growling of the sea breaking on a rocky shore. He was almost on the rocks before he saw them; on a night less calm he would have been shattered against them. With his remaining strength he dragged himself from the swirling waters. Jagged crags appeared to jut up into the opaqueness; he forced himself upward, hand over hand. Gasping, his hands raw, he reached a flat place at the top. Dense jungle came down to the very edge of the cliffs. What perils that tangle of trees and underbrush might hold for him did not concern Rainsford just then. All he knew was that he was safe from his enemy, the sea, and that utter weariness was on him. He flung himself down at the jungle edge and tumbled headlong into the deepest sleep of his life.

When he opened his eyes he knew from the position of the sun that it was late in the afternoon. Sleep had given him new vigour; a sharp hunger was picking at him.

He looked about him, almost cheerfully.

"Where there are pistol shots, there are men. Where there are men, there is food," he thought. But what kind of men, he wondered, in so forbidding a place? An unbroken front of snarled and ragged jungle fringed the shore.

He saw no sign of a trail through the closely knit web of weeds and trees; it was easier to go along the shore, and Rainsford floundered along by the water. Not far from where he had landed, he stopped.

Some wounded thing, by the evidence a large animal, had thrashed about in the underbrush; the jungle weeds were crushed down and the moss was lacerated; one patch of weeds was strained crimson. A small, glittering object not far away caught Rainsford's eye and he picked it up. It was an empty cartridge.

"A twenty-two," he remarked. "That's odd. It must have been a fairly large animal too. The hunter had his nerve with him to tackle it with a light gun. It's clear that the brute put up a fight. I suppose the first three shots I heard was when the hunter flushed his quarry and wounded it. The last shot was when he trailed it here and finished it."

He examined the ground closely and found what he had hoped to find—the print of hunting boots. They pointed along the cliff in the direction he had been going. Eagerly he hurried along, now slipping on a rotten log or a loose stone, but making headway; night was beginning to settle down on the island.

Bleak darkness was blacking out the sea and jungle when Rainsford sighted the lights. He came upon them as he turned a crook in the coast line, and his first thought was that he had come upon a village, for there were many lights. But as he forged along he saw to his great astonishment that all the lights were in one enormous building—a lofty structure with pointed towers plunging upward into the gloom. His eyes made out the shadowy outlines of a palatial chateau; it was set on a high bluff, and on three sides of it cliffs dived down to where the sea licked greedy lips on the shadows.

"Mirage," thought Rainsford. But it was no mirage, he found, when he opened the tall spiked iron gate. The stone steps were real enough; the massive door with a leering gargoyle for a knocker was real enough; yet about it all hung an air of unreality.

He lifted the knocker, and it creaked up stiffly, as if it had never before been used. He let it fall, and it startled him with its booming loudness. He thought he heard steps within; the door remained closed. Again Rainsford lifted the heavy knocker, and let it fall. The door opened then, opened as suddenly as if it were on a spring, and Rainsford stood blinking in the river of glaring gold light that poured out. The first thing Rainsford's eyes discerned was the largest man Rainsford had ever seen—a gigantic creature, solidly made and black-bearded to the waist. In his hand the man held a long-barrelled revolver, and he was pointing it straight at Rainsford's heart.

Out of the snarl of beard two small eyes regarded Rainsford.

"Don't be alarmed," said Rainsford, with a smile which he hoped was disarming. "I'm no robber. I fell off a yacht. My name is Sanger Rainsford of New York City."

The menacing look in the eyes did not change. The revolver pointed as rigidly as if the giant were a statue. He gave no sign that he understood Rainsford's words, or that he had even heard them. He was dressed in uniform, a black uniform trimmed with gray astrakhan.

"I'm Sanger Rainsford of New York," Rainsford began again. "I fell off a yacht. I am hungry."

The man's only answer was to raise with his thumb the hammer of his revolver. Then Rainsford saw the man's free hand go to his forehead in a military salute, and he saw him click his heels together and stand at attention. Another man was coming down the broad marble steps, an erect, slender man in evening clothes. He advanced to Rainsford and held out his hand.

In a cultivated voice marked by a slight accent that gave it added precision and deliberateness, he said: "It is a very great pleasure and honour to welcome Mr. Sanger Rainsford, the celebrated hunter, to my home."

Automatically Rainsford shook the man's hand.

"I've read your book about hunting snow leopards in Tibet, you see," explained the man. "I am General Zaroff."

Rainsford's first impression was that the man was singularly handsome; his second was that there was an original, almost bizarre quality about the general's face. He was a tall man past middle age, for his hair was a vivid white; but his thick eyebrows and pointed military mustache were as black as the night from which Rainsford had come. His eyes, too, were black and very bright. He had high cheekbones, a sharp-cut nose, a spare, dark face, the face of a man used to giving orders, the face of an aristocrat. Turning to the giant in uniform, the general made a sign. The giant put away his pistol, saluted, withdrew.

"Ivan is an incredibly strong fellow," remarked the general, "but he has the misfortune to be deaf and dumb. A simple fellow but, I'm afraid, like all his race, a bit of a savage."

"Is he Russian?"

"He is a Cossack," said the general, and his smile showed red lips and pointed teeth, "So am I.

"Come," he said, "we shouldn't be chatting here. We can talk later. Now you want clothes, food, rest. You shall have them. This is a most restful spot."

Ivan had reappeared, and the general spoke to him with lips that moved but gave forth no sound.

"Follow Ivan, if you please, Mr. Rainsford," said the general. "I was about to have my dinner when you came. I'll wait for you. You'll find that my clothes will fit you, I think."

It was to a huge, beam-ceilinged bedroom with a canopied bed big enough for six men that Rainsford followed the silent giant. Ivan laid out an evening suit, and Rainsford, as he put it on, noticed that it came from a London tailor who ordinarily cut and sewed for none below the rank of duke.

The dining room to which Ivan conducted him was in many ways remarkable. There was a medieval magnificence about it; it suggested a baronial hall of feudal times with its oaken panels, its high ceiling, its vast refectory table where two score men could sit down to eat. About the hall were the mounted heads of many animals—lions, tigers, elephants, moose, bears; larger or more perfect specimens Rainsford had never seen. At the great table the general was sitting, alone.

"You'll have a cocktail, Mr. Rainsford," he suggested.

The cocktail was surpassingly good; and, Rainsford noted, the table appointments were of the finest—the linen, the crystal, the silver, the china.

They were eating *borsch*, the rich, red soup with whipped cream so dear to Russian palates. Half apologetically General Zaroff said: "We do our best to preserve the amenities of civilization here. Please forgive any lapses. We are well off the beaten track, you know. Do you think the champagne has suffered from its long ocean trip?"

"Not in the least," declared Rainsford. He was finding the general a most thoughtful and affable host, a true cosmopolite. But there was one small trait of the general's that made Rainsford uncomfortable. Whenever he looked up from his plate he found the general studying him, appraising him narrowly.

"Perhaps," said General Zaroff, "you were surprised that I recognized your name. You see, I read all books on hunting published in English, French, and Russian. I have but one passion in my life, Mr. Rainsford, and it is the hunt."

"You have some wonderful heads here," said Rainsford as he ate a particularly well-cooked filet mignon. "That Cape buffalo is the largest I ever saw."

"Oh, that fellow. Yes, he was a monster."

"Did he charge you?"

"Hurled me against a tree," said the general. "Fractured my skull. But I got the brute."

"I've always thought," said Rainsford, "that the Cape buffalo is the most dangerous of all big game."

For a moment the general did not reply; he was smiling his curious red-lipped smile. Then he said slowly: "No. You are wrong, sir. The Cape buffalo is not the most dangerous big game." He sipped his wine. "Here in my preserve on this island," he said in the same slow tone, "I hunt more dangerous game."

Rainsford expressed his surprise. "Is there big game on this island?"

The general nodded.

"The biggest."

"Really?"

"Oh, it isn't here naturally, of course. I have to stock the island."

"What have you imported, general?" Rainsford asked. "Tigers?"

The general smiled. "No," he said. "Hunting tigers ceased to interest me some years ago. I exhausted their possibilities, you see. No thrill left in tigers, no real danger. I live for danger, Mr. Rainsford."

The general took from his pocket a gold cigarette case

and offered his guest a long black cigarette with a silver tip; it was perfumed and gave off a smell like incense.

"We will have some capital hunting, you and I," said the general. "I shall be most glad to have your society."

"But what game—" began Rainsford.

"I'll tell you," said the general. "You will be amused, I know. I think I may say, in all modesty, that I have done a rare thing. I have invented a new sensation. May I pour you another glass of port, Mr. Rainsford?"

"Thank you, general."

The general filled both glasses, and said: "God makes some men poets. Some He makes kings, some beggars. Me He made a hunter. My hand was made for the trigger, my father said. He was a very rich man with a quarter of a million acres in the Crimea, and he was an ardent sportsman. When I was only five years old he gave me a little gun, specially made in Moscow for me, to shoot sparrows with. When I shot some of his prize turkeys with it, he did not punish me; he complimented me on my marksmanship. I killed my first bear in the Caucasus when I was ten. My whole life has been one prolonged hunt. I went into the army—it was expected of noblemen's sons—and for a time commanded a division of Cossack cavalry, but my real interest was always the hunt. I have hunted every kind of game in every land. It would be impossible for me to tell you how many animals I have killed."

The general puffed at his cigarette.

"After the debacle in Russia I left the country, for it was imprudent for an officer of the Czar to stay there. Many noble Russians lost everything. I, luckily, had invested heavily in American securities, so I shall never have to open a tea-room in Monte Carlo or drive a taxi in Paris. Naturally, I continued to hunt—grizzlies in your Rockies, crocodiles in the Ganges, rhinoceroses in East Africa. It was in Africa that the Cape buffalo hit me and laid me up for six months. As soon as I recovered I started for the Amazon to hunt jaguars, for I had heard they were unusually cunning. They weren't." The Cossack sighed. "They were no match at all for a hunter with his wits about him, and a high-powered rifle. I was bitterly disappointed. I was lying in my tent with a splitting headache one night when a terrible thought pushed its way into my mind. Hunting was beginning to bore me! And hunting, remember, had been my life. I have heard that in America businessmen often go to pieces when they give up the business that has been their life."

"Yes, that's so," said Rainsford.

The general smiled. "I had no wish to go to pieces," he

said. "I must do something. Now, mine is an analytical mind, Mr. Rainsford. Doubtless that is why I enjoy the problems of the chase."

"No doubt, General Zaroff."

"So," continued the general, "I asked myself why the hunt no longer fascinated me. You are much younger than I am, Mr. Rainsford, and have not hunted as much, but you perhaps can guess the answer."

"What was it?"

"Simply this: hunting had ceased to be what you call 'a sporting proposition.' It had become too easy. I always got my quarry. Always. There is no greater bore than perfection."

The general lit a fresh cigarette.

"No animal had a chance with me any more. That is no boast; it is a mathematical certainty. The animal had nothing but his legs and his instinct. Instinct is no match for reason. When I thought of this it was a tragic moment for me, I can tell you."

Rainsford leaned across the table, absorbed in what his host was saying.

"It came to me as an inspiration what I must do," the general went on.

"And that was?"

The general smiled the quiet smile of one who has faced an obstacle and surmounted it with success. "I had to invent a new animal to hunt," he said.

"A new animal? You're joking."

"Not at all," said the general. "I never joke about hunting. I needed a new animal. I found one. So I bought this island, built this house, and here I do my hunting. The island is perfect for my purposes—there are jungles with a maze of trails in them, hills, swamps—"

"But the animal, General Zaroff?"

"Oh," said the general, "it supplies me with the most exciting hunting in the world. No other hunting compares with it for an instant. Every day I hunt, and I never grow bored now, for I have a quarry with which I can match my wits."

Rainsford's bewilderment showed in his face.

"I wanted the ideal animal to hunt," explained the general. "So I said: 'What are the attributes of an ideal quarry?' And the answer was, of course: 'It must have courage, cunning, and, above all, it must be able to reason'."

"But no animal can reason," objected Rainsford.

"My dear fellow," said the general, "there is one that can."

"But you can't mean—" gasped Rainsford.

"And why not?"

"I can't believe you are serious, General Zaroff. This is a grisly joke."

"Why should I not be serious? I am speaking of hunting."

"Hunting? Good God, General Zaroff, what you speak of is murder."

The general laughed with entire good nature. He regarded Rainsford quizzically. "I refuse to believe that so modern and civilized a young man as you seem to be harbours romantic ideas about the value of human life. Surely your experiences in the war—"

"Did not make me condone cold-blooded murder," finished Rainsford stiffly.

Laughter shook the general. "How extraordinarily droll you are!" he said. "One does not expect nowadays to find a young man of the educated class, even in America, with such a naive, and, if I may say so, Mid-Victorian point of view. It's like finding a snuffbox in a limousine. Ah, well, doubtless you had Puritan ancestors. So many Americans appear to have had. I'll wager you'll forget your notions when you go hunting with me. You've a genuine new thrill in store for you, Mr. Rainsford."

"Thank you, I'm a hunter, not a murderer."

"Dear me," said the general, quite unruffled, "again that unpleasant word. But I think I can show you that your scruples are quite ill-founded."

"Yes?"

"Life is for the strong, to be lived by the strong, and, if need be, taken by the strong. The weak of the world were put here to give the strong pleasure. I am strong. Why should I not use my gift? If I wish to hunt, why should I not? I hunt the scum of the earth—sailors from tramp ships—lascars, blacks, Chinese, whites, mongrels—a thoroughbred horse or hound is worth more than a score of them."

"But they are men," said Rainsford hotly.

"Precisely," said the general. "That is why I use them. It gives me pleasure. They can reason after a fashion. So they are dangerous."

"But where do you get them?"

The general's left eyelid fluttered down in a wink. "This island is called Ship Trap," he answered. "Sometimes an angry god of the high seas sends them to me. Sometimes, when Providence is not so kind, I help Providence a bit. Come to the window with me."

Rainsford went to the window and looked out toward the sea.

"Watch! Out there!" exclaimed the general, pointing into the night. Rainsford's eyes saw only blackness, and then, as the general pressed a button, far out to sea Rainsford saw the flash of lights.

The general chuckled. "They indicate a channel," he said, "where there's none: giant rocks with razor edges crouch like a sea monster with wide-open jaws. They can crush a ship as easily as I crush this nut." He dropped a walnut on the hardwood floor and brought his heel grinding down on it. "Oh, yes," he said, casually, as if in answer to a question, "I have electricity. We try to be civilized here."

"Civilized? And you shoot down men?"

A trace of anger was in the general's black eyes, but it was there for but a second, and he said, in his most pleasant manner: "Dear me, what a righteous young man you are! I assure you I do not do the thing you suggest. That would be barbarous. I treat these visitors with every consideration. They get plenty of good food and exercise. They get into splendid physical condition. You shall see for yourself tomorrow."

"What do you mean?"

"We'll visit my training school," smiled the general. "It's in the cellar. I have about a dozen pupils down there now. They're from the Spanish bark *San Lucar* that had the bad luck to go on the rocks out there. A very inferior lot, I regret to say. Poor specimens and more accustomed to the deck than to the jungle."

He raised his hand, and Ivan, who served as waiter, brought thick Turkish coffee. Rainsford, with an effort, held his tongue in check.

"It's a game, you see," pursued the general blandly. "I suggest to one of them that we go hunting. I give him a supply of food and an excellent hunting knife. I give him three hours' start. I am to follow, armed only with a pistol of the smallest calibre and range. If my quarry eludes me for three whole days, he wins the game. If I find him"— the general smiled—"he loses."

"Suppose he refuses to be hunted?"

"Oh," said the general, "I give him his option, of course. He need not play that game if he doesn't wish to. If he does not wish to hunt, I turn him over to Ivan. Ivan once had the honour of serving as official knouter to the Great White Czar, and he has his own ideas of sport. Invariably, Mr. Rainsford, invariably they choose the hunt."

"And if they win?"

The smile on the general's face widened. "To date I have not lost," he said.

Then he added, hastily: "I don't wish you to think me a braggart, Mr. Rainsford. Many of them afford only the most elementary sort of problem. Occasionally I strike a tartar. One almost did win. I eventually had to use the dogs."

"The dogs?"

"This way, please. I'll show you."

The general steered Rainsford to a window. The lights from the windows sent a flickering illumination that made grotesque patterns on the courtyard below, and Rainsford could see moving about there a dozen or so huge black shapes; as they turned toward him, their eyes glittered greenly.

"A rather good lot, I think," observed the general. "They are let out at seven every night. If anyone should try to get into my house—or out of it—something extremely regrettable would occur to him." He hummed a snatch of song from the *Folies Bergères*.

"And now," said the general, "I want to show you my new collection of heads. Will you come with me to the library?"

"I hope," said Rainsford, "that you will excuse me tonight, General Zaroff. I'm really not feeling at all well."

"Ah, indeed?" the general inquired solicitously. "Well, I suppose that's only natural, after your long swim. You need a good, restful night's sleep. Tomorrow you'll feel like a new man, I'll wager. Then we'll hunt, eh? I've one rather promising prospect—"

Rainsford was hurrying from the room.

"Sorry you can't go with me tonight," called the general. "I expect rather fair sport—a big, strong black. He looks resourceful—Well, good night, Mr. Rainsford; I hope you have a good night's rest."

The bed was good, and the pajamas of the softest silk, and he was tired in every fibre of his being, but nevertheless Rainsford could not quiet his brain with the opiate of sleep. He lay, eyes wide open. Once he tought he heard stealthy steps in the corridor outside his room. He sought to throw open the door; it would not open. He went to the window and looked out. His room was high up in one of the towers. The lights of the chateau were out now, and it was dark and silent, but there was a fragment of sallow moon, and by its wan light he could see, dimly, the courtyard; there, weaving in and out in the pattern of shadow, were black, noiseless forms; the hounds heard him at the window and looked up, expectantly, with their green eyes. Rainsford went back to the bed and lay down. By many methods he tried to put himself to sleep. He had achieved a doze when, just as morning began to come, he heard, far off in the jungle, the faint report of a pistol.

General Zaroff did not appear until luncheon. He was dressed faultlessly in the tweeds of a country squire. He was solicitous about the state of Rainsford's health.

"As for me," sighed the general, "I do not feel so well. I am worried, Mr. Rainsford. Last night I detected traces of my old complaint."

To Rainsford's questioning glance the general said: "Ennui. Boredom."

Then, taking a second helping of crêpes suzette, the general explained: "The hunting was not good last night. The fellow lost his head. He made a straight trail that offered no problems at all. That's the trouble with these sailors; they have dull brains to begin with, and they do not know how to get about in the woods. They do excessively stupid and obvious things. It's most annoying. Will you have another glass of Chablis, Mr. Rainsford?"

"General," said Rainsford firmly, "I wish to leave this island at once."

The general raised his thickets of eyebrows; he seemed hurt. "But, my dear fellow," the general protested, "you've only just come. You've had no hunting—"

"I wish to go today," said Rainsford. He saw the dead black eyes of the general on him, studying him. General Zaroff's face suddenly brightened.

He filled Rainsford's glass with venerable Chablis from a dusty bottle.

"Tonight," said the general, "we will hunt—you and I."

Rainsford shook his head.

"No, general," he said. "I will not hunt."

The general shrugged his shoulders and delicately ate a hothouse grape. "As you wish, my friend," he said. "The choice rests entirely with you. But may I not venture to suggest that you will find my idea of sport more diverting than Ivan's?"

He nodded toward the corner to where the giant stood, scowling, his thick arms crossed on his hogshead of chest.

"You don't mean—" cried Rainsford.

"My dear fellow," said the general, "have I not told you I always mean what I say about hunting? This is really an inspiration. I drink to a foeman worthy of my steel—at last."

The general raised his glass, but Rainsford sat staring at him.

"You'll find this game worth playing," the general said enthusiastically. "Your brain against mine. Your woodcraft against mine. Your strength and stamina against mine. Outdoor chess! And the stake is not without value, eh?"

"And if I win—" began Rainsford huskily.

"I'll cheerfully acknowledge myself defeated if I do not find you by midnight of the third day," said General Zaroff. "My sloop will place you on the mainland near the town."

The general read what Rainsford was thinking.

"Oh, you can trust me," said the Cossack. "I will give you my word as a gentleman and a sportsman. Of course you, in turn, must agree to say nothing of your visit here."

"I'll agree to nothing of the kind," said Rainsford.

"Oh," said the general, "in that case—But why discuss that now? Three days hence we can discuss it over a bottle of Veuve Cliquot, unless—"

The general sipped his wine.

Then a businesslike air animated him. "Ivan," he said to Rainsford, "will supply you with hunting clothes, food, a knife. I suggest you wear moccasins; they leave a poorer trail. I suggest too that you avoid the big swamp in the southeast corner of the island. We call it Death Swamp. There's quicksand there. One foolish fellow tried it. The deplorable part of it was that Lazarus followed him. You can imagine my feelings, Mr. Rainsford. I loved Lazarus; he was the finest hound in my pack. Well, I must beg you to excuse me now. I always take a siesta after lunch. You'll hardly have time for a nap, I fear. You'll want to start, no doubt. I shall not follow till dusk. Hunting at night is so much more exciting than by day, don't you think? Au revoir, Mr. Rainsford, au revoir."

General Zaroff, with a deep, courtly bow, strolled from the room.

From another door came Ivan. Under one arm he carried khaki hunting clothes, a haversack of food, a leather sheath containing a long-bladed hunting knife; his right hand rested on a cocked revolver thrust in the crimson sash about his waist. . . .

Rainsford had fought his way through the bush for two hours. "I must keep my nerve. I must keep my nerve," he said through tight teeth.

He had not been entirely clearheaded when the chateau gates snapped shut behind him. His whole idea at first was to put distance between himself and General Zaroff, and, to this end, he had plunged along, spurred on by the sharp rowels of something very like panic. Now he had got a grip on himself, had stopped, and was taking stock of himself and the situation.

He saw that straight flight was futile; inevitably it would bring him face to face with the sea. He was in a picture with a frame of water, and his operations, clearly, must take place within that frame.

"I'll give him a trail to follow," muttered Rainsford, and he struck off from the rude path he had been following into the trackless wilderness. He executed a series of intricate loops; he doubled on his trail again and again, recalling all the lore of the fox hunt, and all the dodges of the fox. Night found him leg-weary, with hands and face lashed by the branches, on a thickly wooded ridge. He knew it would be insane to blunder on through the dark, even if he had the strength. His need for rest was imperative and he thought: "I have played the fox, now I must play the cat of the fable." A big tree with a thick trunk and outspread branches was near by, and taking care to leave not the slightest mark, he climbed up to the crotch, and stretching out on one of the broad limbs, after a fashion, rested. Rest brought him new confidence and almost a feeling of security. Even so zealous a hunter as General Zaroff could not trace him there, he told himself; only the devil himself could follow that complicated trail through the jungle after dark. But, perhaps, the general was a devil—

An apprehensive night crawled slowly by like a wounded snake, and sleep did not visit Rainsford, although the silence of a dead world was on the jungle. Toward morning when a dingy grey was varnishing the sky, the cry of some startled bird focussed Rainsford's attention in that direction. Something was coming through the bush, coming slowly, carefully, coming by the same winding way Rainsford had come. He flattened himself down on the limb, and through a screen of leaves almost as thick as tapestry, he watched. The thing that was approaching was a man.

It was General Zaroff. He made his way along with his eyes fixed in utmost concentration on the ground before him. He paused, almost beneath the tree, dropped to his knees, and studied the ground. Rainsford's impulse was to hurl himself down like a panther, but he saw that the general's right hand held something metallic—a small automatic pistol.

The hunter shook his head several times, as if he were puzzled. Then he straightened up and took from his case one of his black cigarettes; its pungent incenselike smoke floated up to Rainsford's nostrils.

Rainsford held his breath. The general's eyes had left the ground and were travelling inch by inch up the tree. Rainsford froze there, every muscle tensed for a spring. But the sharp eyes of the hunter stopped before they reached the limb where Rainsford lay; a smile spread over his brown face. Very deliberately he blew a smoke ring into the air; then he turned his back on the tree and walked carelessly away, back along the trail he had come. The swish of the underbrush against his hunting boots grew fainter and fainter.

The pent-up air burst hotly from Rainsford's lungs. His first thought made him feel sick and numb. The general could follow a trail through the woods at night; he could follow an extremely difficult trail; he must have uncanny powers; only by the merest chance had the Cossack failed to see his quarry.

Rainsford's second thought was even more terrible. It sent a shudder of cold horror through his whole being. Why had the general smiled? Why had he turned back?

Rainsford did not want to believe what his reason told him was true, but the truth was as evident as the sun that had by now pushed through the morning mists. The general was playing with him! The general was saving him for another day's sport! The Cossack was the cat; he was the mouse. Then it was that Rainsford knew the full meaning of terror.

"I will not lose my nerve. I will not."

He slid down from the tree, and struck off again into the woods. His face was set and he forced the machinery of his mind to function. Three hundred yards from his hiding place he stopped where a huge dead tree leaned precariously on a smaller, living one. Throwing off his sack of food, Rainsford took his knife from its sheath and began to work with all his energy.

The job was finished at last, and he threw himself down behind a fallen log a hundred feet away. He did not have to wait long. The cat was coming again to play with the mouse.

Following the trail with the sureness of a bloodhound, came General Zaroff. Nothing escaped those searching black eyes, no crushed blade of grass, no bent twig, no mark, no matter how faint, in the moss. So intent was the Cossack on his stalking that he was upon the thing Rainsford had made before he saw it. His foot touched the protruding bough that was the trigger. Even as he touched it, the general sensed his danger and leaped back with the agility of an ape. But he was not quite quick enough; the dead tree, delicately adjusted to rest on the cut living one, crashed down and struck the general a glancing blow on the shoulder as it fell; but for his alertness, he must have been smashed beneath it. He staggered, but he did not fall; nor did he drop his revolver. He stood there, rubbing his injured shoulder, and Rainsford, with fear again gripping his heart, heard the general's mocking laugh ring through the jungle.

"Rainsford," called the general, "if you are within sound of my voice, as I suppose you are, let me congratulate you. Not many men know how to make a Malay mancatcher. Luckily, for me, I too have hunted in Malacca. You are proving interesting, Mr. Rainsford. I am going now to have my wound dressed; it's only a slight one. But I shall be back. I shall be back."

When the general, nursing his bruised shoulder, had gone, Rainsford took up his flight again. It was flight now, a desperate, hopeless flight, that carried him on for some hours. Dusk came, then darkness, and still he pressed on. The ground grew softer under his moccasins; the vegetation grew ranker, denser; insects bit him savagely. Then, as he stepped forward, his foot sank into the ooze. He tried to wrench it back, but the muck sucked viciously at his foot as if it were a giant leech. With a violent effort, he tore his foot loose. He knew where he was now. Death Swamp and its quicksand.

His hands were tight closed as if his nerve were something tangible that someone in the darkness was trying to tear from his grip. The softness of the earth had given him an idea. He stepped back from the quicksand a dozen feet or so and, like some huge prehistoric beaver, he began to dig.

Rainsford had dug himself in in France when a second's delay meant death. That had been a placid pastime compared to his digging now. The pit grew deeper; when it was above his shoulders, he climbed out and from some hard saplings cut stakes and sharpened them to a fine point. These stakes he planted in the bottom of the pit with the points sticking up. With flying fingers he wove a rough carpet of weeds and branches and with it he covered the mouth of the pit. Then, wet with sweat and aching with tiredness, he crouched behind the stump of a lightning-charred tree.

He knew his pursuer was coming; he heard the padding sound of feet on the soft earth, and the night breeze brought him the perfume of the general's cigarette. It seemed to

Rainsford that the general was coming with unusual swiftness; he was not feeling his way along, foot by foot. Rainsford, crouching there, could not see the general, nor could he see the pit. He lived a year in a minute. Then he felt an impulse to cry aloud with joy, for he heard the sharp crackle of the breaking branches as the cover of the pit gave way; he heard the sharp scream of pain as the pointed stakes found their mark. He leaped up from his place of concealment. Then he cowered back. Three feet from the pit a man was standing, with an electric torch in his hand.

"You've done well, Rainsford," the voice of the general called. "Your Burmese tiger pit has claimed one of my best dogs. Again you score. I think, Mr. Rainsford, I'll see what you can do against my whole pack. I'm going home for rest now. Thank you for a most amusing evening."

At daybreak Rainsford, lying near the swamp, was awakened by a sound that made him know that he had new things to learn about fear. It was a distant sound, faint and wavering, but he knew it. It was the baying of a pack of hounds.

Rainsford knew he could do one of two things. He could stay where he was and wait. That was suicide. He could flee. That was postponing the inevitable. For a moment he stood there, thinking. An idea that held a wild chance came to him, and, tightening his belt, he headed away from the swamp. The baying of the hounds drew nearer, then still nearer, nearer, ever nearer. On a ridge Rainsford climbed a tree. Down a water-course, not a quarter of a mile away, he could see the bush moving. Straining his eyes, he saw the lean figure of General Zaroff; just ahead of him Rainsford made out another figure whose wide shoulders surged through the tall jungle weeds; it was the giant Ivan, and he seemed pulled forward by some unseen force; Rainsford knew that Ivan must be holding the pack in leash.

They would be on him any minute now. His mind worked frantically. He thought of a native trick he had learned in Uganda. He slid down the tree. He caught hold of a springy young sapling and to it he fastened his hunting knife, with the blade pointing down the trail; with a bit of wild grapevine he tied back the sapling. Then he ran for his life. The hounds raised their voices as they hit the fresh scent. Rainsford knew now how an animal at bay feels.

He had to stop to get his breath. The baying of the hounds stopped abruptly, and Rainsford's heart stopped too. They must have reached the knife.

He shinned excitedly up a tree and looked back. His pursuers had stopped. But the hope that was in Rainsford's brain when he climbed died, for he saw in the shallow valley that General Zaroff was still on his feet. But Ivan was not. The knife, driven by the recoil of the springing tree, had not wholly failed.

Rainsford had hardly tumbled to the ground when the pack took up the cry again.

"Nerve, nerve, nerve!" he panted, as he dashed along. A blue gap showed between the trees dead ahead. Ever nearer drew the hounds. Rainsford forced himself on toward that gap. He reached it. It was the shore of the sea. Across a cove he could see the gloomy grey stone of the chateau. Twenty feet below him the sea rumbled and hissed. Rainsford hesitated. He heard the hounds. Then he leaped far out into the sea. . . .

When the general and his pack reached the place by the sea, the Cossack stopped. For some minutes he stood regarding the blue-green expanse of water. He shrugged his shoulders. Then he sat down, took a drink of brandy from a silver flask, lit a perfumed cigarette, and hummed a bit from "Madame Butterfly."

General Zaroff had an exceedingly good dinner in his great panelled dining hall that evening. With it he had a bottle of Pol Roger and half a bottle of Chambertin. Two slight annoyances kept him from perfect enjoyment. One was the thought that it would be difficult to replace Ivan; the other was that his quarry had escaped him; of course the American hadn't played the game—so thought the general as he tasted his after-dinner liqueur. In his library he read, to soothe himself, from the works of Marcus Aurelius. At ten he went up to his bedroom. He was deliciously tired, he said to himself, as he locked himself in. There was a little moonlight, so before turning on his light, he went to the window and looked down at the courtyard. He could see the great hounds, and he called: "Better luck another time," to them. Then he switched on the light.

A man, who had been hiding in the curtains of the bed, was standing there.

"Rainsford!" screamed the general. "How in God's name did you get here?"

"Swam," said Rainsford. "I found it quicker than walking through the jungle."

The general sucked in his breath and smiled. "I congratulate you," he said. "You have won the game."

Rainsford did not smile. "I am still a beast at bay," he said, in a low, hoarse voice. "Get ready, General Zaroff."

The general made one of his deepest bows. "I see," he said. "Splendid! One of us is to furnish a repast for the hounds. The other will sleep in this very excellent bed. On guard, Rainsford." . . .

He had never slept in a better bed, Rainsford decided.

# CLOSE UP

1. Draw a map of General Zaroff's island. Mark all the places mentioned in the story and the traps Zaroff laid for Rainsford.

   **or**

   Draw a storyboard that shows how Rainsford survives the hunt. Exchange pictures with another student and write captions for her or his work. If you have access to a computer and a graphics program, you could use them to draw the storyboard or the map.

2. Look back over the story and make notes under the following headings:

   a) words that create suspense;

   b) words that enhance fear;

   c) phrases that heighten the mystery of the island.

3. You are going to produce a movie version of "The Most Dangerous Game." Make a list of the actors you would cast for each character in the story, and beside each name jot down one or two traits the actor should know in order to play that role. You may choose to cast females in any or all of the roles.

4. In no more than twenty-five words, summarize the argument that Zaroff uses to justify his hunt. In another paragraph, state how you feel about his argument.

# WIDE ANGLE

1. Working in a small group, write the script for an advertisement promoting a movie version of "The Most Dangerous Game." Record the advertisement on audio or video tape and play it for your classmates.

2. Working with a partner, write the story of the next week in Rainsford's life, beginning with when he wakes up in General Zaroff's bed in the morning. You may wish to answer some of these questions: Does Rainsford get off the island, and if so, how does he do it? What happens to the sailors imprisoned in the basement of Zaroff's castle? What does Rainsford do with Zaroff's island and his possessions? Revise your draft with your partner's help.

# ANTARCTIC ORDEAL
## by John Trevaskis and Patrick Pringle

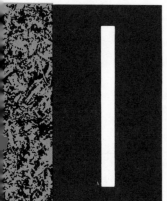

T SEEMED that he had to choose between being frozen to death and being gassed.

The temperature outside the hut was minus 59°, and he could hear his breath freezing as it left his mouth. Inside the hut the oil froze in his instruments, the ink in his pen. All he had for warmth was an oil-stove that leaked poisonous fumes.

It had been poisoning him for some time before he realized it. His companions in the expedition had not the faintest idea of it when they left their leader in his lonely outpost at latitude 80° South.

Richard E. Byrd had chosen himself for this scientific vigil through the seven months of the Antarctic winter. Headaches and a feeling of sickness had given him his first warning of danger, but by the time he knew the cause of the trouble there was no chance of a relief party getting through. The long Polar night had begun.

Byrd turned the stove off, and the temperature in the hut quickly fell. He went outside and walked briskly into the darkness, drawing icy but pure air into his lungs. His head had cleared and he no longer felt sick when he went back inside. He left the stove unlit until he was half-frozen. Then he again turned on the life-giving heat—and the death-dealing fumes.

The walk outside became a daily routine. Not that there was any daylight, for in the Antarctic winter the sun never rises. One fine evening he decided to go farther than usual, and planted flagged bamboo poles in the snow to mark the way. When he had put in the last pole he walked in what he thought was a circle before going back.

It was not a circle, for it did not bring him back to the last bamboo pole. The stick and the flag had disappeared. He could see nothing anywhere except ice and snow.

Fighting down fear, Byrd shone his flashlight on the snow. He hoped to follow his footprints back. The hope died immediately, for his boots had made no marks on the hard snow. Then he was in a panic, and wanted to run blindly. With an effort he forced down his alarm and began a methodical search for the flags.

First he kicked up loose snow and made a pile. Then he took a line from the stars and walked a hundred paces. There was no sign of the poles or flags. He turned and marched back, continually checking with the stars to keep in the same line. After his hundredth pace he still could not see his snow-pile.

Again he panicked and wanted to run. He forced himself to take only a few short steps, shining his flashlight all around—and the light picked out the snow-pile.

He took another line from the stars, and walked a hundred paces in a different direction. This time he got back more easily to his starting point. He went on, all around the compass—without seeing any bamboo poles or flags.

Therefore, they were more than a hundred paces from the pile of snow. They could be in any direction, and that was a horrifying thought. The desire to run blindly was almost irresistible. Tired and very cold now, Byrd knew he could not go on very much longer.

"I must increase the radius." He took another hundred paces, kicked up a second pile of snow and took thirty paces more. On the twenty-ninth step his flashlight showed a fluttering flag.

Then Byrd ran, wild not with fear but with joy. He reached the pole and grasped it, and followed the line of bamboos back to the hut. Half-frozen, he lit the stove to thaw his body—and to go on poisoning his lungs.

# CLOSE UP

1. Write five exciting headlines for a newspaper article on Richard Byrd's experience.
2. Draw the chart below. Fill in all the decisions Byrd made and the consequences of his decisions. In the last column, check off whether his decisions were wise or foolish.

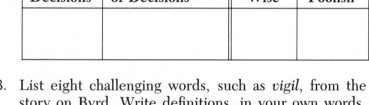

| Decisions | Consequences of Decisions | Decisions Were | |
|---|---|---|---|
| | | Wise | Foolish |
| | | | |

3. List eight challenging words, such as *vigil*, from the story on Byrd. Write definitions, in your own words, beside them. On a separate sheet create a match-up game using the words you chose. Exchange games with a partner and see if you can solve his or her game.

# WIDE ANGLE

1. Imagine that you are Byrd. Write a diary entry for the evening you returned to the hut after being lost in the snow. Knowing that your diary may one day be published, check your writing carefully; the Checklist for Proofreading (p. 182) will guide your review.
2. With the help of your librarian, research the story of Richard Byrd. Tell the class what happened to him in the Antarctic.

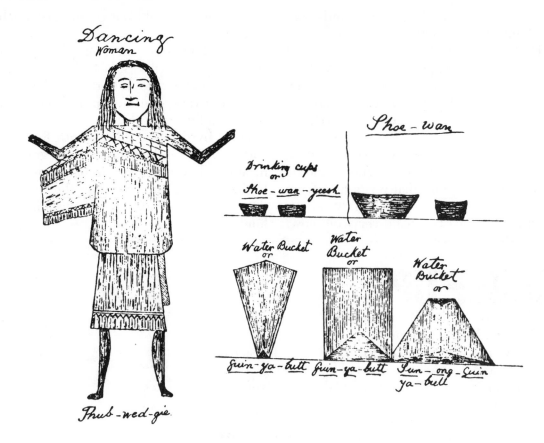

Dancing Woman

Phub-wed-gie.

Shoe-wan

Drinking cups or Shoe-wan-yeesh

Water Bucket or

Water Bucket or

Water Bucket or

Guin-ya-butt    Guin-ya-butt    Gun-ong-Guin ya-butt

# SHANADITHIT
## *from a longer poem by Al Pittman*

What I know of you
is only what my grade seven history book
told me
that you were young when they caught you
that your people lived in deerhide houses
that you drew lovely pictures
that they changed your name to nancy
that you died soon after
that you were the last of the Beothucks

you probably didn't know that
did you
that you were the last of your people
that when you went
there was no one to take your place
I suppose you died
thinking there were uncles and cousins
with toothaches and babies
that there were hunters

young men you'd like to be with
coming home game-laden to campfires
on the shore of the lake
your executioners call Red Indian
you didn't know you'd end up
in my grade seven history book
did you

and when you died your lonely death
when the white disease put an end to you
you didn't know
that one out of a generation of poets
would have given his soul
to be with you
to tell you he wouldn't forget
you didn't know that I would have kissed you
and cried when you went

did you

# CLOSE UP

1. "What I know of you/is only what my grade seven history textbook/told me." In a small group, discuss some of the ways in which the poem would be different from accounts of Shanadithit that appear in textbooks. Write the story of Shanadithit as it might have appeared in the poet's history book.
2. Brainstorm the possible meaning of the phrases "white disease" and "your executioners," and write your explanations in your own words. Suggest reasons why Shanadithit was the last of her people and what happened to them.
3. Re-read the poem once or twice, and then write a letter to Shanadithit telling her what you as a teenager today would have in common with her despite the differences in your worlds.

# WIDE ANGLE

1. A ballad is a poem that tells a story; ballads are often put to music. With your teacher's help, look for several ballads and read them aloud with three or four partners. Using one of the ballads as a guide, write "The Ballad of Shanadithit." Tape your ballad, using your own music if possible, and then play it for the class.
2. With the help of your librarian, or history teacher, research the story of the Boethucks of Newfoundland and how they became extinct. Share your findings with the class. Have those students who did Close Up #2 compare their predictions with your findings.
3. Imagine that you could go back in time and warn Shanadithit about what is happening to her tribe. With a partner playing the part of Shanadithit, role-play the conversation you would have as the two of you tried to think of ways to save the Beothucks.

*Epilogue from*

# I NEVER SAW ANOTHER BUTTERFLY

*by Jiri Weil*

I N Czechoslovakia, there is a strange place called Terezín, some 60 kilometres from Prague. It was founded by order of Emperor Joseph II of Austria 200 years ago and named after his mother, Maria Theresa. This walled-in fortress was constructed on plans drafted by Italian military engineers and has 12 ramparts which enclose the town in the shape of a star. It was to have been a fortress and it became a sleepy army garrison dominated by the barracks, where the homes of the inhabitants were a necessary nuisance. There were homes, taverns, a post office, a bank and a brewery. There was a church as well, built in a sober style and belonging to the barracks as part of the army community. The little town seemed to have been forced onto the countryside, a lovely countryside without either high mountains or dizzy cliffs, without deep ravines or swift rivers . . . only blue hills, green meadows, fruit trees, and tall poplars.

Today, a shadow still lingers above this little town as though funeral wagons still drive along its streets, as though the dust still eddies in the town square, stirred by a thousand footsteps. Today, it seems sometimes as though from every corner, from every stairway and from every corridor, peer human faces, gaunt, exhausted, with eyes full of fear.

During the war years, Terezín was a place of famine and of fear. Somewhere far away, in Berlin, men in uniforms had held meetings. These men decided to exterminate all the Jews in Europe, and because they were used to doing things thoroughly with the calculated, cool passion of a murderer, they worked out plans in which they fixed the country, the place and the timetable as well as the stopping-places on that road to death. One of these stopping places was Terezín.

It was meant to be a model camp which foreigners could be shown, and it was termed a ghetto. At first, Jews from Bohemia and Moravia were brought to Terezín, but finally they came from all over Europe and from hence were shipped further east to the gas chambers and ovens. Everything in this small town was false, invented, every one of its inhabitants was condemned in advance to die. It was only a funnel without an outlet. Those who contrived this trap and put it on their map, with its fixed timetable of life and death, knew all about it. They knew its future as well. Those who were brought here in crowded railroad coaches and cattle cars after days and days of cruelty, of humiliation, of offence, of beatings and of theft, knew very little about it. Some of them believed the murderers' falsehoods, that they could sit out the war here in quiet safety. Others came to Terezín already crushed, yet with a spark of hope that even so, perhaps they might escape their destiny. There were also those who knew that Terezín was only one station on a short timetable and that is why they tried so hard to keep at least themselves alive and perhaps their family. And those who were good and honourable endeavoured to keep the children alive, the aged and the ailing. All were finally deceived and the same fate awaited all of them.

But the children who were brought here knew nothing. They came from places where they had already known humiliation; they had been expelled from the schools. They had sewn stars on their hearts, on their jackets and blouses, and were only allowed to play in the cemeteries. That wasn't so bad, if you look at it with the eyes of a child, even when they heard their parents' lamentations, even when they heard strange words charged with horror such as mapping, registration and transport. When they were herded with their parents into the ghetto, when they had to sleep on the concrete floors in crowded garrets or clamber up three-tiered bunks, they began to look around and quickly understood the strange world in which they had to live. They saw reality, but they still maintained their childish outlook, an outlook of truth which distinguishes between night and day and cannot be confused with false hopes and the shadowplay of an imaginary life.

And so they lived, locked within walls and courtyards. This was their world, a world of colour and shadow, of hunger and of hope.

The children played in the barracks yard and the courtyards of the one-time homes. Sometimes they were permitted to breathe a little fresh air upon the ramparts. From the age of 14, they had to work, to live the life of an adult. Sometimes they went beyond the walls to work in the gardens and they were no more considered to be children. The smaller ones acted out their fairy tales and even children's operas. But they did not know that they too, as well as the grown-ups, had been used deceitfully, in an effort to convince a commission of foreigners from the Red Cross that Terezín was a place where adults and children alike could live. Secretly, they studied and they drew pictures. Three months, half a year, one or two years, depending on one's luck, because transports came and went continually, headed east into nothingness.

From these 15,000 children, which for a time played and drew pictures and studied, only 100 came back. They saw everything that grown-ups saw. They saw the endless queues in front of the canteens, they saw the funeral carts used to carry bread and the human beings harnessed to pull them. They saw the infirmaries which seemed like a paradise to them and funerals which were only a gathering up of coffins. They saw executions too and were perhaps the only children in the world who captured them with pencil and paper. They listened to a speech made up of a hodgepodge of expressions like bonke, shlajska, shahojista, and they learned to speak this language. They heard the shouts of the SS-men at roll call and the meek mumblings of prayer in the barracks where the grown-ups lived.

But the children saw too what the grown-ups didn't want to see—the beauties beyond the village gates, the green meadows and the bluish hills, the ribbon of highway reaching off into the distance and the imagined road marker pointing toward Prague, the animals, the birds, the butterflies—all this was beyond the village walls and they could look at it only from afar, from the barracks windows and from the ramparts of the fort. They saw things too that grown-ups cannot see—princesses with coronets, evil wizards and witches, jesters and bugs with human faces, a land of happiness where for an admission of one crown, there was everything to be had—cookies, candy, a roast pig stuck with a fork from which milk and sodapop trickled. They saw too the rooms they'd lived in at home, with curtains at the window and a kitten and a saucer of milk. But they transported it to Terezín. There had to be a fence and a lot of pots and pans, because there was supposed to be food in every pot and pan.

All this they drew and painted and many other things besides; they loved to paint and draw, from morning till evening.

But when they wrote poems, it was something else again. Here one finds words about "painful Terezín", about "the little

girl who got lost". These told of longings to go away somewhere where there are kinder people; there are old grandfathers gnawing stale bread and rotten potatoes for lunch, there was a "longing for home" and fear. Yes, fear came to them and they could tell of it in their poems, knowing that they were condemned. Perhaps they knew it better than the adults.

There were 15,000 of them and 100 came back. You are looking at their drawings now after many years, when that world of hunger, fear and horror seems to us almost like a cruel fairy tale about evil wizards, witches and cannibals. The drawings and poems— that is all that is left of these children, for their ashes have long since sifted across the fields around Oswiecim. Their signatures are here and some of the drawings are inscribed with the year, and the number of their group. Of those who signed their names, it has been possible to find out a few facts: the year and place of their birth, the number of their transport to Terezín and to Oswiecim and then the year of their death. For most of them, it was 1944, the next to last year of World War II.

But their drawings and their poems speak to us; these are their voices which have been preserved voices of reminder, of truth and of hope.

We are publishing them not as dry documents out of thousands such witnesses in a sea of suffering, but in order to honour the memory of those who created these colours and these words. That's the way these children probably would have wanted it when death overtook them.

# THE BUTTERFLY
*by Pavel Friedmann*

The last, the very last,
So richly, brightly, dazzlingly yellow.
  Perhaps if the sun's tears would sing
  against a white stone . . .

Such, such a yellow
Is carried lightly 'way up high.
It went away I'm sure because it wished to
  kiss the world goodbye.

For seven weeks I've lived in here,
Penned up inside this ghetto
But I have found my people here.
The dandelions call to me
And the white chestnut candles in the court.
Only I never saw another butterfly.

That butterfly was the last one.
Butterflies don't live in here,
  In the ghetto.


# I'D LIKE TO GO ALONE
*by Alena Synková*

I'd like to go away alone
Where there are other, nicer people,
Somewhere into the far unknown,
There, where no one kills another.

Maybe more of us,
A thousand strong,
Will reach this goal
Before too long.

# CLOSE UP

1. Write five questions you would like to ask Pavel Friedmann and Alena Synková about Terezin and what it was like to be there. Form a small group and compare your questions.
2. "In Czechoslovakia there was a strange place called Terezin." Working with a partner, make a list of the horrors of Terezin. Give an appropriate heading to your list.
3. Referring to the poems and the article, in a small group discuss how the young people escaped the misery around them. Put this list beside the list you made in Close Up #2, using the heading "Escape."
4. Look back to the statement in Focussing #4 and write a sentence explaining how it applies to the children of Terezin.
5. You are an illustrator and your job is to provide the artwork for the two poems "The Butterfly" and "I'd Like to Go Alone" when they are published in a magazine. Display your work in the class.

# WIDE ANGLE

1. Invite a guest speaker from your community (perhaps a rabbi or a student of Jewish history) to talk to the class about the Holocaust. Before the speaker visits the class, brainstorm a series of questions that you wish to ask her or him. Ask for volunteers to introduce and thank the guest.
2. Visit a resource centre in your school or community and read or view another account of some aspect of the Holocaust. Prepare a brief report on your findings and share it with a small group. You and your classmates may wish to combine all your information to create a booklet on the Holocaust that can be put in the school library.
3. You are an artist and you have been asked to design a memorial to the children who died in Terezin. It may be in any form you choose—a building, a statue, a plaque, a storyboard for a documentary, or a ballad, for example. Write a few sentences about the children to accompany your design.

# KALEIDOSCOPE

1. The people in the stories, poems, and articles in this cluster experienced events that threatened their lives. After reviewing the cluster, fill in the chart below:

| Person(s) | Threatening Situation | How the Person (or His/ Her Memory) Survived |
|---|---|---|
|  |  |  |

2. Imagine a dangerous situation: it could be a car accident, a set of rapids encountered on a canoe trip, or an oncoming tornado. Create a word-search game involving the items or skills required for survival in the situation you have chosen. Make enough copies to send to another class, then challenge the students to a timed contest. There are computer programs for making word-search games. If your class has such a program, you could use it to design and print your game.

3. Write a speech you could read to people who were taking a survival course to prepare for the emergency you imagined in #2. Include some of the words you put into your word-search game.

4. A city, town, or community has monuments that keep alive the memory of important people or events. Research the monuments in your community. Create a journal of photographs entitled "In Remembrance . . ." Label the photographs so a reader would know what the pictures refer to, and place your photo-journal in your school library.

# WHAT A BOY WANTS

*by Richard Macaulay*

**T**HE BOY WAS about 15. He was reasonably tall for his age—about 5'10"—but he was very thin and wore thick, silver-rimmed glasses. Even under his full-length sleeves, the skinniness of his arms could be sensed. He was so preoccupied that he didn't notice the Jordan automobile that stopped at the curb beside the lot, much less the man behind the wheel who was watching him with a mixture of curiosity and pity.

The boy had just regathered a dozen baseballs beside a wooden slab that was a rough approximation of a pitching rubber. Five of the dozen balls had long ago lost their covers and were bound with heavy, black bicycle tape. The seven others were in various stages of disrepair, ranging from heavily scuffed to a couple of balls actually flapping at a seam.

He was throwing at a curious contrivance. It was a wire frame mounted over a heavily pitted home plate, long abandoned by some amateur team finally able to afford a new one. The frame itself was just about the dimensions of the average strike zone. Within this major frame was an adjustable small one, about six inches square. Just behind the plate, about where the catcher might have been, was the blank brick wall of a factory building.

Working very deliberately, the boy was trying to pitch through the six-inch-square frame. Of the dozen balls, he got two through it, and his last pitch hit the wire of the smaller frame and bent it out of shape.

If the boy had been able to be impervious to the man in the Jordan, he could not very well ignore the well-set-up young man who had stopped on the sidewalk and had watched with amusement his last few pitches. This young man, all of 16 despite his six feet and 180 pounds, asked amusedly, "What're you doing, Randy—getting ready for the White Sox?"

Randy turned and answered, "Sure—or the Cubs, whichever want me first."

The other boy, Mel Baker, snickered and said, "I wouldn't want to stand on my head waiting for that to happen."

Randy stood looking resentfully after the departing Mel, who was tabbed as Traymont High's probable next All-City at football, basketball and baseball. Then he went methodically around the lot to retrieve the balls, which had caromed off the bricks in several different directions and distances, depending on their condition.

While Randy was doing this, the man in the Jordan got out and walked into the lot. He was very tall, perhaps as much as 6′4″, but in spite of near middle age was still quite slender. He felt a compassion for the boy, because this was Chicago in the early '20s, and there was no Little League, Pony League or American Legion League. There were only the unorganized sandlots.

"Son," the man said kindly, "just exactly what are you getting ready for?"

Randy looked behind him, startled, then said, "Only to try out for a highschool team, sir—Traymont High."

"A little early for that, isn't it?" the man asked dryly. It was an early August evening, and a hot one at that.

"Well," Randy said, reassured by the man's kindly manner, "I have a lot to make up for. I'll have to work harder and longer than anyone else."

"As a matter of fact," the man said, looking Randy over appraisingly, "you don't look much like an athlete. Do you play any other sports?"

"No, sir," Randy answered, adding honestly, "I'm too light for football and too clumsy and slow for basketball."

The man said, "Let me tell you something, son. Most pitchers aren't athletes. They're just specialized freaks who can't bat, play the outfield or infield or do any good at any other sport. All they can do while they're young is just pitch that ball up there very fast or very accurately." His eyes twinkled. "I ought to know. My name's Jimmy Lennon, by the way."

Randy gulped and, behind the thick lenses of his glasses, his eyes protruded. He finally gasped, "You mean Jimmy Lennon who pitched for Detroit and Cleveland?"

"And a few other places on the way up," Jimmy Lennon said. "What's your name?"

Randy gasped, "Randy Johnson," as Lennon took his hand.

"Well, Randy," Lennon said, "I'll be by tomorrow night at about the same time if you'll be here."

"Boy!" Randy said fervently. "Will I be here!"

When Lennon drove up in his Jordan the next evening, Randy

was there all right. Lennon got out of the car and carried with him a catcher's mitt and a baseball. It wasn't a completely new baseball, but it was the newest that Randy ever had handled, bearing only a few minor scuffs and abrasions.

The first thing Lennon did after handing Randy the ball was to remove the wire frame, which already had been set up. Lennon said, "Son, you've had a good idea here. You're never going to have a big fast ball, so you figured you'd be able to pitch the ball where you want it. That's all right, but in a game they don't give you a wire frame around the strike zone. You shoot for this." He put on the mitt and pounded the pocket with his right fist. "Now warm up for a while."

Randy did. After a while, Lennon walked out to him and said, "You haven't got a bad natural motion, but it can be better. Like I told you, you're never going to have a real hot fast ball, but you can get it faster than it is. Now look, you're a fairly tall kid with long legs, but you're not using them. You're not stepping out enough. You're not following through on your delivery. Watch this."

Lennon, without ball, demonstrated with a beautifully fluid motion. He went through it a couple of more times, then went back behind the plate, put on his mitt and said, "Now you try it."

Randy tried it and after a few pitches started to get the hang of it.

Lennon said, "Now let's see your curve. Have you got one?"

"A little one," Randy admitted.

He threw it. It was a little curve, but it definitely bent. Furthermore, it was natural. He didn't have to think about snapping his wrist or anything. He just had to throw with his natural motion, releasing the ball between his thumb and his index finger, and it curved.

Lennon said, "O.K., son. The curve will get a little better when you get just a little faster. It's going to be your big pitch." He put his glove just over the outside corner of the plate, about knee-high. "Now put that curve in here. Just imagine that the little square of wire is a little ahead of the mitt."

Lennon didn't move his mitt, and Randy hit it right in the pocket. Lennon looked pleased. He said, "When you get a real curve and can do that, you're in. Most of the right-handed batters you'll ever face for a long time can't hit that one. Now let's say it's a left-handed batter." He threw the ball back and gave as a target the same position on the other corner of the plate. This time Lennon had to move his mitt a little, but not much.

August ran into September, and school started, but Randy continued to work out on the lot with Jimmy Lennon at least three or four times a week. His fast ball improved, but, as Lennon had said, he would never overpower batters with it.

"You'll use it as your change of pace," Lennon told him. "It will look relatively fast beside the other stuff you're throwing." Starting to work on the knuckle ball, Lennon said, "I'm going to teach you pitches that a fast-ball thrower wouldn't be learning until he was 30."

When the cold winds of October came, they moved inside to a small gym in the neighbourhood, where they worked out all winter. Sometimes Randy had Mr. Lennon—he always thought of him and addressed him as "Mr. Lennon"—over to the house for dinner. In a neighbourhood already sprouting with apartment houses, Randy Johnson's folks still maintained a large, old, comfortable house, in which the elder Johnson had a room then known as a "den."

It was outside this room that Randy, on one of the dinner occasions, eavesdropped. He didn't mean to—but who can resist listening when the subject of the conversation is himself?

His father, a thick, muscular man who had been a pretty good athlete, asked, "But don't you think, Lennon, that you're giving the boy false hopes? To my mind he's just not built for it, and he's in for a bad letdown."

There was a clink of bottle on glass before Lennon answered, "Johnson, there's no telling where a boy who wants something that much might go." Pause. "I'll admit he hasn't got the physical equipment, but he does have a brain. What he wants is *right now*. I think he has a chance of making his high-school squad next spring. After that, if he goes on to college, he might even play a little college ball. But the boy gets good marks in school, and by that time he may have decided to be an engineer or something. At any rate, no harm done."

Randy turned around blindly in the darkened hallway, tears streaming behind his thick glasses, and ran to his room. He didn't hear Lennon continuing, "Even so, I think he has a sort of talent for pitching, a sense for it. He'll never break any of Alexander's records, but he's got something—and he's learning."

Randy didn't show up at the gym the next day, but the day after that he did, with a mumbled apology to Lennon about some extra school chores. That day he worked harder than ever, with a certain grimness that puzzled Lennon.

On a cold day in April, that, in Chicago, could easily have been mistaken for one of the milder days of February or March, the

Traymont High School baseball team came out for its first practice. In the dim, moldy, 40-year-old locker room Randy was issued an old uniform too short for him, but also too full.

A bitter wind whipped across the scraggly, rocky old playing field, which was used only for practice, football or baseball. No self-respecting opponent would have played on that surface.

Things started out badly almost immediately. The coach, Corny Huggins, scattered some boys in the rock-strewn outfield. Randy, shivering in the cold, happened to be standing nearest to him. Huggins, a short, squat man, had once got up as far as Moline, in the Three-I-League. His face was hard and wore a perpetual expression of bitter disappointment, perhaps because at an early age he had reached the backwater of Traymont High instead of the line-up of the Yankees.

Huggins suddenly tossed a fungo bat to Randy, who promptly fumbled it. Looking at him doubtfully, Huggins said, "Hit out some fungoes." He tossed Randy a ball, which was also fumbled. Trembling with embarrassment and nervousness, Randy tossed the ball in the air, took a mighty swing—and missed the ball. Now, in a complete panic, he missed again and, on the third try, topped the ball and hit a trickling roller that came to rest about halfway to the fielders.

Huggins merely looked at him as if he'd crawled out of a wall, took the bat away from him and gave it to another boy. This fellow promptly hit a towering fly, and the coach walked away.

*Well*, Randy thought, *I'm a pitcher. I'm not supposed to be an expert with the fungo bat.*

After a couple of days things started to sort out. Positions were assigned, truncated games were played. Randy felt very good. He had put on a little weight, and he had been throwing indoors all winter. His arm felt good, and he was ready to go. But no one asked him to. Most of the time he couldn't even get one of the catchers to receive him. More often than not he threw to a neglected first baseman or outfielder. Two or three times he pitched batting practice, but with no umpire to call strikes, the batters just stood there and ignored his low stuff until he laid in something they liked.

He realized he was being ignored, but he could see he was better than the other pitcher candidates, and he was sure that one day Coach Corny Huggins would discover him.

It was on Friday after practice that Huggins called them all together in the locker room. He had a list in his hand and intoned,

"Those on the following list report as usual Monday. If your name isn't on the list, turn in your suit and better luck next year."

The list was read, and Randy's name wasn't on it. He stood there in stunned incredulity, trying to prevent the tears from forming in his eyes. He sat down and kept his head low so that no one could see his face. He felt a hand on his shoulder, and turning reluctantly, his tear-drowned eyes perceived Mr. Grimslaw, the principal. Mr. Grimslaw was a sports fan who attended all school contests and as many practice sessions as he could.

"Don't take it so hard, Johnson," the principal said. "As the coach remarked, you have another year."

"Mr. Grimslaw," Randy said bitterly, "I wouldn't play under Coach Huggins if it meant I never played baseball again."

Huggins, who was passing by and heard this, said, "Gee, that'll be tough for the team. And here I'd been figuring on another championship next year."

Randy didn't answer. He finished undressing, took his shower and dressed. He turned in his uniform and shoved into his briefcase the special pair of pitcher's baseball shoes with the toe plate and the glove his parents had given him at Christmastime.

Once at home Randy locked himself in his room and tossed the glove and the spikes on a top closet shelf with other old junk he didn't expect to be using in the future. Then he lay on the bed and let the tears and sobs come. Finally he lay quiet and eventually dozed.

He was awakened by a knocking at his door. His mother's voice said, "Randy, Mr. Lennon is here to see you."

Randy didn't feel like seeing anyone, but he was a normally polite boy and he eventually said, "All right, ask him to come in here."

He tried to wipe away evidences that he had been crying, then unlocked the door. Jimmy Lennon entered the room, closed the door behind him and looked at Randy carefully. Lennon finally said, "Your mother told me you brought your spikes and glove home with you."

Randy said shortly, "I was cut."

"Why?"

"You tell me." Randy's voice was bitter. "I never pitched to a batter in a practice game. The coach never saw me pitch at all. He never even stood behind me while I threw to a catcher."

Lennon murmured, "Doesn't seem very fair, does it?"

"No!" Randy was having a hard time keeping the tears from coming back to his eyes, and he looked resentfully at Lennon.

Wasn't this the man who had caused him to work like a dog, who had buoyed his hopes?

"Look, Randy," Lennon finally said, "I've taken over the management of a team a little west of here. The fellows are a little older than you, but if you'd like to work out with us, you can."

"Work out for what?" Randy asked.

Lennon shrugged. "Maybe we can see exactly how good you are. Then, depending how it comes out, maybe we can find a place for you—or else you can hang up your spikes for good." He patted Randy on the shoulder. "Be out at Pilot Field at about 12:30 Saturday."

He left the room, and Randy stared after him, puzzled.

Randy was amazed at Pilot Field. To begin with, it had covered wooden stands that extended down both foul lines almost to the outfield fences and seated almost 10,000 people. The infield had grass inside the skinned base paths, and the outfield looked smooth and green. There was a real pitcher's mound, instead of the unraised slab that Randy had been used to, and home plate looked new and white.

Under the stands was the clubhouse, and there Lennon got Randy a uniform that fitted fairly well. Then, before going out on the field, Lennon told him, "Randy, the Pilots are a semipro team. We play the big industrial teams from Racine, Kenosha and Beloit, as well as other semipro teams here in Chicago. We also play teams from the Negro League, like the Kansas City Monarchs and the American Giants. Some of the fellows on the squad make more money playing than they would in Class C organized ball, although they all have other jobs. Beginning soon we play every Saturday and Sunday, and around June we start playing in the Twilight League on Tuesday and Thursday evenings." As Randy blinked behind his thick glasses, Lennon added, "I'm telling you this now, Randy, so you won't expect too much of yourself. A couple of the fellows have been in the majors, and a few more have played Double-A ball. There are others, younger ones, who could step onto a Class-B team right now."

That day Randy just threw idly to a succession of catchers, while the rest of the squad engaged in infield practice, shagged fly balls and took batting practice.

However, the next day, Sunday, Lennon had enough men out so that, loosely speaking, he was able to get two teams together. He said to Randy, "You're pitching for the outs. Samson will be your catcher. Get your signals worked out with him."

As Randy finished warming up and walked out to the mound he felt dizzy and light-headed. Lennon was umpiring from behind the pitcher's box. "Remember," he told Randy, "keep your strikes low and outside."

But Randy had never thrown from an elevated mound before, and his pitches kept coming in too high. He was nervous, and the balls he was throwing up there were too fat, catching too much of the plate. The first five batters all nearly tore the cover off the ball, and Randy, badly shaken, finally retired the side only by virtue of three long line drives pulled down after heroic runs by outfielders. Four runs had poured across the plate.

It wasn't much of a game. Except for two or three men who had been playing basketball, the players were favouring winter-stiffened muscles. After the first inning Randy did somewhat better, but not enough to evaporate his feeling of discouragement. After five innings the game was called.

As he undressed, Randy was surprised when Lennon said to him, "Be back next Saturday, same time." Noting the look of astonishment on Randy's face, Lennon added, "You didn't do bad at all, considering. The next time, just keep thinking of that wire frame you used to practice with."

Randy did better than think of the frame. He got it out, and during the next week he went every evening to the vacant lot and practised with it. He could still lay the ball through that little six-inch square of wire more often than not, but he now knew, from sore experience, that pitching to batters was a totally different thing, the notable difference being that the wire frame couldn't drive the ball to left centre for two bases.

On the following Saturday, as Randy and the regular Pilots were suiting up in the clubhouse, Lennon said, "Fellows, we're going to play a game today. It shouldn't extend you very much, but maybe it'll be fun."

"How much?" an old pro asked.

"For free," Lennon answered. "The other team are amateurs, and there won't be any box office." He turned to Randy and said, "Boy, you're going to pitch. Let's shave that plate thin and keep the ball low. I want you to warm up way out in the left-field corner. Don't come in until the team takes the field."

The players looked curiously at Randy and puzzledly at each other. It was customary at Pilot Field for the home starting pitcher to warm up on the sidelines between home and third base.

Before the other team came onto the field, Randy already was down in the left-field corner with his catcher, Samson, a burly, older man who once had been up with the Washington Senators for a year. Randy produced from his glove a ball heavily wrapped with black bicycle tape. He lobbed it easily to Samson, who exclaimed, "What the devil is this?"

"It's a taped ball," Randy said carefully. "Furthermore, I've had it soaking in a bucket of water all week."

"What's the idea?" Samson asked.

Randy answered firmly, "The same principle as a batter walking up to the plate swinging two bats. By the time I get a real baseball in my hand, it will feel like a feather."

"I thought I'd seen everything," Samson shrugged, "but this is the first time I ever saw a pitcher warm up by shot putting."

He threw the ball back to Randy, and it landed with a heavy, wet plunk in his glove. Randy threw it back, and the warm-up went on. It was an unseasonably warm day for Chicago in April, a month that has brought blizzards to the city. The good, warm sweat began to trickle down Randy's back and pitching arm. It felt fine, like a benevolent lubricant.

The bell finally rang, just as in a big-league park. Randy threw one final pitch to Samson, then turned toward the diamond for the first time since he'd started to warm up. Samson joined him, mumbling, "Something's screwy here. I didn't get any batting practice."

As he got out to the mound, the second-string catcher rolled him the ball from behind the plate and filled in while Samson donned his tools of ignorance. It was a brand-new ball, the first such that Randy ever had handled in his life. Jubilantly he weighed it. Beside the black-taped monstrosity he'd been throwing, it felt like a tennis ball, only smoother. Carefully he tried three curves. Then, through sheer joy, he used his last two warm-up pitches throwing hard ones over the heart of the plate. He felt as if he could have thrown the ball clear through the backstop.

As the first batter approached the plate, Randy was looking at him only with the detached interest of a pitcher sizing up a hitter he'd never faced before. It was only a delayed reaction that telegraphed to his mind the letters on the batter's shirt. They read, "Traymont." The second mind telegram told him the batter was Wally Trumbo, a senior who had made the All-City team as a junior.

Startled, Randy looked toward the first-base dugout. There he saw "Traymont" on many shirt fronts—and kneeling in front of the dugout was Coach Corny Huggins. All of them were staring out at him with mixed expressions of astonishment and amusement.

Randy returned his attention to the batter, Trumbo, who had now stepped into the box. Trumbo's expression was one of supercilious merriment. Randy, feeling very calm, peered near-sightedly at his catcher and caught the sign for a curve. Without a windup Randy threw it in there, knee-high and just over the outside corner. The properly blue-clad umpire threw up his right hand—"Strike!"

The next sign was for a fast ball. Randy aimed it for approximately the bill of Trumbo's cap, and Trumbo sat down. "Ball." The next call was for a curve again, and once more Randy broke it low over the outside corner. Trumbo hesitated, then swung wildly, missing by a foot. One and two.

Another fast ball called for, Randy knew he ought to drive Trumbo back again; but, with supreme confidence, he blew the ball over the inside corner, just above the knees. Trumbo took it and was called out.

The next man went down without ever taking the bat off his shoulder. Third man up was the same Mel Baker who had teased him so often as he practised in the vacant lot. Baker let two curve balls over the outside corner go by for strikes and then went down swinging on a knuckle ball that actually bounced on the plate. Randy walked into the dugout feeling confident and good.

The game was called in the fifth inning, with the Pilots still batting. The score was a horrendous 23-0. Randy's happiness was somewhat marred by the fact that he felt a little sorry for the sheepish, disgusted Traymont team.

As he walked in from second base, where he had been stationed as the result of an unexpected base-clearing double, he passed Lennon, who had stopped to talk to Corny Huggins. He heard Lennon saying to Huggins, "You might be all right with pros, but you ought never to coach boys. You don't even know what a boy wants."

"And what does a boy want?" Huggins snarled.

"A chance," Lennon said quietly. "Just a chance."

Before he could pass into the dugout and through into the clubhouse, Randy was intercepted by Mr. Grimslaw, the principal of Traymont High. "Well, Johnson," Mr. Grimslaw said, "revenge is sweet, isn't it?"

"Yes, sir," Randy answered honestly.

The principal smiled and said, "If you were to come out for the Traymont team again, I believe that Coach Huggins would look on you with new eyes."

"Thank you, sir," Randy said earnestly, "but that won't be possible. You see, sir, the Pilots are a semi-professional team, and I wouldn't be eligible for interscholastic activities now."

"Quite right," Mr. Grimslaw murmured. "I'd forgotten that for the moment. Good luck, Johnson."

Mr. Grimslaw walked away, and Randy ducked through the tunnel door that led into the clubhouse. Randy undressed and took a leisurely shower. Standing there with the hot water sluicing down his body, he thought that he'd never felt better. He'd had a glorious moment such as few boys his age would ever know.

Back in front of his locker he dressed slowly and methodically. When he had finished combing his hair in front of the cracked wall mirror, he took his spikes and his glove from his locker and turned to go. He faced into Lennon. "Thank you very much, Mr. Lennon," he said. "But I still don't see how you set it up."

"That was easy," Lennon said, shrugging. "At the risk of sounding vain, I'll say that Huggins was flattered that I'd look him up. Secondly, he was glad for his boys to play in a real ball park instead of those piles of cinders they usually play on."

"Well," Randy said, "thank you anyway. It made a big minute for me."

He extended his hand, but Lennon refused it. "Where are you taking that glove and those spikes?" Lennon asked.

Surprised, Randy answered, "Home."

"What for?" Lennon demanded gruffly. "You'll be needing them here tomorrow."

"Tomorrow?" Randy asked blankly.

"Yes, tomorrow. We start to work on teaching you to field your position so you won't be bunted silly—so that when you should be backing up third base, you won't be standing out there on the mound with your teeth hanging out. Twelve o'clock." He started away, then turned back smiling. "By July, if you keep learning, I may start using you in relief. By September you might even start a game." He put his hand on Randy's shoulder and said softly, "There aren't many pitchers who can throw a ball through a six-inch square of wire."

As Lennon walked off, Randy found himself trying to blink back those awful tears, which so often threatened his dignity. Only this time they were happy tears.

# FOCUSSING

1.  a) Find two reports of recent sports events in your local newspaper. Bring them to class and read them to a partner. Write down the three most important pieces of information contained in each report.

    b) Attend a school sporting event with your partner and together write a report for your school newspaper on the game. Use one of the stories you have read in (a) as a model. Before you submit it to the paper, revise and proofread your article together using the checklists on pp. 181-183.

2.  In your journal explore some of the following topics:
    * my favourite sports and why I like them;
    * the sports I dislike and why I dislike them;
    * why it is important for me to be involved in sports;
    * why I would rather be a spectator than a participant;
    * my sports heroes (female or male).

    Read your journal entry to a partner and listen to hers or his.

3.  Work in a group of three and choose two sports you all know how to play. Prepare a list of the five basic rules of each sport and, without mentioning the name of the sport, read the rules to the class or another group and see how quickly they can guess the name of the sport. Invite the other group to edit your description of the rules to make them clearer. You may wish to choose several sets of rules that you all agree are clear and well-written and compile them for your physical education teacher to post in the gymnasium or the changerooms.

4.  In groups of four or five, make three tableaux from three different sports. To make each tableau, you and your partners should talk about the action in the scene, begin acting it out, and freeze at an exciting moment. Give each tableau a descriptive title. Show your tableaux to the rest of the class and let them guess your titles.

5.  Make a sports collage using newspaper and magazine headlines and photographs. Work in pairs and focus on your favourite sports.

# GREATZKY

## by Scott Young

**W**HEN I watch Wayne Gretzky play, even in one-sided games, I am often reminded of another night long ago. It was Toronto against Boston. On one play, Frank Mahovlich of the Leafs streaked at full speed around the Boston goal, braked to a dead stop behind the net and in a flash pulled the puck back and tucked it into the corner that both he and the goalie had just left. Lynn Patrick was the Boston general manager then. When someone remarked later that it hadn't been much of game, Patrick set him straight. "That one play of Frank's alone was worth the price of admission," he said. "You won't see that done again so well if you watch every night for years."

I felt that way watching Gretzky against Toronto late last year (1984) when he was still more than two dozen points short of reaching 1,000 in his NHL career. He achieved that eminence almost twice as fast as the previous leader, Guy Lafleur, who took 720 games to get there. Gretzky took 424.

At the time of the Toronto game, in fact, Gretzky still had not even had his first five-goal game of the season! (He ran that one, third of his career, at the paying customers on December 15 in St. Louis, along with an assist, to move his points total from 992 to 998 in one blistering evening.) One assist in New Jersey a couple of nights later set up a return to the home folks in Edmonton on a Wednesday, Dec. 19. He needed only the single point to reach the promised land. He actually had to wait 101 seconds before his rebound off the Los Angeles goalpost was slapped straight back in by his left wing,

Mike Krushelnyski, and Gretzky had his 1,000. Just to make sure, he picked up two goals and three more assists to run his total to 1,005 before the night, or at least the hockey part of it, was over. The NHL points record is 1,850, set by Gordie Howe in 1,767 games spanning 26 seasons. Gretzky has said he doesn't think anyone will break Howe's record. Howe laughed at that and said the only Howe record Wayne won't break is playing six years with his sons, as Gordie did.

It was another whole 10 days, believe it or not, before Gretzky assaulted the NHL record book once more—to victimize Detroit with his 32nd NHL hat trick and tie Phil Esposito and Mike Bossy in that department.

How does he do it? It isn't because everybody else in the league is content to go down in history chiefly as a grand audience for the Gretzky show.

Let us take that game in Toronto as an example. Dan Maloney and his fellow big-domes of Leafs' strategy board knew he was coming. The strategy was: 1, forecheck the Edmonton defence before it could move the puck up to Gretzky; 2, shut down the middle of the ice so that Gretzky couldn't cavort and freewheel there in his usual manner but would have to operate (sob) from the wings; 3, watch especially for long passes that might set Gretzky free on breakaways.

It was a good plan. Leafs are not the Eighth Army, but there was no lack of try that night, and even, sometimes, of execution.

Except that on the first shift after a face-off in the Edmonton zone, Gretzky got the puck and handled it a couple of times while

speeding (he can speed) into the Toronto end, where he wound up on the right-wing side. The puck was over by the left boards. Gretzky took the direct route to get there— skating right through the Toronto crease and into the scramble, where he snagged the puck and passed in front of Krushelnyski, who shot. The point-blank rebound landed at defender Borje Salming's stick. However, this happened just as Gretzky arrived again from the left corner, lifted Salming's stick off the puck, and poked it under goalie Ken Wregget. The time: 71 seconds into the game.

For the rest of the period, he helped kill penalties, twice made passes for shots on goal, and for a while eased the crowding on the Edmonton bench by sitting on a stool with his back against the wall, sometimes grinning and exchanging comments with teammates. With two minutes to go he went out for a power play. He lost the first draw to Billy Derlago. But a little later Gretzky made his way down left wing, crossed to right wing at the lower edge of the face-off circle, turned, and faked a big slapshot— except that when his stick came down, the faked shot turned into a deadly accurate pass across for a shot, I think by Randy Gregg, the rebound coming to Krushelnyski, who scored.

A period later Gretzky gave the puck to Jari Kurri, his right wing, and cruised through the right side of the slot looking for a return pass. But when it came he made an interesting move. I thought Gretzky could have had that pass. His stick moved as if to take it but he didn't. One could almost imagine his split-second decision. Wregget was ready for him then, and if he let the puck go by to Krushelnyski on his left wing, Wregget would have to move to cover that side. Wregget dutifully slid across the goal. Gretzky moved to the corner of the crease at Wregget's left, with Wregget now facing away from him. When Krushelnyski's quick pass came back, all Gretzky had to do was tap it into the open corner—which he, of course, did.

On the same shift, same minute, Charlie Huddy broke up a Leaf attack at the Edmonton defence. The moment he did so, Huddy passed to Paul Coffey. Coffey instantly sent it up to Gretzky, in full flight, in the clear. Taking the pass and going in alone on Wregget, Gretzky drifted to his left away from the pursuit and held the puck—and held it and held it—until he seemed too far in for a good shot. At that point, Wregget had to come in tight to the short-side post. Gretzky's shot from that difficult angle just caught the inside of the far post.

Three goals in a 7-1 win, each bearing a special Gretzky label.

To my mind, it was not that the Leafs were bad. They had their chances. The good ones played hard and the others were not just passengers.

After the second period on my way to seats behind the Leaf bench, I passed Rick Vaive standing with his back against the wall. When our glances met, he rolled his eyes eloquently.

Others in the league often put such frustration into words. Brian Engblom of Los Angeles Kings, a good defenceman, is one of those who credit Gretzky with a sixth sense: "He has a radar in his brain, even if you're coming at him from behind."

A different angle on that idea from Bobby Orr: "How many times have you seen a player line up Gretzky? You figure the guy has Gretzky trapped. Next thing you know, Gretzky has given the puck to somebody you figure he couldn't even see. He has such exceptional vision that he seems to know where his teammates are all the time."

Calgary coach Bob Johnson: "Most of his goals come after he takes the puck away from somebody. I tell my players the secret is to not play one on one with him. I don't care who you are or how good you are, don't test him. He'll beat you."

St. Louis coach Jacques Demers, after Gretzky's five-goal performance there (on only five shots in the whole game): "Nobody in hockey can cover Gretzky. Tonight the people in St. Louis saw one of the greatest athletes in any sport. He's just incredible."

Edmonton coach Glen Sather, after the same game: "Just when you think you've seen it all, Wayne Gretzky comes up with a couple of new moves like he did tonight. He scores goals nobody else even dreams about."

Before we all faint dead away with the wonder of it all, there is another side to Wayne Gretzky—the human side. Broadcaster and author Peter Gzowski once said of him, "He's a really nice young guy who just happens to be the world's greatest hockey player." That opinion stands up, although everyone with any sense should understand that being a nice young guy in this context does not mean he doesn't require protection from his fame. He needs privacy—what he calls "free time"—in which he can keep his batteries charged, spend time with his girl friend or his family, go out for a few hours with his team-mates or sometimes just sit at home alone watching television.

The management of Edmonton Oilers knows this full well. When I was trying to line up an interview and suggested Pittsburgh or New Jersey, I was told Pittsburgh would be fine, New Jersey next to impossible. "The New York media has been lining up for weeks to get at him there—everybody. TV, newspapers, radio, magazines, commercial people. You name it," said the club's PR director, Bill Tuele.

I got into the Pittsburgh Hyatt on a Monday afternoon and asked at the desk if the Oilers were in. "Expected soon," the man said. His own word "soon" made him jump. "Gotta lay out the keys," he said hurriedly to another man. Quickly he carried a table to a place directly in front of the main revolving door and began to lay out keys in envelopes identified by name and room number. He arranged them in alphabetical order so that when the mighty Edmontons came through the door each could grab a key and be at the elevator in seconds.

A few minutes later the Oilers streamed through the door, grabbing keys and heading for their rooms. I chatted with a couple of people, friends of Wayne's father, Walter, in town to see the game. Eventually one of them said to me, "There's your man."

I looked up. Gretzky and two other players were heading rapidly for the door to the street. For a beer, a movie, a walk, who knows. I got up and said, "Wayne."

I saw his look when he stopped. His expression, I thought, said "Dammit!" He told me later he hadn't felt that way, but that is the look I saw. He's taller than I'd imagined him to be—six feet and 170 pounds, the record books say. A little taller and about the same weight as Rocket Richard. I mentioned that I'd called Bill Tuele about talking to him here. "When would

be a good time?"

"How about tomorrow after we practise?" he said.

"Sure. See you then."

The next day the papers were full of Gretzky. I walked across to the Arena to watch the game-day skates. Pittsburgh Penguins were on the ice first. One film crew was following Mario Lemieux, but two or three others sat back to wait for the Oilers. They straggled to the ice in twos and threes. Gretzky, about the middle of the arrivals, was dressed in a red shirt. As he reached the ice he glided on one skate while he lifted the other and peered at the blade. He did this to each skate, then flipped a blooper into the net from well out. As the Oilers skated circuits he was just one man, calling back and forth with the others, talking like any hockey player, with a few censorable expressions along the way; laughing a lot and often with a big grin showing below his long, straight nose. Sometimes he burst into that angular skating style that earned him the nickname Pretzel when he was a junior in Sault Ste. Marie. I recalled he once said, "You know the only place where I can go to get away from it (the pressure) during the season, the only place I can totally relax? On the ice." He was relaxing. Once he fanned on a slapshot. Once when Glen Sather was feeding out pucks for line rushes, he whistled Gretzky's line back, dissatisfied, and started it again. You could hear Wayne's call, "What happened?" Sather didn't answer. There was no impression at all that one man was the game's greatest star.

When it was over, Gretzky was first to the gate leading off the ice. I was sitting nearby. The corridor led to the Oilers' dressing room. Gretzky caught my eye, and jerked his head. It had to be fast. Other reporters and film crews were coming for him from all directions. I pushed open the dressing room door. Wayne beckoned me through the main room into a smaller area between the dressing room and the showers. He closed the door. He hadn't undressed or showered but sat on a settee beside me. Others coming through to the showers closed the door behind them to keep the room a little more private. A ghetto-blaster roared rock music from across the room. It isn't the kind of music Wayne goes for, incidentally. He likes anything that's easy to listen to, he said, but that's when he's at home, not when he's in a place where others might have different tastes.

There is a lot that no one has to ask Gretzky. That's the past. There are not many, even those who do not follow hockey, who are unaware of what he had done long before he turned 24, on January 26. His 50-goal weekend as a kid. His playing with 10-year-olds when he was five (but could already out-skate many twice his age). The Gretzky backyard rink in Brantford, Ont., where Walter Gretzky taught the boy what he could, which was plenty, not only in hockey technique but in attitudes—including the one toward hard work. His time as a junior, when he scored 70 goals in 64 games with Sault Ste. Marie while also working to improve his checking. His multi-million dollar contract which he wrote out himself and signed in an airplane to turn pro at 17. His amazing play with the Oilers in the old World Hockey Association when some NHL'ers tended to say right out loud that the kid would never do that stuff in a stronger league. His proving to everybody that he could do it anywhere the game was played, 51 NHL goals and a tie for the league points-scoring Championship, the Hart and Byng trophies, and centre on the second all-star team the winter he turned 19, his first in the NHL. His record 91 goals and 212 total points the year he turned 21. His girl friend Vickie Moss who has her own career as a cabaret singer. His closeness to his parents, Walter and Phyllis, and to his brothers and sister. His reverence for his grandmother and her small farm near Brantford, where he is loved as a grandson, not as the world's greatest hockey player.

(Once he said that he would rather spend a free afternoon at her farm than go out and do something else that would make him $20,000). His long list of national and international awards, including that of Officer of the Order of Canada, and Sports Illustrated's Sportsman of the Year. In the same short period he also became the greatest media star ever in hockey.

Yet all along he has been evolving, changing. He has admitted that as the pressures on him get stronger he's found himself less and less patient. How did the shorter fuse operate?

The ghetto-blaster blared, keeping the conversation private because no voice could be heard from more than a couple of feet away. "Well, it's just," he all but sighed, "I'm at the point now where I've played five years in the National Hockey League and for a while all the things that were said about Wayne Gretzky didn't bother me at all. But now after all that's happened—fortunate enough to play for a great hockey club, won a Stanley Cup—some of those things are still being said and written about me, about my skating, my checking, my speed. It's beginning to bother me a little bit when those things are inaccurate and pointless."

I mentioned feeling in the hotel lobby that he'd been annoyed at being interrupted in his dash for open country.

"Well, I didn't know you at first—but I know I have a responsibility not only to the team but to the league to promote the game as much as I can. Where I'm different now is that if I have free time, it stays free time. Before, if somebody came up to me and asked me to do something in what I'd counted on as free time, I'd maybe not be happy but I'd give it up to do this or that. Not any more. Now things are set up in advance. If things aren't set up, that's my free time and I won't change it, it's too valuable. Not that it wasn't important a couple of years ago, but it means a lot more to me than it used to, to be able to just go out with the guys, or be at home by myself. Before I go on a trip, Bill Tuele comes down to the room and we go over everything that's been lined up, and I know exactly what my free time is. It takes an awful lot to make me give it up."

Did crowds ever do anything that bugged him?

He thought over that one, then nodded. "Yes. When a guy gets hurt and the crowd cheers. I hate that."

We switched then to more personal things. Home, for Gretzky, is a 3,000 square-foot, two-storey penthouse in midtown Edmonton. Talking about life there, he seemed to relax, smiling as he thought about it. "I have my routines. I like it that way. On the day of a game I'm up at nine and have a cup of tea and some toast, then head down to the rink for the practice. I come back late in the morning and turn on TV and cook my own dinner." He laughed. "It's always the same when I'm home, steak and cheese perogies, the Polish kind. Wish I could get them on the road, too. Then I'll watch TV for a while and have a sleep until about four. When I get up, I have half a cup of tea and then head out. I usually get to the rink by quarter to five, for a 7:30 game."

Most pro athletes like the familiar routine of a dressing room. Gretzky sounded as if he felt good just to talk about that feeling of a good team in the privacy of its two hours before a game.

What does he like to read?

"I'm not a big reader. I'm a bad reader, to be honest. Now and then I read books given to me, like at Christmas. But I have read two books in the last little while, my Dad's and Tiger Williams' book."

After we'd been talking a while, Glen Sather came along. He joined the conversation for a minute, then asked, "How long do you think you'll be?" and, to Wayne, "There's a lot of guys waiting for you in the other room."

Wayne: "What guys?"

"Reporters."

"Let them talk to the other guys."

Sather, patiently: "Well, they're waiting for you."

When they did come in, Gretzky was ready for them, as well. There would always be reporters after practices. And after games. And in between.

One last thing from the talk in Pittsburgh. I mentioned his long-term relationship with the talented Vickie Moss. They met in a cabaret in Edmonton where she was singing. She is also very much her own person, busy with gigs both in the East and the West. I asked Wayne what he thought about marriage. As he answered, one could hear, unspoken, a lot about his own life.

"There's no question in my mind that marriage is what we all live for," he said. "I think it's the greatest thing in the world to be married and have kids. I see how my mom and dad are, how happy they are with their kids, and without question when you're ready, then it's great. If you're not ready, then it's not worth doing. Right now I have my career that I'm more concerned about than marriage and Vickie has her career and is away quite a bit. So I guess you say, you sow your own oats. She has her ambitions and I have my ambitions and it's not that we don't work well together, but I think it's better that we as individuals do what we want to do before we combine it into one."

In his father's book he says a little more. He'd like to have a son and go skating with him and "hold his toes and make the cold go away, just like my Dad did for me." I bring this up with some diffidence, but Wayne is 24 now. Gordie Howe was 26 when his first son, Marty, was born, and 27 when Mark came along. They all did play together in the NHL. In the interest of science, and while suggesting nothing, I must point out that it is still at least a mathematical possibility that this Howe record could be broken too.

## N.H.L. Records/ Jan. 1985
### INDIVIDUAL RECORDS

1. HIGHEST GOALS-PER-GAME AVERAGE, CAREER: .906 (356 goals, 393 games, 1979-84)
2. HIGHEST ASSISTS-PER-GAME AVERAGE, CAREER: .1.420 (558 assists, 393 games, 1979-84)
3. HIGHEST POINTS-PER-GAME AVERAGE, CAREER: .2.326 (914 points, 393 games, 1979-84)
4. MOST GOALS, ONE SEASON: .92 (1981-82)
5. MOST ASSISTS, ONE SEASON: .125 (1982-83)
6. MOST POINTS, ONE SEASON: .212 (1981-82)
7. MOST GAMES SCORING AT LEAST THREE GOALS, ONE SEASON: .10 (twice—1981-82, 1983-84)
8. HIGHEST ASSISTS-PER-GAME AVERAGE, ONE SEASON: .1.59 (118 assists, 74 games, 1983-84)
9. HIGHEST POINTS-PER-GAME AVERAGE, ONE SEASON: .2.77 (205 points, 74 games, 1983-84)
10. MOST GOALS, ONE SEASON, INCLUDING PLAYOFFS: .100 (87 in regular season, 13 in playoffs, 1983-84)
11. MOST ASSISTS, ONE SEASON, INCLUDING PLAYOFFS: .151 (125 in regular season, 26 in playoffs, 1982-83)
12. MOST POINTS, ONE SEASON, INCLUDING PLAYOFFS: .240 (205 in regular season, 35 in playoffs, 1983-84)
13. MOST GOALS, ONE SEASON, BY A CENTRE: .92 (1981-82)
14. MOST ASSISTS, ONE SEASON, BY A CENTRE: .125 (1982-83)
15. MOST POINTS, ONE SEASON, BY A CENTRE: .212 (1981-82)
16. MOST SHORTHANDED GOALS, ONE SEASON: .12 (1983-84)
17. MOST GOALS, 50 GAMES FROM START OF SEASON: .61 (twice—1981-82, 1983-84)
18. LONGEST CONSECUTIVE POINT-SCORING STREAK FROM START OF SEASON: .51 games, Oct. 5, 1983—Jan. 27, 1984 (61 goals, 92 assists)
19. LONGEST CONSECUTIVE POINT-SCORING STREAK: .51 games (1983-84)
20. LONGEST CONSECUTIVE ASSIST-SCORING STREAK: .17 games (38 assists, 1983-84)
21. MOST ASSISTS, ONE GAME: .7 (vs. Washington, Feb. 15, 1980; tied with Billy Taylor)
22. MOST ASSISTS, ONE GAME, BY A ROOKIE: .7 (vs. Washington, Feb. 15, 1980)
23. MOST GOALS, ONE PERIOD: .4 (vs. St. Louis, Feb. 18, 1981; tied with six others)

### STANLEY CUP RECORDS

24. MOST POINTS, ONE PLAYOFF YEAR: .38 (12 goals, 26 assists, 16 games, 1983)
25. MOST SHORTHANDED GOALS, ONE PLAYOFF YEAR: .3 (1983; tied with 3 others)
26. MOST ASSISTS, ONE PLAYOFF YEAR: .26 (16 games, 1983)
27. MOST POINTS, ONE GAME: .7 (four goals, three assists vs. Calgary, April 17, 1983)
28. MOST SHORTHANDED GOALS, ONE GAME: .2 (vs. Winnipeg, April 6, 1983; tied with two others)
29. MOST GOALS, ONE PERIOD: .3 (vs. Winnipeg, April 6, 1983; tied with 14 others)
30. MOST ASSISTS, ONE PERIOD: .3 (twice, vs. Montreal, April 8, 1981 and vs. Chicago, April 24, 1983; tied with 26 others)
31. FASTEST GOAL FROM START OF PERIOD (OTHER THAN FIRST): .9 seconds (vs. Winnipeg, April 6, 1983; tied with seven others)

### ALL-STAR RECORDS

32. MOST GOALS, ONE GAME: .4 (1983)
33. MOST POINTS, ONE GAME: .4 (1983)
34. MOST GOALS, ONE PERIOD: .4 (1983)
35. MOST POINTS, ONE PERIOD: .4 (1983)

# CLOSE UP

1. "Greatzky" is a good title for an article about Wayne Gretzky. Work with a partner to prepare three different statements to support this idea.
2. Wayne Gretzky is a very famous person. With a partner, make two lists, one showing the advantages of being so famous and one showing the disadvantages. Using the list, one partner should write a paragraph arguing that the advantages outweigh the disadvantages. The other partner should write the opposite argument. Trade arguments and read them persuasively out loud to each other.

# WIDE ANGLE

1. The statistics showing Gretzky's N.H.L. Records were compiled in 1985. Do some research in your school or public library and bring the statistics up to date.
2. This article is based on an interview with Wayne Gretzky. Imagine that you have set up an interview with Wayne but you want to ask him about things this article does not cover. Work with two or three others and prepare six questions you would ask Wayne.
3. The next time Wayne's team is on television, watch the game and pay special attention to how Wayne plays. Write a description of Wayne's performance. Share your description with a small group and ask for their opinions about your work.

# BOBBIE ROSENFELD

*by Robert Livesey*

OBBIE Rosenfeld's favourite sport was hockey, which she learned on the corner lots playing with the boys. Constance Hennessey, founding member of the Toronto Ladies Athletics Club, described her abilities as follows:

*"She was a fine hockey player—she checked hard and she had a shot like a bullet. On the basketball court she drove with the ball if she had it, she drove after it if someone else had it. She was just the complete athlete."*

The wiry, aggressive woman had arrived in Canada as a baby in the arms of her Russian parents and grew up in Barrie, Ontario. She excelled in so many sports during her athletic career that she was selected as best Canadian woman athlete of the half-century.

Bobbie was unknown until the day she was playing with her girls' softball team at a picnic in Beaverton, Ontario. Her friends coaxed her to run in the ninety metre dash at the small track meet that was being held. She won. To her surprise, a gentleman in-. troduced himself to her after the race as Elwood Hughes, manager of the Canadian National Exhibition, and informed her that she had just beaten Rosa Grosse, the champion Canadian sprinter.

Young Bobbie went on to play on several championship basketball teams in Ontario and Eastern Canada. In 1924, she was the champion tennis player at the Toronto grass courts. In 1925, she was the only entry representing the Patterson Athletic Club in the Ontario Ladies Track and Field Championship, yet she won the total-points title single-handedly for her club when she came first in the discus, the running broad jump, the 110 m low hurdles and the 200 m, as well as placing second in the javelin throw and the ninety metre dash.

During the Amsterdam Olympics in 1928, Bobbie was put in the 800 m race not because she had trained for the event, but to give moral support to seventeen-year-old Jean Thompson. On the stretch down the track, Bobbie sprinted from ninth position to run right on the heels of the younger girl from Canada. Jeannie began to falter, but Bobbie coaxed her on, refusing to pass her. The youngster finished fourth and Bobbie accepted fifth position for herself. In the ninety metre dash, Bobbie was neck and neck with the American runner, collecting a silver medal for her efforts, and in the relay team with Ethel Smith, Jane Ball, and Myrtle Cook, she helped win a gold medal for Canada.

Then, in 1929, arthritis struck, leaving her in bed for eight months and on crutches for a year afterward. By 1931, she was back in athletics, however, playing in the leading softball league as an outstanding hitter and fielder, and that winter she became the top Ontario hockey player in women's competition.

The career of Canada's best woman athlete ended sadly in 1933, when arthritis returned to retire her permanently from active sports.

# ETHEL CATHERWOOD

*by Robert Livesey*

SIX young women, decked out in cloth hats and bobbed hair, squeezed together on the platform of a railroad observation car to have their photographs taken. They were the greatest track and field team Canada ever sent to the Olympics. In Amsterdam in 1928, they triumphed over the United States women, twenty-six to twenty, to give the Canadian women's team an overall victory.

The tallest of the group was "The Saskatoon Lily". One Toronto sportswriter explained how she received her nickname:

*"From the instant this tall, slim, graceful girl from the prairies tossed aside her long flowing cloak of purple and made her first leap, the fans fell for her. A flower-like face of rare beauty above a long, slim body simply clad in pure white . . . she looked like a tall strange lily— and she was immediately christened by the crowd, "The Saskatoon Lily".*

Beautiful Ethel Catherwood, nineteen years old, had to face twenty-three jumpers, including Caroline Gisolf, a Dutch athlete and the world record holder, who was cheered on by a home-town crowd. Only competitors were allowed on the large field, which left Ethel, Canada's only entry in the high jump, alone. When the opportunity came, her co-ordinated body slipped gracefully over the bar at a height of 159 cm and Ethel had won an Olympic gold medal.

# CLOSE UP

1. Make up a statistics sheet for the Canadian Women's Team in the 1928 Olympics. Write the names of the six members of the team, the events in which they competed, and how they placed. (Be sure to include all three events for Bobbie Rosenfeld.)

| Name | Event | Finish/Medal |
|------|-------|--------------|
|      |       |              |

2. Role-play with a partner the conversation Bobbie Rosenfeld and Jean Thompson would have had after the 800 m race. You may want to take turns on a word processor to write the dialogue. You could write the lines for one of the athletes and your partner could write the lines for the other. Make brief notes on some of the things they might have said to each other before you begin writing.

3. Pretend that you are Ethel Catherwood that day in 1928 when you won the Olympic gold medal for high jumping. Write a letter to your parents at home in Saskatoon describing the scene at the stadium and your feelings before and after winning. Have a partner help you revise the letter.

SYLVIE BERNIER

BOBBIE ROSENFELD

# SYLVIE BERNIER

*by Janet Brooks*

LOS ANGELES—In her mind, it was all there. Sylvie Bernier had imagined over and over the scene at the Olympic swim stadium, the feeling of being alone on the springboard and the resounding cheers that would greet the American divers.

Before the competition even started, Bernier knew the ending.

"I knew I was going to be on that podium," the 20-year-old native of Ste. Foy told a news conference yesterday (Aug. 7, 1984), a day after winning the gold medal in the women's three-metre springboard competition—Canada's first Olympic diving gold.

"It was a deja vu. It was like I was in a dream and it was finally true. All the training and all the pain was finally worth the effort. It's a moment I'll never forget."

Bernier's Olympic gold was also the first medal won by a Quebec woman, an achievement quickly recognized by Premier Rene Levesque in a telegram.

"Quebec is proud of you, of your exploits, of this gold medal that is the crowning touch on all that relentless work that led to excellence," the telegram said.

In the Bernier home in Ste. Foy, Sylvie's achievement was watched on television by three of the family's five children. Her parents are with her in L.A.

"There was a lot of tension among us, especially after the last dive," recalled brother Denis, 17.

"When we saw that Sylvie had won, we all jumped into the air."

They toasted her victory with beer. "The champagne is for when she comes back home."

There'll also be a civic reception.

Denis said his sister started to get interested in diving when she was about eight or nine years old.

"She went with some friends to dive for fun. But she was good, and my parents enrolled her in diving courses."

At 12, she began competing, and "during the last five or six years, she trained five or six hours a day," Denis said.

Sylvie, who had been living and training in Montreal until recently, studied health sciences at CEGEP Andre-Grasset.

She plans to return home Aug. 17, and will probably study pharmacology at Laval University this fall, Denis said.

At the Claude Robillard Sports Centre in Montreal, where Sylvie trained for the past two years, there was jubilation yesterday.

Marc Filion, 24, coaches members of Sylvie's club, the Club Aquatique de Montreal Olympique, and has also coached her.

"She's a young woman with a goal: the Olympic Games. When she came to train here, she always had first place in mind.

"And she has enormous personal discipline," Filion said.

Winning the gold medal became a realistic objective for Bernier in the past two years, after she began to achieve success in international competition.

She won the Can-Am-Mex competition last year and placed third at both the World University Games and the Pan-American Games. Earlier this year, she won the Fort Lauderdale International.

# ELASTIC GIRL

*By Larry Wood*

LOS ANGELES—Canadian swimming's Elastic Girl seemed stunned by the news she had become the first Canadian female gold medal winner in the history of Olympic Games swimming (July 1984).

"I knew George Hodgson was the last gold medal winner, but I never thought about the woman's angle," Anne Ottenbrite said.

"I do know that I was this close to tears when they raised that flag and gave me the medal."

The Ottenbrite story is another of those Cinderella tales in a town that will be choked with them over the next two weeks. She wrenched her knee in a freak accident prior to the Canadian team trials and was forced to forego that action.

"Actually, she's only been using her kick in training the past two weeks," said coach Deryk Snelling. "Prior to that she had been working strictly by arm strength."

"And," the Whitby, Ont., teenager added, "I have weak arms."

So how does a kid rebound so fast to win an Olympic gold medal?

"She had two things going for her," said Snelling. "The fastest girl in the world in 200 breaststroke over the past couple of years swimming right beside her, and the fact that she had something to prove. She wanted it badly because she was included on the team in spite of missing the trials.

"There wasn't a controversy over it, but it had never happened before, either."

And, something else.

"I've been feeling real good lately, like I'm ready to swim," she said. "Before the trials I didn't know where I stood. I didn't know if I'd even be here. It just feels good to, well, feel good, you know?"

Snelling says that Japan's swift Hiroko Nagasaki, who hid in the grass during the qualifying heat and then came out bombing in the final, "actually gave Anne the pacesetting lift she needed".

But, realistically, Snelling admits he figured Ottenbrite for a bronze or silver at best yesterday.

"It was a very tough race," he admitted. Her response was outstanding. She swam a tactically perfect race.

"She has come a long way quickly. Her starts and turns aren't the greatest. And there used to be a lot of controversy surrounding her technique. She's been disqualified a couple of times in international races for her high, undulating stroke. Some judges have seen it as illegal.

"She's a very flexible person. Capable of all sorts of physical contortions. And that's why she hurt herself this spring. She twisted her foot in her shoes and did something to her knee."

Ottenbrite agrees she has worked hard to make "the magic corrections".

"It's strictly a feel thing, off the start and on the turns. I don't know how to explain it but the changes have been working."

Above the pool, and the stands with a seating capacity of 16,000, a wildly cheering group is waving the Canadian flag atop a nearby building, part of the University of California's Olympic Village.

"This is a great team," said Elastic Girl, craning her neck to a 50 degree angle. "Look at those guys. They know we've just begun. We're going to win some more gold medals before this is over."

# CLOSE UP

1. Read through the two newspaper articles and with a partner find the qualities Sylvie and Anne possess that give them the competitive edge that helped win gold medals in 1984. Make a list of these qualities and file it in your writing folder.
2. Imagine that you are either Sylvie or Anne and write a monologue expressing what is going through your mind as you stand on the podium accepting your gold medal and listening to the national anthem. Ask a partner to help you polish your work. Tape your monologue with "O Canada" playing softly in the background. Share your tape with another group, then file it with the written copy of your monologue in your Polished Writing File (see p. 181).

# WIDE ANGLE

1. Research the 1928 Olympics in Amsterdam or the 1984 Olympics in Los Angeles to find out how other Canadian men and women did. Give a brief oral report on your findings to the class.
2. Make a bulletin board on *Canadian Women Athletes of the Twentieth Century*. Ask your physical education teacher if you may use the bulletin board in the gymnasium or in the health room. Include short biographies, statistics, newspaper clippings, pictures, or your own drawings. You might want to write to Fitness and Amateur Sport Canada in Ottawa for further information.
3. Ask your school or public librarian to help you research the origins of the Olympic Games. Your history teacher might also be able to help you. Try to find out the following information:
   - when the games began;
   - where the first games were held;
   - the events;
   - the prizes; and
   - who could compete.

   **or**

   Research the modern Olympic Games. Try to find out
   - when women were first allowed to participate;
   - which new events were introduced for men and women in 1984; and
   - which athlete has won more medals than anyone else.

   Summarize the information you gather on a poster. You may want to include illustrations.

**ANNE OTTENBRITE**

## I LOVE ALL
## GRAVITY DEFIERS
*by Lillian Morrison*

The vaulter suspended
on a slender pole
hangs in the air
before his fall.

The trapeze artist
tumbles through space
in split-second rescues
from the abyss.

Kids on swings
pumping to the sky
in a pendulum of pleasure,
fly.

Ski-jumpers, speed-propelled,
extended in flight

loop down
to land upright.

Hail gravity defiers,
jumpers, broad and high
and all non-jumpers
who will not drop, who try.

Somersaulters
on the trampoline,
battered boxers
up at the count of nine.

Springboard athletes
jackknifing as they dive
and people who stand straight
and stay alive.

# CLOSE UP

1. a) Discuss with a partner the concept of gravity. Jot down notes on your understanding of the concept.

   b) Ask your science teacher to explain gravity to you, or look for an encyclopedia article in your school or public library. Add any new information to your original notes.

   c) Using your notes, explain in your own words what it means to defy gravity. Compare your explanation with a partner's, and put the best features together to make one explanation.

2. In a group of three or four, consider the last two lines of the poem and discuss

   (a) how "people who stand straight/and stay alive" defy gravity; and

   (b) why the poet loves these and other "gravity defiers" so much. Share your explanations with the other groups.

3. Make an illustration for one stanza of this poem. Be sure to show the athlete defying gravity. Post your illustration and accompany it with a caption.

# WIDE ANGLE

1. Write a poem entitled "I Love All Barrier Defiers" modelled on this poem. Think of as many athletes as you can who set new records, and incorporate five of the athletes into your poem. Form a small group and read your poems for each other in a way that captures the mood of what you are saying.

2. Form a small group and go to the library to find two newspaper or magazine articles on the achievements of disabled athletes. Brainstorm a list of the special qualities that disabled athletes possess. If you did Close Up #1, on p. 257, compare the two lists. Do disabled athletes have qualities different from those that Sylvie and Anne have? With the other members of your group, write a paragraph that explains how disabled athletes are gravity defiers.

# KALEIDOSCOPE

1. FIRST SKATER

   Leaving behind
   at every turning
   scratched circles
   of delicious joy

   *by Raymond Souster*

   Using the above poem as a model, write your own poem about a sport you enjoy. As in this poem, focus on some action in the sport you choose. Together with four or five others make a big poster of your poems. Decorate the poster with illustrations.

2. Interview a coach and an athlete about training, diet, and motivation. You and your partner should take notes during the interview, then condense the information into a brochure that could be given to young athletes who are just starting their training.

3. Watch a movie or a television program that involves sports. Prepare a short talk for a small group giving your reactions to the movie or program and telling what you learned from it.

4. Invent a sport! Work in a group of four or five. Decide on the equipment needed, the number of players, the rules, and so on. Demonstrate or explain your sport for the class. You may wish to do the demonstration in the gymnasium.

5. Imagine that you are a sports commentator for a television network covering a final game in the World Series, the Stanley Cup, the World Cup of Soccer, or an event in the Olympics. Write and then record on tape the play-by-play of a thrilling play or series of plays in the game. You may wish to use sound effects. Share your recording in a small group.

# THE TURN OF THE TIDE

*by C. S. Forester*

SLADE WAS glad it was such a tempestuous night. It meant that, more certainly than ever, there would be no one out in the lanes, no one out on the sands when he disposed of young Spalding's body.

Back in his drawing-room, Slade looked at the clock. There was still an hour to spare; he could spend it in making sure his plans were all correct.

He looked up the tide tables. Yes, that was right enough. Spring tides. The lowest of low water on the sands. There was not so much luck about that; young Spalding came back on the midnight train every Wednesday night, and it was not surprising that, sooner or later, the Wednesday night would coincide with a spring tide. But it was lucky that this particular Wednesday night should be one of tempest: luckier still that low water should be at one-thirty, the most convenient time for him.

He opened the drawing-room door and listened carefully. He could not hear a sound. Mrs. Dumbleton, his housekeeper, must have been in bed some time now. She was as deaf as a post, anyway, and would not hear his departure. Nor his return, when Spalding had been killed and disposed of.

The hands of the clock seemed to be moving very fast. He must make sure everything was correct. The plough chain and the other iron weights were already in the back seat of the car; he had put them there before old Matthews arrived to dine. He slipped on his overcoat.

From his desk, Slade took a curious little bit of apparatus: eighteen inches of strong cord, tied at each end to a six-inch length of wood so as to make a ring. He made a last close examination to see that the knots were quite firm, and then he put it in his pocket; as he did so, he ran through, in his mind, the words—he knew them by heart—of the passage in the book about the Thugs of India, describing the method of strangulation employed by them.

He could think quite coldly about all this. Young Spalding was a pestilent busybody. A word from him, now, would bring ruin upon Slade, could send him to prison, could have him struck off the rolls.

Slade thought of other defaulting solicitors he had heard of, even one or two with whom he had come into contact professionally. He remembered his brother-solicitors' remarks about them, pitying or contemptuous. He thought of having to beg his bread in the streets on his release from prison, of cold and misery and starvation. The shudder which shook him was succeeded by a hot wave of resentment. Never, never would he endure it.

What right had young Spalding, who had barely been qualified two years, to condemn a gray-haired man twenty years his senior to such a fate? If nothing but death would stop him, then he deserved to die. He clenched his hand on the cord in his pocket.

A glance at the clock told him he had better be moving. He turned out the lights and tiptoed out of the house, shutting the door quietly behind him. The bitter wind flung icy rain into his face, but he did not notice it.

He pushed the car out of the garage by hand, and, contrary to his wont, he locked the garage doors, as a precaution against the infinitesimal chance that, on a night like this, someone should notice that his car was out.

He drove cautiously down the road; of course, there was not a soul about in a quiet place like this. The few streetlamps were already extinguished.

There were lights in the station as he drove over the bridge; they were awaiting, there, the arrival of the twelve-thirty train. Spalding would be on that. Every Wednesday he went over to his subsidiary office, sixty miles away. Slade turned into the lane a quarter of a mile beyond the station, and then reversed his car so that it pointed towards the road. He put out the sidelights, and settled himself to wait; his hand fumbled with the cord in his pocket.

The train was a little late. Slade had been waiting a quarter of an hour when he saw the lights of the train emerge from the cutting and come to a standstill in the station. So wild was the night that he could hear nothing of it. Then the train moved slowly out again. As soon as it was gone, the lights in the station began to go out, one by one; Hobson, the porter, was making ready to go home, now that his turn of duty was completed.

Next, Slade's straining ears heard footsteps.

Young Spalding was striding down the road. With his head bent before the storm, he did not notice the dark mass of the motorcar in the lane, and he walked past it.

Slade counted up to two hundred, slowly, and then he switched on his lights, started the engine, and drove the car out into the road in pursuit. He saw Spalding in the light of the headlamps—the rain making silver streaks in the beam—and drew up alongside.

"Is that Spalding?" he said, striving to make the tone of his voice as natural as possible. "I'd better give you a lift, old man, hadn't I?"

"Thanks very much," said Spalding. "This isn't the sort of night to walk two miles in."

He climbed in and shut the door. No one had seen. No one would know. Slade let in his clutch and drove slowly down the road.

"Bit of luck, seeing you," he said. "I was just on my way home from bridge at Mrs. Clay's when I saw the train come in and remembered it was Wednesday and you'd be walking home. So I thought I'd turn a bit out of my way to take you along."

"Very good of you, I'm sure," said Spalding.

"As a matter of fact," said Slade, speaking slowly and driving slowly, "it wasn't altogether disinterest. I wanted to talk business to you, as it happened."

"Rather an odd time to talk business," said Spalding. "Can't it wait till tomorrow?"

"No, it cannot," said Slade. "It's about the Lady Vere trust."

"Oh, yes, I wrote to remind you last week that you had to make delivery."

"Yes, you did. And I told you, long before that, that it would be inconvenient, with Hammond abroad, and so on."

"I don't see that," said Spalding. "I don't see that Hammond's got anything to do with it. Why can't you just hand over and have done with it? I can't do anything to straighten things up until you do."

"As I said, it would be inconvenient."

Slade brought the car to a standstill at the side of the road.

"Look here, Spalding," he said desperately. "I've never asked a favour of you before. But now I ask you, as a favour, to forgo delivery for a bit. Just for three months, Spalding."

But Slade had small hope that his request would be granted. So little hope, in fact, that he brought his left hand out of his pocket holding the piece of wood, with the loop of cord dangling from its ends. He put his arm around the back of Spalding's seat.

"No, I can't, really I can't," said Spalding. "I've got my duty to my clients to consider. I'm sorry to insist, but you're quite well aware of what my duty is."

"Yes," said Slade. "But I beg you to wait. I implore you to wait, Spalding. There! Perhaps you can guess why, now."

"I see," said Spalding, after a long pause.

"I only want three months," pressed Slade. "Just three months."

Spalding had known of other men who had had the same belief in their ability to get straight in three months. It was unfortunate for Slade—and for Spalding—that Slade had used those words. Spalding hardened his heart.

"No," he said. "I can't promise anything like that. I don't think it's any use continuing this discussion. Perhaps I'd better walk home from here."

He put out his hand to the latch of the door, and, as he did so, Slade jerked the loop of the cord over his head. A single turn of Slade's wrist—a thin, bony old man's wrist, but as strong as steel in that wild moment—tightened the cord about Spalding's throat. Slade swung round in his seat, getting both hands to the piece of wood, twisting madly. His breath hissed between his teeth with the effort, but Spalding never drew breath at all. He lost consciousness long before he was dead. Only Slade's grip of the cord round his throat prevented the dead body from falling forward, doubled up.

Nobody had seen, nobody would know. And what that book had stated about the method of assassination practised by Thugs was perfectly correct.

Slade had gained, now, the time in which he could get his affairs into order. With all the promise of his current speculations, with all his financial ability, he would be able to recoup himself for his past losses. It only remained to dispose of Spalding's body, and he had planned to do that very satisfactorily. Just for a moment Slade felt as if all this were only some heated dream, some nightmare, but then he came back to reality and went on with the plan he had in mind.

He pulled the dead man's knees forward so that the corpse lay back in the seat, against the side of the car. He put the car in gear, let in his clutch, and drove rapidly down the road—much faster than when he had been arguing with Spalding. Low water was in three-quarters of an hour's time, and the sands were ten miles away.

Slade drove fast through the wild night. There was not a soul about in those lonely lanes. He knew the way by heart—he had driven repeatedly over that route recently in order to memorize it.

The car bumped down the last bit of lane, and Slade drew up on the edge of the sands.

It was pitch dark, and the bitter wind was howling about him, under the black sky. Despite the noise of the wind, he could hear the surf breaking far away, two miles away, across the level sands. He climbed out of the driver's seat and walked round to the other door. When he opened it the dead man fell sideways, into his arms.

With an effort, Slade held him up, while he groped into the back of the car for the plough chain and the iron weights. He crammed the weights into the dead man's pockets, and he wound the chain round and round the dead man's body, tucking in the ends to make it all secure. With that mass of iron to hold it down, the body would never be found again when dropped into the sea at the lowest ebb of spring tide.

Slade tried now to lift the body in his arms, to carry it over the sands. He reeled and strained, but he was not strong enough— Slade was a man of slight figure, and past his prime. The sweat on his forehead was icy in the icy wind.

For a second, doubt overwhelmed him, lest all his plans should fail for want of bodily strength. But he forced himself into thinking clearly; he forced his frail body into obeying the vehement commands of his brain.

He turned around, still holding the dead man upright. Stooping, he got the heavy burden on his shoulders. He drew the arms round his neck, and, with a convulsive effort, he got the legs up round his hips. The dead man now rode him pick-a-back. Bending nearly double, he was able to carry the heavy weight in that fashion, the arms tight round his neck, the legs tight round his waist.

He set off, staggering, down the imperceptible slope of the sands towards the sound of the surf. The sands were soft beneath his feet—it was because of this softness that he had not driven the car down to the water's edge. He could afford to take no chances of being embogged.

The icy wind shrieked round him all that long way. The tide was nearly two miles out. That was why Slade had chosen this place. In the depth of winter, no one would go out to the water's edge at low tide for months to come.

He staggered on over the sands, clasping the limbs of the body close about him. Desperately, he forced himself forward, not stopping to rest, for he only just had time now to reach the water's edge before the flow began. He went on and on, driving his exhausted body with fierce urgings from his frightened brain.

Then, at last, he saw it: a line of white in the darkness which indicated the water's edge. Farther out, the waves were breaking in an inferno of noise. Here, the fragments of the rollers were only just sufficient to move the surface a little.

He was going to make quite sure of things. Steadying himself, he stepped into the water, wading in farther and farther so as to be able to drop the body into comparatively deep water. He held to his resolve, staggering through the icy water, knee deep, thigh deep, until it was nearly at his waist. This was far enough. He stopped, gasping in the darkness.

He leaned over to one side, to roll the body off his back. It did not move. He pulled at its arms. They were obstinate. He could not loosen them. He shook himself, wildly. He tore at the legs round his waist. Still the thing clung to him. Wild with panic and fear, he flung himself about in a mad effort to rid himself of the burden. It clung on as though it were alive. He could not break its grip.

Then another breaker came in. It splashed about him, wetting him far above his waist. The tide had begun to turn now, and the tide on those sands comes in like a racehorse.

He made another effort to cast off the load, and when it still held him fast, he lost his nerve and tried to struggle out of the sea. But it was too rough for his exhausted body. The weight of the corpse and of the iron with which it was loaded overbore him. He fell.

He struggled up again in the foam-streaked, dark sea, staggered a few steps, fell again—and did not rise. The dead man's arms were round his neck, throttling him, strangling him. Rigor mortis had set in and Spalding's muscles had refused to relax.

# FOCUSSING

1. The words listed below are often found in mystery stories:

autopsy     forensic science     private eye
clue     motive     sleuth
confession     murder     suspect
culprit     mystery     suspense
deduction     perpetrator     victim
detective     police line-up     witness

Work in a group of three and divide the words among you. Check the meanings of your words in a dictionary and exchange definitions with your partners. Add any other mystery words that you can think of to the list. Compile the group's words into a *Crime Dictionary* and decorate it with illustrations if you wish. Be sure to design a cover, too. If you store your dictionary on a computer disc, the "find" command of the word processor will allow you to look up the word you want.

2. A witness to a crime is helpful only if he or she can clearly remember details. Here are two ways to find out if you are an observant witness:

a) Bring six or seven small objects to class and display them on your desk. Let a partner look at the objects for one minute and then, while your partner covers his or her eyes, remove one or two objects. See if your partner can name and describe the missing object(s). Switch roles with your partner and repeat the procedure.

**or**

b) Show your partner a magazine picture or a colour photograph of someone he or she does not know. Let your partner examine the picture or photograph for one minute, and then remove it from his or her view. Ask your partner to describe the person's physical characteristics and clothing and the background of the picture. Switch roles with your partner and repeat the process.

3. Detective stories are very popular on television and in films. List the television and film mysteries that you have seen recently and note the following information for one or two of them:

● name of show ● name of police officer or private detective ● type of crime committed ● name of victim(s) ● clues ● suspects ● name of perpetrator of crime

Form a small group and look over all your findings together. Make note of any patterns you detect.

# THE MIDNIGHT VISITOR

*by Elsie Katterjohn, based on a short story by Robert Arthur*

## CHARACTERS

ADAMS,
*an American secret agent*

FOWLER,
*a young American writer*

MAX,
*a foreign agent*

HENRI,
*a Frenchman*

### THE SCENE:

*A small, sixth-floor room in a gloomy hotel in Paris. The room is dark except for a shaft of light from a partly open transom above the door to the hall at stage right. The dim light reveals the usual collection of shabby hotel-room furniture. At stage left are two doors: one at left centre is closed and blocked off by a desk placed squarely against it; the closet door at lower left is slightly ajar. At upper centre are shabby velveteen curtains that hide all but a narrow vertical strip of the window behind. Traffic noises from the street six stories below sound faintly in the background.*

### THE TIME:

*The present. It is nearly midnight.*
*As the curtains open, a dark figure moves stealthily about the room. He holds a small flashlight which he shines into the closet, among the papers on the desk, and into the chest of drawers across the room. After a moment, footsteps and voices are heard in the hall. Suddenly alert, the dark figure snaps off his flashlight. His form is seen once against the darker black of the window; then he disappears into the closet.*
*Through the open transom is heard a jingling of keys. As the door opens, Adams is talking. He wheezes as he talks.*

ADAMS (*ushering his companion into the room ahead of him*): Of course you are disappointed! You were told that I was a secret agent, a spy—that I deal in espionage and danger. You wanted to meet me because you are a writer—and young and romantic. (*He presses a light switch inside the door. When the stage is lighted, Adams is seen to be very fat and his wrinkled business suit is badly in need of cleaning. He looks anything but a secret agent.*) No doubt you expected mysterious figures in the night, the crack of pistols, maybe even drugs in the wine. (*Closing the door, he chuckles at the embarrassment of his guest, a good-looking, neatly dressed young man who seems more boyish than his 28 years.)*

**FOWLER:** No, not really. Well—*(with a self-conscious laugh)* a couple of mysterious figures, maybe.

**ADAMS** *(tossing his battered hat onto the bed)*: Instead, you have spent a dull evening in a second-rate music hall with a sloppy fat man.

**FOWLER** *(protesting)*: Oh, it wasn't so bad.

**ADAMS:** And do I get messages slipped furtively into my hand by dark-eyed beauties? On the contrary, all I get is one ordinary telephone call making an appointment in my room. Admit it, my friend, you have been bored.

**FOWLER:** No, not bored—just a bit—

**ADAMS:** Ah yes, you are completely disillusioned. An evening wasted and you have nothing to write about—not even a small paragraph to put into that notebook of yours. *(Fowler looks at the notebook he is still holding in his hand, smiles sheepishly, and puts it into his pocket.)* But take cheer, my friend. After all, this is Paris. You may yet see some drama tonight.

But come—see my view—even from a shabby hotel room on the sixth floor it is still quite a view. *(He walks to a window and pulls open the draperies a few more inches. The night presses blackly against the glass.)* Oh, too bad, the fog is even thicker now. But still you can make out the Eiffel tower in the distance there. *(chuckling)* Even a foggy night in Paris is better than a clear night in Des Moines, no?

**FOWLER** *(taking a few steps toward the window and glancing only briefly at the distant view)*: Mr. Adams, excuse me if I am prying, but—you mentioned—well—that phone call . . .

**ADAMS:** Ah, Mr. Fowler, you are observant. Very observant. And such devotion to your work shall not go unrewarded. Was that phone call important? Yes, my friend, it was very important. That is why we have cut short a bit our evening on the town, and why, in fact, I have brought you back here with me. Perhaps I will show you that I do not waste my time completely. Yes, the call had to do with a certain paper—a very important paper—for which several men have risked their lives. You shall see this paper presently. It will come to me here in the next-to-last step of its journey into official hands. *(confidentially)* You realize, of course, that I could not let you witness this event if it were not for your uncle's very persuasive letter. But how can one disappoint a dear old friend? *(closing the draperies and returning to a position*

ADAMS

*down centre)* Some day soon this paper may well affect the course of history. Now in this thought there is drama, is there not?

*(Suddenly, the door to the closet opens and out steps a man with a small automatic in his hand. He is slender, not very tall, and his rather pointed features suggest the crafty expression of a fox.)*

**ADAMS:** Max!

**MAX** *(speaking with an indefinable European accent)*: Good evening, Mr. Adams.

**ADAMS** *(wheezing)*: Max, you gave me a start! I thought you were in Berlin. What are you doing here? *(He backs away.)*

**MAX:** I was in Berlin, yes. But I, too, had a telephone call—earlier in the week. So here I am. I will have your weapon, please. *(Adams puts on a look of innocence.)* Your gun, please, which I know you are never without. Give it to me. *(Adams shrugs, hands over gun he takes from shoulder holster. Fowler looks amazed, not having suspected that Adams was armed.)* Thank you. Now—the report— *(Again Adams pretends innocence.)* The report on our new missiles that is being delivered to you tonight? *(with exaggerated politeness)* We merely thought it would be safer in our hands than in yours.

**ADAMS:** But—even I didn't know until the phone call tonight—*(He smiles weakly, then shrugs.)* Well, you always were known for your timing—

**MAX** *(with a tight smile)*: Just so. Please sit down. We may as well be comfortable. You, too, young man. *(He shrewdly appraises Fowler, who remains standing, still dazed at the turn of events.)*

**ADAMS** *(backs to armchair at centre stage and sinks down heavily)*: Max, I just can't get over your being here. *(to Fowler)* As you may have gathered, Max and I have known each other a long time. In fact, I might say *(glances at Max)* we are old business associates. *(Fowler smiles nervously, nods.)* Max, I'm sorry not to be more hospitable, but I can't say I am exactly happy to see you. The last time we met—two years ago, wasn't it? In Geneva? *(Adams is obviously playing for time.)* I was expecting you then—but now—why, I don't even have comfortable accommodations to offer you—certainly nothing like that delightful little villa in Geneva. You remember it—the one with the stained glass windows and the balconies?

**MAX:** Yes, I recall your hospitality at that villa—including the gendarmes. Thank you! But this room will serve for our transaction.

FOWLER

ADAMS: Oh, well, I suppose the quarters *(indicating room)* are adequate, but really, the management here is impossible! *(to Fowler)* I was assured—*assured* that this hotel was safe, and yet this is the second time in a month—the *second* time, mind you—that somebody has gotten into my room off that confounded balcony!

MAX: Balcony? No *(taking key from pocket and holding it up)*, I used a passkey. I did not know about the balcony. It might have saved me some trouble had I known.

ADAMS *(in surprise and irritation)*: A passkey? A passkey! Well, that is the limit. Max, I'm truly annoyed. I expected the balcony, but a passkey—why, this is ridiculous. At least the balcony called for a little ingenuity. The ironic thing is that it is not even my balcony: It belongs to the next apartment. *(glancing toward Fowler)* This room, you see, used to be part of a larger unit, and that door there *(indicates sealed door)* used to connect with the living room. *It* had the balcony, which extends under *my* window, too. You can get onto it from the empty room two doors down—and someone did, last month. Nothing was lost that time—but the management promised me they would block it off. *(Shrugs wearily.)* But they haven't done it. No matter, I guess—

MAX: As you say, no matter. *(Glancing at Fowler, who stands stiffly a few feet from Adams, Max waves the gun with a commanding gesture.)* Please sit down. *(Fowler perches on edge of bed.)* We have a wait of half an hour at least, I think.

ADAMS: Thirty-one minutes. The appointment was for twelve-thirty. *(moodily)* I wish I knew how you learned about that report, Max.

MAX *(smiling, but only with his mouth)*: I may say, the interest is mutual. We would like to know how the report was gotten out of our country. However, no harm has been done. I will have it back.

*(There is a sudden rapping on the door. Fowler jumps.)*

MAX *(sharply)*: Who—?

ADAMS *(calmly)*: The gendarmes. I thought that so important a paper as the one we are waiting for might well be given a little extra protection tonight—from the police.

MAX *(in an angry whisper, flourishing the gun)*: You—! *(Bites his lip uncertainly as the rapping is repeated.)*

ADAMS: What will you do now, Max? If I do not answer, they have instructions to enter anyway. The door is unlocked. And they will not hesitate to shoot. *(Max starts toward closet door.)* Nor will they neglect to search the room. You would be quite a prize for . . .

MAX

**MAX** *(interrupting in a sharp whisper)*: Quiet!
*(His face twisted with rage, Max has been glancing about the room. He abruptly changes direction and backs swiftly toward window at upper centre. The gun in his right hand is still levelled at the other two. With his left arm, he reaches behind him and pushes open the window. Then he swings his left leg over the sill. The street noises are louder now.)*

**MAX**: Don't move till I'm gone! You have outsmarted me this time—but we haven't seen the last of each other, I think! *(smugly)* So thoughtful of you to inform me of this convenient exit. Au revoir!

*(The rapping on the door becomes louder, more insistent.)*

**HENRI** *(from outside)*: M'sieu! M'sieu Adams!

*(Max, who has twisted his body so that his gun still covers the fat man and his guest, grasps the window frame with his left hand and then swings his right leg up and over the sill. He pushes free with his left hand and drops out of sight.*

*Adams' body relaxes visibly. With seeming casualness, he goes to the window and closes it, then crosses the room and opens the door.)*

**ADAMS**: Ah, Henri—
*(A waiter enters with a tray on which are a bottle and two glasses.)*

**HENRI**: Pardon, M'sieu, the cognac you ordered for when you returned. *(He sets the tray on a small table and deftly uncorks the bottle.)*

**ADAMS**: Merci, Henri. *(Hands him a coin.)*

**HENRI**: Merci, M'sieu. *(He leaves.)*

**FOWLER** *(staring after him, stammering)*: But—the police—

**ADAMS**: There were no police. Only Henri, whom I was expecting.

**FOWLER**: But the man on the balcony—Max—won't he—?

**ADAMS**: No, he will not return. *(He reaches for the bottle of cognac.)* You see, my young friend, there is no balcony.

*(Fowler stands frozen as the meaning of this last statement sinks in; then he dashes to the window, flings it open, and looks down. Among the street noises that filter up through the open window, an ambulance siren rises and grows steadily louder.)*

**ADAMS** *(filling the glasses)*: Come, have your drink. Maybe now, after all, you have something to write about.

*(He raises his glass as the CURTAINS CLOSE.)*
*THE END*

HENRI

# CLOSE UP

1. Adams outsmarts Max by casually telling him two lies. Identify the lies, write two sentences describing them, and, in your own words, tell what happens when Max believes them.
2. With a partner make a list of the qualities Adams has that make him a good secret agent.
3. Make a recording of the play; include as many sound effects as you can. Rehearse your reading before you record it, putting as much emotion into your character as you can. You will need three readers and one or two sound-effects technicians.

# WIDE ANGLE

1. Imagine that you are Fowler, and write a letter to your uncle telling him about your meeting in Paris with his dear old friend Adams. Be sure to express your feelings about some of the events of that night. Read your letter to a partner and have him or her help you revise it. When it has been proofread, file it with the rest of your polished writing.
2. You are the *gendarme* (police officer) investigating the death of Max. You go up to Adams' room and find him drinking cognac with Fowler. Working with a partner, write out the questions you will ask Adams and Fowler, and then write the answers you think they would make. Before you begin to write, you will have to decide whether or not Adams and Fowler will cover up the truth. Read your dialogue for another pair of students and then listen to their work.

# ELEMENTS OF A MYSTERY

*by Karen Hubert*

IRST THINGS first. There must be a crime, or at least a crime-in-the-making. The crime may be against a person: a murder, a rape, a mugging, a hold-up, blackmail, or a kidnapping. Or it may be against an object, usually one that has special value or meaning to its owner: a jewel, a vase, a manuscript, a good-luck charm, a car with important documents hidden in its glove compartment. A crime may also be committed against a place: a church or park vandalized; a tennis club destroyed; a house bombed; a patch of land or beach booby-trapped.

The crime, or crime-in-the-making, must be discovered. Without discovery there would be no mystery story. Who discovers the crime, and how does the discovery take place? The discoverer may be an innocent bystander who later becomes the prime suspect, a relative, a maid, the narrator, a detective, the police, a child. Any one of them may force open a locked door and find a body crumpled up nearby, routinely open a safe to find a diamond tiara gone, take a dip in a pool and encounter a corpse fully dressed at the bottom with rocks in his pockets.

After the crime has been discovered, the mystery solver steps onto the scene. He may be a police officer, detective, private citizen, curious neighbour, or relative. His motive for taking on the case may be personal interest, love, familial responsibility, curiosity, money, or sentiment.

The mystery solver first tries to ascertain whether anyone has seen anything that might be relevant to the case. Enter the witnesses. Witnesses are accidental or purposeful observers who have seen a crime or a very suspicious occurrence. Very rarely does a witness see the crime as it happened. More often she sees or hears part of it: sees a leg as the criminal runs out the door, hears a loud noise and happens to look at her watch. Witnesses observe with varying degrees of accuracy. What they think they have seen they may not have. A witness may not tell the truth because she is protecting herself or someone else. Or she may simply have seen or heard in a faulty or partial manner.

Next come the suspects, those seemingly guilty characters any one of whom had motive and opportunity enough to commit the crime. Some suspects seem more obviously guilty than others, but there is no way of identifying the real culprit from outward appearances alone. A character becomes a suspect because she is found near or at the scene of the crime, or because she has no alibi at the time the crime was committed. But, most important, she must have a motive. Motive and suspect are inextricably entwined.

As I said earlier, the mystery story is much more psychological in nature than the other genres because of its concern with motive. Motive is in a sense nothing less than a case history, a study in human behaviour. A character's motives stem from her "secret self," that part of the personality which readers and viewers of the mystery

love to see exposed. It is never enough to know how a crime was done and by whom: we want to know why it was done. Some writers attempt to give the motive behind the motive: *X* killed his father because *X* hated his father. Why did *X* hate his father? Because he was cut out of his father's will. Why? Because *X* had married against the old man's wishes. Why? *X* was rebelling against the old man. Motives may include revenge, jealousy, lust, greed, altruism, fear of blackmail, fear of exposure of one's past, abnormality.

The criminal in a mystery story never succeeds entirely in covering up his tracks. The detective finds clues that implicate, or lead him to, the criminal. Clues may be objects that belong to the criminal or that are in some way associated with him. A lighter left behind at the scene of the crime may bear his initials, for example. The murder weapon itself may provide a clue, as may a set of fingerprints, a piece of clothing, a comb, a handkerchief, a heel off a shoe. Some clues may be in the form of information or statements provided by suspects, witnesses, or other characters.

The mystery solver follows suspects and is himself often followed. Almost always a chase of some sort takes place that moves the story to a high pitch of excitement and adventure. In some novels, the chase lasts all book long. A chase is usually physical but may also have aspects of a contest in which criminal and mystery solver try to outwit each other.

The mystery ends with a confession, which the criminal may make voluntarily or at the point of a gun. Through it the true story emerges and loose ends are cleared up.

The mystery is commonly thought of as sensational, but it does not necessarily have to make the hair stand on end. Its prime satisfaction is intellectual: the reader takes part in the mystery solver's mental gymnastics and may even compete with him by trying to reach a solution before he does.

# CLOSE UP

1. Each paragraph in this piece of writing contains a word or phrase that sums up the topic of the paragraph, e.g., *crime* in paragraph one, and *discovery* in paragraph two. Working with a partner, list the key word or phrase for the remaining paragraphs.
2. In your own words, explain to a partner what quality the mystery story has that makes it different from most other types of stories. Your clue is in the last paragraph. Listen to your partner's explanation.

# WIDE ANGLE

1. Motive is an important element in a mystery story. In your local newspaper, find two short articles about crimes. In a group of three, take turns reading your articles aloud. For each crime try to figure out what the motive(s) might have been.
2. You are a video game manufacturer and you want to invent a new video game. Your game should include the following elements: a crime, a victim, a mystery solver, clues, witnesses, a chase, and a perpetrator. Give the game an attention-grabbing title and draw what the video screen would look like. Share your drawing with a small group, and explain how your game would work if it were built.

   b) If your class has a computer and a games program, form a small group and design your own computer mystery game. Use the program to create a game that features at least five of the elements of a mystery. When your game is finished, invite another group to play it.
3. Find a mystery or suspense novel in your school or public library. Read it and make brief notes on it using the topics you identified in Close Up #1. Write an outline of the plot that would summarize the book for someone who had never read it. Join with three or four partners, show them your work, and share your reaction to the novel.

# DEATH OF A DIETER

*by Colleen Kobe*

H ER NERVOUSNESS affected Ellen worst in her stomach, but she held it in as best she could. The fifteen-year-old, delicate-featured black woman clasped her hands firmly in her lap in an attempt to calm herself.

She sat in a small room, about the size of a bedroom, that was completely unfurnished for the occasion save for the chair upon which she sat, the plain wooden table before her, and the folding chair on the opposite side of the table. Upon the table squatted a cathode ray tube computer terminal, whose screen at the moment was blank. The only window in the uncarpeted room was off to Ellen's left, leaving the screen in shadow. Late morning winter sun streamed nakedly into the room, without benefit of softening by a lacy curtain or two.

She drew a deep breath, as Louisa had shown her, checked her watch once more, and, as she slowly expelled it, typed into the terminal, "I'm ready."

After a moment, the screen filled with a not-unpleasant array of amber-on-black paragraphs. She knew by heart already what they said, but she read again the paragraphs of the final test.

*You're a finalist in the competition to become a member of the Mystery-Solver's Club of Earth (it read). Congratulations for getting this far!*

*You are now about to solve the last mystery we have so cleverly arranged for you. To refresh your memory, here are the ground rules.*

*1. You will receive a brief description of the (possible) crime or event and a list of the persons involved. Your task (should you decide to accept it) is to determine if a crime has been committed, and if so, by whom and why.*

*2. You may interview any of the persons involved with the case as many times as you like.*

*3. You may perform your task in any legal fashion you like.*

*4. You may ask once, and only once, if you have enough information to solve your task. We will answer either "yes" or "no." Subsequent questions will be ignored.*

5. *When you feel you have accomplished your task, enter your reasoning into this terminal; your statements will be immediately transmitted to us.*

  *a. If your conclusions are incorrect, you may reapply for membership at any time.*

  *b. If your conclusions are correct, you will become a member of the MSCE.*

6. *You may not leave the room until one of these conditions is fulfilled:*

  *a. You have accomplished your task.*

  *b. You feel you cannot accomplish your task.*

  *c. The four-hour time limit, begun the moment you request the case history, has been exceeded.*

7. *Failure to follow these rules will result in immediate disqualification and a suspension of the privilege of joining the MSCE for a period of ten years.*

*Press any key to produce the case history.*

Ellen breathed deeply again. It's now or never, she thought. Maybe I should just go home. I can always try again later. Then again, if I make it I *will* become a member and then that stupid Simon Parker will have to pay up. He'll *have* to. Louisa saw us shake hands and she'll tell his mama if he doesn't. What I could do with twenty dollars—

With a short, almost spastic flick of her finger, she hit the space bar. The screen cleared instantly. She checked her watch: nine fifteen on the nose. She had until one fifteen to solve the case—if there was anything to solve.

The screen filled again with amber words. She made herself review them carefully.

*Susan Hartshaw, a wealthy twenty-four-year-old woman, died of malnutrition today. She had been riding a tandem side-by-side bicycle with her husband when she collapsed. The medical examiner's report says that she weighed seventy-four pounds when she died, and that her death was primarily due to starvation.*

*The people involved with the case are:*

  *a. Bradley Hartshaw, Susan's husband*

  *b. Amanda Cathcart, Susan's best friend*

  *c. Louetta Hartshaw, Susan and Bradley's daughter*

  *d. Christopher Hartshaw, Bradley's son from a previous marriage*

  *e. Wilbur Succint, Susan's lawyer*

Susan read and reread the screen. The cursor blinked impatiently as she typed, "Please send in Bradley Hartshaw."

Into the room strode a tall, swarthy man, about thirty years old. His olive-coloured skin contrasted neatly with his black hair and eyes; his belly threatened to explode from beneath his tight, but fashionable, sweat suit. At the moment his features were contorted in grief: his lips were pressed firmly together, his eyes avoided her gaze. He slumped into the folding chair.

Not quite sure where to begin, Ellen faltered. "Mr. Hartshaw?" she said tentatively. "I'm very sorry about your wife's death."

He shrugged listlessly. "Can't change anything now." He seemed to gather courage: he lifted his head and tried to smile, but it quickly faded into a grimace. He looked away. Ellen marveled at the man's acting.

"I'm sorry, sir, but I'll have to ask you a few questions." Again he shrugged. "How long were you two married?"

"Only two glorious years."

"Any children?"

"One, Louetta, a little over a year old." He smiled.

"I, uh, understand that your wife died of starvation." Instantly the smile vanished. "Was she always so thin?"

Bradley stared at his toes. "No," he said, looking at her for the first time. "That started after Louetta was born. When we got married, she was a little on the plump side. She's five f— she *was* five feet four and then weighed around one thirty-five. And when she was pregnant with Louetta, she gained about thirty pounds more. But after Louetta was born, the extra weight really started bothering her, so she started to diet. And exercise. Unbeatable combination."

"What kind of exercise did she do, Mr. Hartshaw?"

"Just call me Bradley, honey. Exercise? Name it. Swimming, running, golf, racquetball . . ." He snorted. "I saw this coming, you know," he admitted confidentially.

That startled Ellen. "You did?"

He nodded wisely. "Yeah. I've seen pictures of those people with that disorder. Anorexia nervosa, that's what it's called, right? Arms and legs like sticks, chests like a washboard. Horrible. Hard to understand why being cool means looking like that." He shook his head, looking away.

Suddenly he rose and paced the floor. "But what are you supposed to do? You can't make them eat 'cause they'll just run to the bathroom and waggle their fingers in their throats and get rid of it. Even Chris saw this coming. Just what are you supposed to *do*?" he ended in a wail.

Ellen hastily consulted her terminal. "Chris is your son, is that right?"

"Yeah."

"How old is he?"

"Thirteen. He's the only good thing my lousy ex-wife left me. Geez. Never get married if you ain't in your twenties yet. It'll never work. Unless you're both masochists."

"How long have you been divorced?"

"Ten years now." He stopped pacing, staring out the window. "Listen, if you don't mind, is that all?"

"One more thing, Mr. Har—Bradley. What do you do for a living?"

He hesitated, smiling crookedly. "I used to be a plumber. Would you believe it? But three years ago, when I turned twenty-eight, I thought to myself, 'Sure, the money's good. But do I want to do this alone, forever?' so that was when I started going out to meet people, and that was when I met Susan . . . Yeah, I met Susan . . . Excuse me." He rubbed his forehead and hurried out of the room.

Ellen glanced at her watch. Nine forty-five. What a quick half hour! She consulted the list of persons and typed into the terminal, "Please send in Amanda Cathcart."

She waited, gazing around the room. Am I doing this right? she wondered. These people—these actors—are very good at this. Surely they wouldn't divulge information freely. I'll have to ask the right person the right question. I wonder how I'll know if I have enough information to make an intelligent decision?

The door opened and a slightly chunky woman walked straight to Ellen, her sneakered feet squeaking loudly on the wooden floor. The expression on her bland face was one of grim determination.

"Ellen?" Amanda snapped briskly, her hand outstretched for Ellen to shake. "I'm Amanda Cathcart. I was Susan's best friend. There was nothing we didn't tell each other. And I want you to know that I think poor, poor Susan was murdered!"

Ellen, taken aback, said soothingly, "Won't you sit down, Ms. Cathcart? Now then, permit me to ask you a few questions, may I? First, how old are you?"

The woman sniffed. "Twenty-four."

"And how long have you known Susan?"

"We've been best friends since grade school. Went to all the parties and other social events together. Everyone always called us Susanda when they wanted both of us." She smiled at the memory.

"So you two were virtually sisters, is that right?"

"Yes."

"Did you share everything?"

"Well, just the things we wanted to share."

"Who do you think killed Susan, and why?"

"It was that no-good husband of hers. Bradley. And as to why—well, look." She tapped a dirty fingernail nervously on Ellen's table as she collected her thoughts. "You know Susan was left with all her parents' money when they were killed?"

"No," said Ellen curiously. "I didn't know they were."

"They died three years ago in a typical car crash. Drunk driving other car, one-way street, head-on collision, everyone dies but the drunk. Nothing anybody could do. So they left all their *substantial* estate to only child Susan, who could easily live on it the rest of her life. At first she moped around all the time, didn't want to do anything, bawled a lot, you know, just generally mourning. Finally I got tired of it and got it into her head that all the grieving in the world wasn't going to bring her parents back. After a while she realized I was right. So she—and I, too, occasionally—started going out to bars and things, to meet some nice guys. After all, she might as well be happy, right?

"Well, not long after that both *my* parents died, also in a wreck involving a drunk driver." Amanda stopped to catch her breath. "The different thing was, my parents were up to the wazoo in debt, and by the time all the bills were paid off there wasn't anything left for yours truly. Ahh, well. Who wants to be rich anyway.

"So now I'm going to Tech to become a mechanical engineer. Doesn't seem like I have the brain for it, does it? But the tests say I do, so I will. Can't stand law, or business, or cutting people up, so what else is there?

"And I started going out with Susan to the bars. And we met guys. And not too long after that, Susan started getting nervous."

"Nervous?" interrupted Ellen.

"Yeah. I mean, how was she to know whether the guy liked her for her money or for herself? How did she know what they *really* wanted, you know? She got a little scared, and only went out with me once in a while. And so she wasn't around when I met Bradley Hartshaw."

"Bradley? You mean her husband?" Ellen exclaimed without thinking.

Amanda glared at her. "Yeah. Her husband, that skunk. Anyway, we went out for a while. 'Cept . . . I don't know. I was head-over-heels for that jerk. Crap." She inspected her fingernails closely. Ellen remained silent.

"So, yeah, we went out a year together. Then I noticed he wasn't coming around so much, and then one day I stopped over at Susan's and his car was in her driveway and there they were on the sofa in the living room making out.

"Didn't see either of them for a week. Finally Susan came over looking guilty as hell and told me they were going to get married. Married!" She paused again. "It was a long time, about a year, just before she had the baby, that we got to be good friends again. Not quite like it used to be, but good." She smiled. "I was there when Louetta was born."

Ellen cleared her throat. "You mentioned that you were in bad shape financially. Why didn't you ask Susan to lend you some? It sounds as if she had more than enough."

Amanda smirked. "I was too proud. She offered over and over again. But I never took any. Funny, huh? But the more engineering I learned, the better I felt about myself. Like, I used to tell myself that sure, maybe Susan had a lot more money than me, but she never did anything to get it except get born. Big deal. But me—I'm earning my Suzybucks. Or I will, this May, when I graduate."

"But why do you think he killed her?" persisted Ellen.

Exasperated, Amanda cried, "Because he's a jerk, that's why! He's a sneak and a greedy lout, and he's smart. He'll have thought out a way to get all her money, don't you worry."

Disappointment creeping in, Ellen asked, "But you have no idea how, no concrete proof . . ."

Amanda grinned maliciously. "That's for *you* to find out, my dear." And she rose and left the room, the door slamming loudly behind her.

Irritated at the woman's abrupt exit, Ellen scowled at the closed door. Remembering her deadline, she looked at her watch again. Ten thirty. She consulted her list and typed into the terminal, "Please send in Christopher Hartshaw."

What should I ask him? she wondered, rising to stretch her muscles a bit. Bradley says he's—what?—thirteen? She swung her arms in wide circles, her hands occasionally breaking the shaft of sunlight streaming through the window. How much does a thirteen-year-old notice?

Presently there was a knock on the door. "Come in." A small, muscular boy with Bradley Hartshaw's black hair and eyes, but with lighter skin, entered and, while smiling politely at Ellen, seated himself. She followed, astounded at how old the boy looked for his age.

"I'm Ellen," she said, extending her hand.

"Pleased to meet you, Ellen. I'm Christopher," replied the boy. His grip was warm and clammy.

"How old are you, Christopher?"

"I'll be fourteen in January."

She shook her head disbelievingly. "My gosh, you look

big for your age. I would swear you look fifteen at the least."

He smiled at what he took to be a compliment. "I lift weights," he said smugly, as if that were all he needed to say.

"So, tell me. How did you and your stepmother get along?"

The cool demeanor flickered for an instant. "Susan and I got along very well. We hardly ever saw each other."

"Does that mean when you did see each other there were personality conflicts?"

He winced. "If you mean did we fight, the answer is yes. She always wanted me to bring other kids home to play with, as if I were a little child. Honestly. Anybody can see that *I* am no little kid. I'm almost fourteen. I don't play those kid games any more."

"You don't? Then what do you do?"

"I do adult, mature things."

"Like what?"

"Well . . . downhill ski, for one thing. And lift weights. And play racquetball, if I can find a partner of my caliber. And watch sports on TV. The Lions did pretty well this year."

Ellen realized they were off the track. "So you and your mother got along fairly well. How about your father?"

"If you mean my *step*mother," snapped Christopher testily, "I guess so. My father and I get along okay, though we do occasionally have a difference of opinion. But who doesn't?"

"What did you do when your stepmother started getting thinner?"

"Nothing. Was I supposed to do something?"

Ellen decided she didn't like this kid. "Your dad mentioned you saw this coming, the starvation that caused her death."

"Of course. It was all the doing of that wench Amanda Cathcart."

"What?"

He shook his head pityingly. "Of course it was. A child could see it. She was still jealous of Susan's taking Father away from her, so she encouraged Susan to lose weight. And lose it. And lose it. Finally, you know, she died."

Confused, Ellen asked, "But how could Amanda persuade Susan to lose weight? Why should Susan have listened?"

"Because she felt guilty for taking Father away from her best friend in the world. Guilt makes people do strange things sometimes," he added airily, flexing a bicep admiringly.

Ellen sat back and thought for a moment, "What do you think of your half-sister Louetta?"

He snorted. "Oh, she's still such a child. We don't have a lot to talk about."

"Talk about? She's a year-old *baby*, Christopher! What do you mean you don't have a lot to talk about?"

Christopher, missing the slur, merely rolled his eyes heavenward. "May I leave now? I have a set of weights that I have to return to the store. They don't weigh in right."

Disgusted, Ellen waved him away. He left. She glanced at her watch: eleven o'clock.

Two people remained on the list that she hadn't seen yet. Louetta seemed unlikely to shed much light on the matter, but then you never knew. Ellen's black hands typed, "Please send in Bradley and Louetta Hartshaw."

In a moment the dark man sat before her, an unhappy baby in his arms. The baby had her father's olive skin, but her hair was probably her mother's colour. She was cranky about something: her little mouth twisted into a scowl and her eyebrows nearly touched, despite Bradley's desperate cooing.

"Aww, isn't she a dumpling?" Ellen marveled for Bradley's sake. He half-smiled, his attention still on Louetta. "May I hold her?"

He looked uneasily at her before he agreed. Gently they transferred the now-wailing infant to Ellen's arms. "Shh," she murmured, remembering all the tricks babysitting had taught her. Before long the child slept peacefully.

"Hey, that's pretty good," exclaimed Bradley softly.

Ellen examined Louetta's unblemished skin. No bruises, or makeup imitating them, so it was unlikely Bradley was supposed to be a child-beater. More likely a neglecter. "What are your plans concerning Louetta?"

"Uh . . . I don't follow you."

"Are you planning to hire a nursemaid, or governess, or whatever they're called?"

He shrugged. "I don't know. I haven't thought about it. Susan's death, you know . . . she always used to take care of Louetta . . . " His voice trailed off. Ellen's lips hardened.

"Tell me, why did you break up with Amanda Cathcart?" she asked innocently.

Immediately a suspicious, guarded look stamped itself on Bradley's face. Then he shrugged. "I didn't love her any more, I guess. It was gone. And Susan, my Susan, was so pretty, just like a dream. I can hardly believe she's gone." He gulped loudly.

Oh, brother, thought Ellen. "Christopher seems to have a definite idea about who killed her."

He perked up. "Who?"

She watched him carefully. "Amanda. For revenge."

He stared at her, then slowly nodded. "It all fits. The rejected lover, the betrayed best friend. She was both. Hey, you know, that's one of the reasons I stopped going out with her. Once her mind was made up, that was it. Totally inflexible. That wench." He scowled blackly. "I hope you can get evidence to prove it."

"So do I, Bradley. Would you mind taking Louetta? I believe I'd like to think for a while." He dutifully retrieved the baby and headed toward the door. "Just a moment, Bradley," she called.

He stiffened and then turned, a pleasant smile on his face. "Yes?"

"Whose idea was the tandem side-by-side?"

He relaxed. "Oh, mine. I wanted to go with her when she was out exercising. Seemed like we were never together. I guess . . . I guess that's how it'll always be now . . . " A sob caught in his throat, and he left.

Ellen stared at the ceiling. Eleven thirty. An hour and forty-five minutes. She wished Louisa were here. Louisa could do anything, just about. Well, maybe her legs weren't so good any more, but she could get along fine in her wheelchair. She sure was smart. Ellen tried to remember what Louisa had told her.

"Now you relax, young lady," she could almost hear the woman saying in her cracked, aging voice. "You're all tensed up, ain't no way your brain's gonna work right. But don't you turn into no sloth, neither. Relax them shoulders! Stand up once in a while—don't let that seat fall asleep!"

What else had she said? thought Ellen, pacing the room slowly, swinging her arms. Oh, yeah. "Ever'body runs by their own set of rules. Only a few people can see beyond the end of their nose." That was *not* Christopher, Ellen grimaced. What a lost cause.

"Afore you tackle the problem," continued the old woman's voice in Ellen's memory, "make sure you got all the information. A picture puzzle ain't nothing without all the pieces. Don't even try to put it together without knowing everything."

Ellen halted. *Did* she know everything she needed to solve the case? No. There was somebody else on the list she hadn't thought about. She crossed back to her table. "Please send in Wilbur Succint."

An old man came in, stooped over with age. "Mr. Succint?" Ellen asked, holding out her hand as she went to greet him. He ignored her and hobbled over to sit down wearily. She crossed back to her own chair, miffed about the handshake. The gentleman's white hair and weathered skin, together with his obviously painful back, gave Ellen the impression he ought to have retired years ago. "Mr. Succint, I'm Ellen, and I'd like to ask—"

"What?" shouted Wilbur, cupping a hand to his ear. "Say, I'm Wilbur Succint. Hope you don't mind me not shaking hands, but they shake fine by themselves." He laughed cheerfully at his own humour, despite the dark side of it. "Besides, the arthritis is hell today. Damned winter."

Relieved that he hadn't meant to hurt her, Ellen relaxed. "You're Susan Hartshaw's lawyer, aren't y—"

"What?"

Feeling uncomfortable at shouting at the old man, Ellen tried again. "You're Susan Hartshaw's lawyer, aren't you?"

"Yes, yes I am. And her parents' before that."

"Could you please tell me who benefits from her death?"

"Well, I don't suppose it's any secret now, if it ever was. Let's see . . . " He fumbled in his suitcoat's inner pockets and produced a folded piece of paper in his gnarled, wrinkled hands. Carefully, trembling a bit, he unfolded it. "This is a copy of the will she made last week," he explained. "It's slightly different from the one she and What's-his-name made when the baby was born. Don't even know if he knows about it."

"Did you say last *week*?"

"What's the matter, hard of hearing? Welcome to the club!" Wilbur laughed easily again. Ellen found herself smiling with him. "Yes, yes, last Wednes—no, must have been Thursday, stopped at the grocer's that afternoon. So Thursday. And here it says . . . " He straightened the trifocals perched precariously on his nose. "Ahhh . . . she left half her estate—that's *after* taxes, of course—to her husband Bradley. Then an eighth each to Christopher and Louetta, not to be given to them till their thirtieth birthdays." He peered over his glasses at her. "Got that one from Ann Landers. Didn't want easy money at an early age to spoil 'em, she said. Smart woman." He returned to the paper. "Then a quarter is to go to her dear childhood friend Amanda Cathcart." Satisfied, he turned back to Ellen.

"What makes this will different from the one she and Bradley made?"

"Why, the amount left to Amanda. There wasn't any before."

"Oh. Well, thank y—"

"What?"

"Thank you, Mr. Succint!" The old man smiled and hobbled out.

*Now* where am I? thought Ellen. It's noon, *everybody* has a motive (inheritance), and I'm frankly not even sure there's been murder here. Louisa, help me!

But Louisa wasn't there.

Ellen was.

And if Ellen was going to get her twenty dollars from stinky Simon Parker—and *not* hear about it the rest of forever—she had better get thinking. *Now.*

She had seventy minutes.

Ellen chewed her fingernails nervously. Now, do I have all the facts? I could ask, but only once. What if I don't? What if I haven't asked the right questions? What if someone has *lied* to me? What if—

Oh, what if, what if. Ellen smacked the table with her palm. I have to know.

"Have I all the clues necessary to solve this case?" she typed fearfully.

After a million-year wait, the one-word reply came back. *Yes.*

Yes, puzzled Ellen. I have all the pieces. I can now solve it myself.

For nearly an hour she paced the darkening room, testing theories, remembering statements, tones of voice, gestures, anything that seemed significant. Several times she grew excited with her own ideas, but each time she was forced to reject them.

Make the *theory* fit the *facts*. Make the *theory* fit the *facts*, she repeated to herself. Finally she typed, "Please send in Christopher Hartshaw."

The boy walked insolently into the room. "Well, what else do you want me to explain to you?"

Gritting her teeth, Ellen said, "You mentioned you lift weights." He nodded. "But you have problems with some of them." Again he nodded. "What were they?"

"Aww—the weights would say something like fourteen point three pounds, but it wasn't really, it was more like forty."

Her heart pounding, Ellen asked, "And how did you know that?"

With exaggerated patience, Christopher answered slowly. "I picked up the dumbbell and weighed myself. Then I put it down and weighed myself. Then I subtracted the smaller number from the bigger number. And the dumbbell weighed what was left. Remember second grade?"

"What was the scale you used?"

"Where are most scales in houses, El—"

"*Where was the scale you used*?"

"In the bathroom, of course."

Ellen felt like singing. "That's enough Christopher. You may leave." Clearly he didn't care much for the dismissal, but Ellen didn't notice as she typed furiously into the terminal. At one twelve, when she was through, she critically reviewed her work.

"Was Susan Hartshaw murdered? Yes," she read.

"By whom? Her husband, Bradley Hartshaw.

"How and why? He wanted money, but he didn't want to work for it. The easiest method, therefore, was to marry it. That's why he courted Amanda, who, although she no longer had money of her own, knew someone who did. Someone available, someone who wouldn't be nervous around a near-sister's boyfriend, someone almost asking to be married.

"So Bradley Hartshaw got to know Amanda, who loved him truly, with all her heart. Then he gradually moved into Susan's territory, winning her over eventually but leaving a scalded Amanda behind. Unconcerned, he married Susan and together they had a child.

"At that point, he decided he was tiring of Susan and her worries and he'd like to be rid of her. So he took advantage of her desire to trim down and encouraged her. With the popularity of the disorder known as 'anorexia nervosa' he was able to pretend that Susan had developed it, to her friends (even though she had none of the preceding symptoms). He vigorously supported her exercise and dieting, for in fact wasn't she walking right into his trap?

"Despite all her fasting and sweating, however, she didn't think she was losing weight very fast. But she was. She never knew exactly how much she weighed—because Bradley *kept misadjusting the bathroom scale*. When she really weighed one hundred thirty pounds, the scale said one forty-one. And so on. So when she died at seventy-four pounds, the scale only read one hundred—which was probably her goal.

"Bradley could possibly have gotten away with it if his son, who took it upon himself to play the role of the idle rich kid, hadn't checked the weights of his dumbbells on the same scale Susan used.

"Is this reasoning correct?"

Ellen waited tensely for the answer. Her time had run out. She fidgeted in her chair, her tushie fallen asleep. Simon Parker's unwelcome mug intruded upon her thoughts, and she pushed it away disdainfully. She thought about what she could do with twenty dollars, and what it would be like without twenty dollars . . . and what it could be like to be a member of a club of people who liked to solve mysteries, too . . . Lost in a daydream, she suddenly noticed the return message that cleared the screen.

*Yes.*

Ellen was just beginning to break into a wide grin when a second message appeared below that.

*Welcome to the club, Ellen.*

# CLOSE UP

1. With the help of a partner, hunt through the story and find five words or phrases that you don't understand. Using dictionaries, encyclopedias, and other reference materials, find out what the "mystery terms" mean. Write the definitions as footnotes that other people could refer to as they read the story.

2. In a small group identify the elements of a mystery that

are present in "Death of a Dieter." (For a summary of the elements, refer to the list you made for Close Up #1, "Elements of a Mystery.") Write notes on the elements that appear in the story. Here is an example of how your notes might begin:

1. Crime: the suspected murder of Susan Hartshaw (starved to death);
2. Discovery: victim collapses while cycling with her husband, Bradley.
3. With a partner, find the question Ellen asked that allowed her to solve the case. On your own, write a brief explanation of why the question was so important to the case. Compare your explanation to your partner's and combine them to make one clear and complete explanation.

# WIDE ANGLE

1. One of Ellen's motives for solving the case is the twenty dollars she can win from "stinky Simon Parker." With a partner, imagine what Ellen would say to Simon in order to enjoy her victory to the fullest. Write a script of the scene and read it to another group that has read "Death of a Dieter."

2. Ellen must pass a difficult test in order to become a member of the Mystery-Solver's Club of Earth. Write a journal entry describing how you feel about tests. You might want to write about
   • why we have tests;
   • the advantages and disadvantages of tests;
   • how students can cope with tests;
   • how teachers can help reduce the anxiety associated with tests; and
   • alternatives to the usual kinds of tests.

3. Ellen refers to "the popularity of the disorder known as 'anorexia nervosa.'" In a group of three, research the following aspects of the disease:
   a) the symptoms;
   b) the victims: who are they and what they have in common;
   c) the causes and the treatment.
   Use your school or public library or ask for information from your school nurse or health teacher. When the three of you have collected all the facts you can, design a poster that will inform people about the disease. After you have revised and proofread it, show the final version of your poster to your health teacher and the school nurse.

# THE CASE OF THE DEAD MILLIONAIRE

*by Donald J. Sobol*

"**I** SEE WILLIE Van Swelte just reached his twenty-first birthday," said Inspector Winters, looking up from his newspaper. "Tomorrow he gets the ten million his father left him."

"Didn't the old man commit suicide twenty years ago?" asked Dr. Haledjian.

"Yes," replied the inspector. "And there was always something that puzzled me about the case. Edgar Van Swelte shot himself below the heart. The bullet passed upward, piercing the heart all right. Death was instantaneous. But why did he aim like that—upward?

"Another thing—no suicide note. Nobody was in the house when he died. I've got a picture of the scene, though."

The inspector drew from his files a manila folder and picked out a glossy print. It showed Edgar Van Swelte dead. His body, seated in the kitchen, had fallen across the kitchen table. His right hand, still clutching the gun, rested on the table close beside the back of his head.

"The cook discovered the body upon returning from the market," continued the inspector. "She claims she telephoned the police promptly. When our photographer snapped this, it was 1 A.M. Edgar had been dead approximately six hours."

Haledjian studied the twenty-year-old photograph. Then he inquired, "How tall was Edgar?"

"Five-feet-eight, but long-legged, so that when he sat down, he appeared much shorter," answered the inspector.

"Then I should say there can be no doubt that he was murdered," announced Haledjian.

*How did Haledjian reach his conclusion?*

# THE CASE OF THE HITCHHIKER

## by Donald J. Sobol

"BOY, THANKS for the lift," exclaimed the young man as he slid off his knapsack and climbed into the front seat of the air-conditioned patrol car beside Sheriff Monahan. "Say, aren't you going to arrest me for bumming a ride?"

"Not today," replied the sheriff. "Too busy."

The young man grinned in relief. He took a chocolate bar from his knapsack, broke off a piece, and offered the rest to the sheriff.

"No, thanks," said the police officer, accelerating the car.

"You chasing someone?" asked the hitchhiker.

"Four men just held up the First National Bank. They escaped in a big black sedan."

"Hey," gasped the hitchhiker. "I saw a black sedan about ten minutes ago. It had four men in it. They nearly ran me off the road. First car I saw in an hour. But they took a left turn. They're headed west, not north!"

Sheriff Monahan braked the patrol car and swung it around. The young man began peeling an orange, putting the rinds tidily into a paper bag.

"Look at the heat shining off the road ahead," said the sheriff. "Must be eighty-five in the shade today."

"Must be," agreed the hitchhiker. "Wait—you passed the turn off—where're you going?"

"To the police station," snapped the sheriff—*How come?*

# CLOSE UP

1. In a small group, brainstorm possible answers to the question at the end of each of the mysteries. Present your solutions to the class. After all the guesses have been heard, appoint a classmate to read aloud the true solutions. The solutions are printed at the end of Kaleidoscope, p. 298.

# WIDE ANGLE

1. Work with a partner or in a small group and write your own two-minute mystery. Read it aloud to another group and ask them to solve it.
2. With a partner, write a script for and dramatize "The Case of the Hitchhiker." Add what happens after the sheriff takes the hitchhiker to the police station for questioning. If you write your script on a word processor, you can print out a copy for each member of the cast.

# KALEIDOSCOPE

1. Many puzzles and games are mysteries of a sort. A crossword puzzle, for example, involves clues and solutions. Working in a small group, brainstorm games you have played that involve keeping secrets or finding out the secrets of other players. Choose one of the games and create an advertisement for it that would make a mystery-lover want to play it.

2. You are the detective in the cartoon below. In your notebook, describe the events leading up to the discovery of the rhinoceros. Make sure you include facts, physical descriptions, dialogue, and the emotions the characters feel. If you like, use the caption as the last line of your description. Have a conference with a partner to revise your writing. Remember to note your corrections on your Personal Usage Sheet.

"The Far Side" cartoons are reprinted by permission of Chronicle Features, San Francisco.

**"Blast! Up to now, the rhino was one of my prime suspects."**

3. Picture in your mind's eye the window of a pawnshop and the items displayed there—a clarinet, some jewellery, a vase, and other objects. One of the items has been stolen from its owner. Draw a picture of the object and write the story of how its owner felt about it, how it was stolen, and how it ended up in the pawnshop.

4. Choose a partner. One of you was discovered at the scene of a crime and apprehended by the police. The other is the police officer. (The two of you will have to agree on the circumstances of the crime.) The suspect claims that she or he is innocent; the police officer holds the opposite opinion. Write an argument for your side of the story, depending on whether you are the suspect or the police officer. Each of you should role-play your argument for a small group, letting them decide who is most believable.

5. Find a mystery that has been recorded on tape—an episode from the Sherlock Holmes radio show, for example. Listen to the cassette in a small group and make notes on the suspects, the clues, and the possible motives. Have someone who has heard the whole mystery turn the tape off just before the solution is given. Brainstorm predictions of the ending and decide which ending is best. Play the end of the mystery and compare your prediction with the real solution.

### Solution to "The Case of the Dead Millionaire"

Had Van Swelte shot himself "from below the heart" while seated, he must have held the gun close to his lap. Since death was "instantaneous," it would have been impossible for him, a short-bodied man, to have lifted the hand with the gun until it "rested on the table" after shooting himself.

### Solution to "The Case of the Hitchhiker"

The hitchhiker quickly confessed to being one of the hold-up gang, left behind to misdirect pursuit. His story was obviously phony, since he "broke off a piece" of chocolate. Standing for more than an hour in eighty-five-degree heat, as he claimed, the chocolate bar would have been soupy.

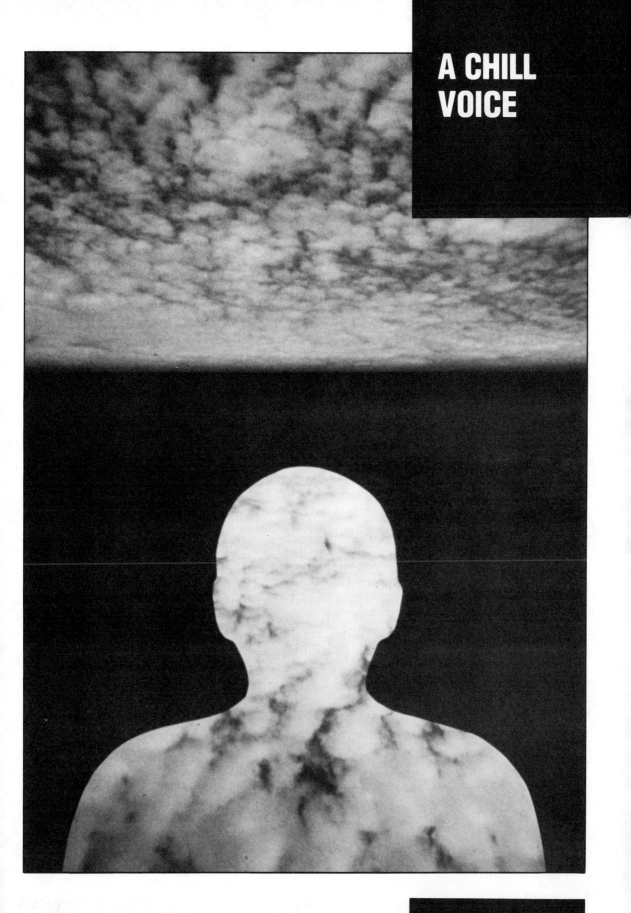

# A CHILL VOICE

# AT THE RIVER-GATES

*by Philippa Pearce*

LOTS OF SISTERS I had (said the old man), good girls, too; and one elder brother. Just the one. We were at either end of the family: the eldest, my brother John— we always called him Beany, for some reason; then the girls, four of them; then me. I was Tiddler, and the reason for that was plain.

Our father was a flour miller, and we lived just beside the mill. It was a water-mill, built right over the river, with the mill-wheel underneath. To understand what happened that wild night, all those years ago, you have to understand a bit about the working of the mill-stream. About a hundred yards before the river reached the mill, it divided: the upper river flowed on to power the mill, as I've said; the lower river, leaving the upper river through sluice-gates, flowed to one side of the mill and past it; and then the upper and lower rivers joined up again well below the mill. The sluice-gates could be opened or shut by the miller to let more or less water through from the upper to the lower river. You can see the use of that: the miller controlled the flow of water to power his mill; he could also draw off any floodwaters that came down.

Being a miller's son, I can never remember not understanding that. I was a little tiddler, still at school, when my brother, Beany, began helping my father in the mill. He was as good as a man, my father said. He was strong, and he learnt the feel of the grain, and he was clever with the mill machinery, and he got on with the other men in the mill—there were only ten of them, counting two carters. He understood the gates, of course, and how to get just the right head of water for the mill. And he liked it all: he liked the work he did, and the life; he liked the mill, and the river, and the long river-bank. One day he'd be the miller after my father, everyone said.

I was too young to feel jealousy about that; but I would never have felt jealous of Beany, because Beany was the best brother you could have had. I loved and admired him more than anyone I knew or could imagine knowing. He was very good to me. He used to take me with him when you might have thought a little boy would have been in the way. He took me with him when he went fishing, and he taught me to fish. I learnt patience, then, from Beany. There were plenty of roach and dace in the river; and sometimes we caught trout or pike; and once we caught an eel, and I was first of all terrified and then screaming with excitement at the way it whipped about on the bank, but Beany held it and killed it, and my mother made it into eel-pie. He knew about the fish in the river, and the little creatures, too. He showed me fresh-water shrimps, and leeches—"Look, Tiddler, they make them-selves into croquet-hoops when they want to go anywhere!" and he showed me the little underwater cottages of caddis-worms. He knew where to get good watercress for Sunday tea—you could eat watercress from our river, in those days.

We had an old boat on the river, and Beany would take it upstream to inspect the banks for my father. The banks had to be kept sound: if there was a breach, it would let the water escape and reduce the water-power for the mill. Beany took Jess, our dog, with him in the boat, and he often took me. Beany was the only person I've ever known who could point out a kingfisher's nest in the river-bank. He knew about birds. He once showed me a flycatcher's nest in the brickwork below the sluice-gates, just above where the water dashed and roared at its highest. Once, when we were in the boat, he pointed ahead to an otter in the water. I held on to Jess's collar then.

It was Beany who taught me to swim. One summer it was hotter than anyone remembered, and Beany was going from the mill up to the gates to shut in more water. Jess was following him, and as he went he gave me a wink, so I followed too, although I didn't know why. As usual, he opened the gates with the great iron spanner, almost as long in the handle as he was tall. Then he went down to the pool in the lower river, as if to see the water-level there. But as he went he was unbuttoning his flour-whitened waistcoat; by the time he reached the pool he was naked, and he dived straight in. He came up with his hair plastered over his eyes, and he called to me: "Come on, Tiddler! Just time for a swimming lesson!" Jess sat on the bank and watched us.

Jess was really my father's dog, but she attached herself to Beany. She loved Beany. Everyone loved Beany, and he was good to everyone. Especially, as I've said, to me. Just sometimes he'd say, "I'm off on my own now, Tiddler," and then I knew better than to ask to go with him. He'd go sauntering up the river-bank by himself, except for Jess at his heels. I don't think he did anything very particular when he went off on his own. Just the river and the river-bank were happiness enough for him.

He was still not old enough to have got himself a girl, which might have changed things a bit; but he wasn't too young to go to the War. The War broke out in 1914, when I was still a boy, and Beany went.

It was sad without Beany; but it was worse than that. I was too young to understand then; but, looking back, I realize what was wrong. There was fear in the house. My parents became gloomy and somehow secret. So many young men were being killed at the Front. Other families in the village had had word of a son's death. The news came in a telegram. I overheard my parents talking of those deaths, those telegrams, although not in front of the girls or me. I saw my mother once, in the middle of the morning, kneeling by Beany's bed, praying.

So every time Beany came home on leave, alive, we were lucky.

But when Beany came, he was different. He loved us as much, but he was different. He didn't play with me as he used to do; he would sometimes stare at me as though he didn't see me. When I shouted "Beany!" and rushed at him, he would start as if he'd woken up. Then he'd smile, and be good to me, almost as he used to be. But, more often than he used to, he'd be off all by himself up the river-bank, with Jess at his heels. My mother, who longed to have him within her sight for every minute of leave, used to watch him go, and sigh. Once I heard her say to my father that the river-bank did Beany good, as if he were sickening for some strange disease. Once one of the girls was asking Beany about the Front and the trenches, and he was telling her this and that, and we were all interested, and suddenly he stopped and said, "No. It's hell." And walked away alone, up the green, quiet river-bank. I suppose if one place was hell, then the other was heaven to him.

After Beany's leaves were over, the mill-house was gloomy again; and my father had to work harder, without Beany's help in the mill. Nowadays he had to work the gates all by himself, a thing that Beany had been taking over from him. If the gates needed working at night, my father and Beany had always gone there together. My mother hated it nowadays when my father had to go to the gates alone at night: she was afraid he'd slip and fall in the water, and, although he could swim, accidents could happen to a man alone in the dark. But, of course, my father wouldn't let her come with him, or any of my sisters, and I was still considered much too young. That irked me.

Well, one season had been very dry and the river level had

dropped. The gates were kept shut to get up a head of water for the mill. Then clouds began to build up heavily on the horizon, and my father said he was sure it was going to rain; but it didn't. All day storms rumbled in the distance. In the evening the rain began. It rained steadily: my father had already been once to the gates to open the flashes. He was back at home, drying off in front of the fire. The rain still drove against the windows. My mother said, "It can't come down worse than this." She and my sisters were still up with my father. Even I wasn't in bed, although I was supposed to have been. No one could have slept for the noise of the rain.

Suddenly the storm grew worse—much worse. It seemed to explode over our heads. We heard a pane of glass in the skylight over the stairs shatter with the force of it, and my sisters ran with buckets to catch the water pouring through. Oddly, my mother didn't go to see the damage: she stayed with my father, watching him like a lynx. He was fidgeting up and down, paying no attention to the skylight either, and suddenly he said he'd have to go up to the gates again and open everything to carry all possible floodwater into the lower river. This was what my mother had been dreading. She made a great outcry, but she knew it was no use. My father put on his tarpaulin jacket again and took his oil lamp and a thick stick—I don't know why, nor did he, I think. Jess always hated being out in the rain, but she followed him. My mother watched him from the back door, lamenting, and urging him to be careful. A few steps from the doorway and you couldn't see him any longer for the driving rain.

My mother's lingering at the back door gave me my chance. I got my boots on and an oilskin cape I had (I wasn't a fool, even if I was little) and I whipped out of the front door and worked my way round in the shelter of the house to the back and then took the path my father had taken to the river, and made a dash for it, and caught up with my father and Jess, just as they were turning up the way towards the gates. I held on to Jess's tail for quite a bit before my father noticed me. He was terribly angry, of course, but he didn't want to turn back with me, and he didn't like to send me back alone, and perhaps in his heart of hearts he was glad of a little human company on such a night. So we all three struggled up to the gates together. Just by the gates my father found me some shelter between a tree-trunk and a stack of drift-wood. There I crouched, with Jess to keep me company.

I was too small to help my father with the gates, but there was one thing I could do. He told me to hold his lamp so that the light shone on the gates and what he was doing. The illumination was very poor, partly because of the driving rain, but at least it was better than nothing, and anyway my father knew those gates by heart. Perhaps he gave me the job of holding the light so that I had something to occupy my mind and keep me from being afraid.

There was plenty to be afraid of on that night of storm.

Directing what light I could on to my father also directed and concentrated my attention on him. I could see his laborious motions as he heaved the great spanner into place. Then he began to try to rack up with it, but the wind and the rain were so strong that I could see he was having the greatest difficulty. Once I saw him stagger sideways nearly into the blackness of the river. Then I wanted to run out from my shelter and try to help him, but he had strictly forbidden me to do any such thing, and I knew he was right.

Young as I was, I knew—it came to me as I watched him—that he couldn't manage the gates alone in that storm. I suppose he was a man already just past the prime of his strength: the wind and the rain were beating him; the river would beat him.

I shone the light as steadily as I could, and gripped Jess by the collar, and I think I prayed.

I was so frightened then that, afterwards, when I wasn't frightened, I could never be sure of what I had seen, or what I thought I had seen, or what I imagined I had seen. Through the confusion of the storm I saw my father struggling and staggering, and, as I peered, my vision seemed to blur and to double, so that I began sometimes to see one man, sometimes two. My father seemed to have a shadow-self besides himself, who steadied him, heaved with him, worked with him, and at last together they had opened the sluice-gates and let the flood through.

When it was done, my father came back to where Jess and I were, and leant against the tree. He was gasping for breath and exhausted, and had a look on his face that I cannot describe. From his expression I knew that he had *felt* the shadow with him, just as I had seen it. And Jess was agitated too, straining against my hold, whining.

I looked past my father, and I could still see something by the sluice-gates: a shadow that had separated itself from my father, and lingered there. I don't know how I could have seen it in the darkness. I don't know. My father slowly turned and looked in the direction that he saw me looking. The shadow began to move away from the gates, away from us; it began to go up the long river-bank beyond the gates, into the darkness there. It seemed to me that the rain and the wind stilled a little as it went.

Jess wriggled from my grasp and was across the gates and up the river-bank, following the vanished shadow. I had made no move, uttered no word, but my father said to me, "Let them go!" I looked at him, and his face was streaming with tears as well as with rain.

He took my hand and we fought our way back to the house. The whole house was lit up, to light us home, and my mother stood at the back door, waiting. She gave a cry of horror when she saw me with my father; and then she saw his face, and her own went quite white. He stumbled into her arms, and he sobbed and sobbed. I didn't know until that night that grown men could cry. My mother led my father indoors, and I don't know what talk they had together. My sisters looked after me, dried me, scolded me, put me to bed.

The next day the telegram came to say that Beany had been killed in action in Flanders.

It was some time after that that Jess came home. She was wet through, and my mother thought she was ill, for she sat shivering by the fire, and for two days would neither eat nor drink. My father said: "Let her be."

I'm an old man: it all happened so many years ago, but I've never forgotten my brother Beany. He was so good to us all.

# FOCUSSING

1. Play a word-association game. Form a group of three or four and appoint one group member to write down all the words and ideas that are brought to mind by the word *ghosts*.

2. Working with a partner, use the words and ideas from #1 above and write a cinquain poem. Transfer your poem onto poster paper, decorate it with artwork, and display it in the classroom.

3. With two partners, conduct a survey to find out how many people believe in ghosts. One of you should focus on people 6–12 years old, another on people 13–19, and another on people 20 and older. Combine your results and summarize them in a report to the class. There are computer programs that can help you tabulate the results of surveys; check with your teacher to see if such a program is available.

4. Write a journal entry describing

   a) whether or not you have ever seen a ghost. If you have, tell how you reacted; if you have not, tell how you might react.

   **or**

   b) any ghost story that you have read or heard, or a ghost film that you have seen, and what you think about it.

5. Gather pictures of eerie settings from magazines and newspapers. Write a paragraph that describes one of the pictures. Have a partner read your description and try to match it to the right picture.

# THE BEST GHOST STORY

## by Daniel Cohen

T HIS IS the best real ghost story that I have ever heard.

The strange events took place on December 7, 1918. World War I had just ended. Lieutenant David McConnell was an eighteen-year-old British trainee pilot. He was stationed at a Royal Air Force (RAF) base in a place called Scampton in the English Midlands. On the morning of December 7, his commanding officer asked him to fly a plane to a field at Tadcaster. Tadcaster was about sixty miles northwest of Scampton.

McConnell was to be accompanied by a second pilot in another plane. He was to leave the plane he flew at Tadcaster and return to Scampton in the second plane. It was a routine mission for moving a plane from one field to another.

At about 11:30 A.M., shortly before he took off, McConnell spoke to his roommate, Lieutenant Larkin. McConnell, Larkin, and a third officer, Lieutenant Garner Smith, had planned to go out that evening. McConnell said he had to deliver a plane to Tadcaster, but he expected to be back the same afternoon. There was no reason to change plans.

During the flight to Tadcaster, Mc-Connell and the second pilot ran into an unexpected heavy fog. They landed their planes in a field and found a house with a telephone. They phoned Scampton for instructions. The commanding officer said they should use their own judgment about whether to go on or not. So the pair took off again in the direction of Tadcaster. The fog got worse. Finally McConnell's companion was forced to make a landing, but McConnell continued the flight.

He reached Tadcaster safely. A witness at the field saw his plane make its approach for landing. But the angle of approach was too steep, and the plane crashed. When witnesses reached the plane they found Lieutenant McConnell dead. He had struck his head on the machine gun mounted in front of the pilot's seat. His watch had also been broken in the crash. It was stopped at exactly 3:25 P.M.

At about the same time that McConnell was killed, Larkin was sitting in the room the two of them shared at Scampton. He was reading a book and smoking. His back was to the door. He heard footsteps coming up the corridor, then he heard the door open and close.

A voice said, "Hello, boy." That was McConnell's usual greeting. Larkin turned and saw McConnell—or what he took to be McConnell—standing in the doorway about eight feet from him. Larkin assumed it was McConnell because of the hat the figure was wearing. McConnell had been in the Naval Air Service before joining the RAF. He was very proud of this. Often he wore a Navy cap instead of the standard flying helmet. The figure in the doorway was wearing a Navy cap.

Larkin, of course, didn't know what had just happened at Tadcaster. He didn't think there was anything odd about his roommate coming in at that moment. He said, "Hello! Back already?" The figure replied, "Yes. Got there all right. Had a good trip." The figure then said, "Well, cheerio!" Then the figure turned and went out, closing the door behind him.

It was a very ordinary scene. Except for one fact. The man Lieutenant Larkin thought he had seen come in the door had just been killed sixty miles away.

A short time later, at 3:45 P.M., Lieutenant Garner Smith entered Larkin's room. He asked about McConnell and said he hoped that he would be back early so the three of them could still go out as planned. Larkin said McConnell was already back. He told Garner Smith that McConnell had come into that very room less than half an hour ago. But we know that McConnell was dead at 3:25. That means that Larkin must have thought he had seen McConnell at almost the exact moment McConnell died.

News of McConnell's death did not reach Scampton immediately. Larkin did not hear of it until early evening when he was eating dinner. An announcement was made over the base loudspeaker. Larkin could hardly believe what he heard. He assumed at first that McConnell had returned to Scampton safely after his mission to Tadcaster. Then he must have taken another plane up. It was during this second flight, Larkin reasoned, that his roommate had been killed.

Only later that evening did Larkin discover the truth. McConnell had been killed at Tadcaster. He died at almost exactly the moment that he had been "seen" in the room they shared at Scampton.

Larkin told other men on the base of his strange experience. Garner Smith confirmed that he had spoken to Larkin at 3:45 P.M., and had been told that McConnell had entered the room within the last half hour.

A short while later McConnell's family heard about the experience. They wrote to Larkin, asking him what had happened. On December 22, he sent them a letter setting down all the details that he could remember. It was a clear, matter-of-fact letter. Lieutenant Larkin did not believe in ghosts before this experience. He was still skeptical about them afterwards. But he could not explain what had happened. All he could do was insist that things happened the way he said they did.

Eventually the story came to the attention of the Society of Psychical Research. An investigator for the Society talked to Larkin and to Garner Smith. They stuck to their original stories.

The tale of the "ghost" of Lieutenant David McConnell is a strange one, I'm sure you will agree. But it is not as strange as many other ghost stories. The ghost did not shriek or moan. It did not rattle any chains. It did not warn about things that were going to happen. It did not even look like a ghost. Yet I said this was the best real ghost story that I have ever heard. Why?

The reason is because the evidence is so very good. Many ghost stories are secondhand. They are told by someone who heard it from someone else. But in this case we have an eyewitness account. Everyone who interviewed Lieutenant Larkin found him to be a reliable, honest, and unhysterical young man. He was not the sort of person who normally went around "seeing things." Nothing like that had ever happened to him before.

Another problem with many "real" ghost stories is that they happened a long time before anyone bothered to write them down. Sometimes it is months or years before a person puts down in black and white the details of his ghostly experience. And time plays tricks with the human memory. Even honest people with good memories can make mistakes about details. The longer the period of time between the event and the telling, the more mistakes will be made.

In ghost stories, details are important, in order to establish what really happened. Larkin wrote down his account a little over two weeks after the experience. It would have been better if he had sat down and written it that very night. But he was not interested in psychical research. He did not think his story was ever going to be used

as evidence to prove that ghosts exist. He wrote it down only because his dead friend's family asked him to.

As far as ghostly evidence goes a two-week gap is not too bad. The investigators for the SPR also checked Larkin's written account with some of the people he had talked to in the days following December 7. They all agreed that what he had written was just what he had told them. This strengthens the case. Larkin's memory of the event seems excellent.

All the times are well established. There was a witness to the time McConnell was killed. The dead pilot's smashed watch, stopped at 3:25 P.M., confirms this.

Probably the most important evidence is Garner Smith's visit. Garner Smith did not see McConnell's ghost or whatever it was. He did not see anything unusual. But at 3:45, less than one half hour after the appearance of the figure, he heard the story. At that moment there was no way in which either he or Larkin could possibly have known that their friend was dead. If Larkin had begun talking about seeing McConnell only after he found out that McConnell was dead, the case would not be nearly as good.

But he told his story at a time when he had no reason to suspect there was anything strange about it.

Does this mean that we have proof that Lieutenant Larkin saw the ghost of his dear friend? Not necessarily. There are several other possible explanations. Let's take a look at them.

The first possible explanation is that the story is a hoax. Many ghost stories that are supposed to be real turn out to be false. People make them up in order to attract attention, or just to have a good story to tell.

If this account is a hoax, then it could not have been Larkin's alone. Garner Smith would have to be in on it.

Considering everything a hoax does not seem very likely in this case. It would mean that two RAF officers were telling lies about the death of their friend and fellow officer. Many, many RAF men had been killed during the war. Death was not the sort of thing that any of them took lightly.

Even if they had wanted to fool the other men at the base, it would have been downright cruel to tell the story to the dead man's family. But Larkin did tell the story to the family. He told them in writing. Garner Smith later confirmed the story to SPR investigators. We cannot prove that this ghost story was not the result of a hoax. But that explanation does not really seem to fit.

Another possible explanation is mistaken identity. Sometimes people think they have seen the ghost of someone dead. Then it turns out that what they have seen is a living person who resembles the dead person.

Larkin did not see the figure he took to be McConnell for long. It was eight feet away, standing in a doorway. The light was not good. He spoke to the figure and the figure answered. But, if you recall, he never addressed the figure as McConnell. Nor did the figure ever say it was McConnell. Larkin just assumed that it was because it looked like McConnell, and had entered the room

he shared with McConnell at about the time he expected McConnell to be there.

The figure was wearing a flight suit. On the base there must have been dozens of young men about the same age and size as McConnell who might have been wearing flight suits at that time. If one of them had wandered into the room, he might have looked very much like McConnell.

He might have—except for the hat. Remember that McConnell usually wore a Navy cap instead of the usual flight helmet. He was the only man on the base to do that. The figure in the doorway was also wearing a Navy cap. Mistaken identity can be ruled out.

There is another possible explanation. Larkin may have dreamed that he saw McConnell. He insists that he was awake. We know he was awake when Garner Smith came into the room. But we cannot be sure that he did not doze off somewhat earlier. Sometimes people who are sitting quietly can fall asleep without knowing it.

Dreams are strange things. When we dream we are not completely cut off from the outside world. We can hear noises and feel sensations. Sometimes we fit these outside noises and sensations into our dreams. Many people begin to dream of fire engines or police sirens when they hear their alarm clocks ringing in the morning. Something of the sort may have happened to Lieutenant Larkin.

It might have happened this way. Larkin was sitting in his room and dozed off. In his sleep he heard footsteps, real ones, in the hall. Then he heard a door slam—not his door, but another one in the building. These sounds may have become part of his dream. McConnell had already told him he would be back that afternoon. Larkin may have been anxious for his roommate to come back in time for them to go out that evening. So when he heard the footsteps, and the door slam in his sleep, he may have dreamed that McConnell had returned.

There is no way of proving the experience happened this way. But the explanation is a possible one.

Another possible explanation is that Lieutenant Larkin had a hallucination. That is, he saw something that was not there while he was wide awake. You don't have to be crazy to have hallucinations. They are much more common than most people suspect.

That brings up an interesting question. What is the difference between a hallucination of this sort and a ghost? Larkin was perfectly normal. He did not go around seeing things that were not there all the time. But on this occasion he did see something that was not there, something that could not possibly be there—his dead roommate. Does it make any difference whether we call this figure a hallucination or a ghost? Hallucination sounds more "scientific" and more "realistic," but is it? Psychical researchers often argue over questions like this.

And even if Larkin had been asleep, and the whole thing was a dream, there is still something very strange. Why was he dreaming about McConnell at what may have been the exact moment that McConnell was killed?

Could it be just coincidence? Perhaps it could be. But it is a very strange coincidence.

Now you see why I have called this the best "real" ghost story I ever heard.

# CLOSE UP

1. Make a list of the four possible explanations for what Larkin saw. Write a few sentences stating which explanation you think is the best and why. You may use your own explanation if you wish.

# WIDE ANGLE

1. Put yourself in Larkin's place and write his letter to the McConnell family, giving all the details you can remember about the incident. (Remember that your letter is being mailed on 22 December, and will arrive around Christmastime.)

2. Pretend that you are a member of the Society of Psychical Research sent to interview Larkin to find out if his story is true. Write out the questions you would ask him and have a partner play the role of Larkin. After the interview, prepare an official report. Revise the report with the help of your partner and write up a polished copy. You and your partner could edit your report on screen if you compose it on a word processor, and then print the polished version on the printer.

# THE MONKEY'S PAW
*by W.W. Jacobs*

## CHARACTERS

NARRATOR

HERBERT WHITE

MR. WHITE

SERGEANT MORRIS

MRS. WHITE

STRANGER

## SCENE 1

**NARRATOR:** It is a cold, wet night outside. We are inside a warm, cozy house. A fire is burning brightly in the fireplace. An old man, Mr. White, and his son, Herbert, are playing chess. Mrs. White is knitting by the fire. They are expecting a visitor—Sergeant Morris, who has just come back from India. There is a knock at the door.

**MR. WHITE:** There he is. I'll let him in.

**NARRATOR:** Mr. White goes to the door and returns with a tall, red-faced man. Sergeant Morris shakes hands with everyone and goes to the fire.

**SERGEANT MORRIS:** Ah, this feels good! It's really cold outside.

**MR. WHITE:** Even with this bad weather, it must be good to get back home to England.

**HERBERT:** I'd love to go to India! It must be interesting. England is so dull. Nothing exciting ever happens here.

**MR. WHITE:** Morris, why don't you tell us more about that monkey's paw we've heard about?

**SERGEANT MORRIS:** There's nothing to it, really. Just some strange old Eastern magic.

**HERBERT:** Oh, please tell us! It's a good night for a story.

**SERGEANT MORRIS:** Well, it looks just like an ordinary paw. Nothing special about it.

**NARRATOR:** He takes a small paw from his pocket and gives it to Herbert.

**MRS. WHITE:** Ugh! Herbert, how can you touch that awful old thing?

**MR. WHITE:** It sure doesn't look like magic. What's so special about it?

**SERGEANT MORRIS:** An old holy man in India put a spell on it. He wanted to show that fate rules people's lives, and that if you mess with fate, you'll get hurt. He put a spell on the paw so that three different men could have three wishes from it.

**MRS. WHITE:** You sound so serious about it! It's just an ugly old paw, after all.

**HERBERT:** Why don't you make three wishes on it, Sergeant Morris?

**SERGEANT MORRIS** (*looking hard at Herbert*): I have. (*He turns pale at the thought.*)

**MRS. WHITE:** Well, did you really get the three wishes?

**SERGEANT MORRIS:** Yes, I did. But let's not talk about it.

**MRS. WHITE:** Has anyone else wished?

**SERGEANT MORRIS:** The first man had his three wishes. I don't know what the first two were. But the third wish was for death. That's how I got the paw.

**HERBERT:** You mean he wished to die, and he did?

**SERGEANT MORRIS:** Yes.

**MRS. WHITE:** So what? It's probably just a coincidence.

**MR. WHITE:** I'm not so sure. If you've had your three wishes, why don't you give the paw to someone else?

**SERGEANT MORRIS:** I thought of selling it, but I don't think I will. It has caused enough trouble already.

**NARRATOR:** Sergeant Morris picks up the paw and throws it on the logs burning in the fireplace.

**MR. WHITE:** Don't do that! (*He snatches the paw from the fire.*) Sergeant Morris, if you don't want the paw, then give it to me.

**SERGEANT MORRIS:** Take it. But you're a fool if you do. And don't blame me for what happens. Listen, be sensible. Burn it.

**MR. WHITE:** No. I want it. How do you make the wishes?

**SERGEANT MORRIS:** Hold it up in your right hand and wish aloud. But I warn you of the result.

**NARRATOR:** Mrs. White gets up to make dinner.

**MRS. WHITE:** Why don't you wish for four pairs of hands for me?

**SERGEANT MORRIS:** If you *must* wish, wish for something sensible. But I think you'll be sorry.

**NARRATOR:** The monkey's paw was forgotten during dinner. For the rest of the evening the Whites listened to Sergeant Morris talk about India.

**SERGEANT MORRIS:** My goodness, it's late. I've talked too much. I must be going. But before I leave, I wish you'd throw the monkey's paw away.

**MR. WHITE:** Don't worry, Sergeant. We'll be careful.

**NARRATOR:** Sergeant Morris puts on his coat, says goodnight, and walks out the door.

**HERBERT** (*looking at the paw*): A magic monkey's paw—how silly! Wish to be a king, Father, then Mother can't boss you around.

**MRS. WHITE** (*laughing*): Wish for 200 pounds to pay off the mortgage.

**MR. WHITE:** Why not? Let's try it. (*He holds up the paw in his right hand.*) I wish for 200 pounds.

**NARRATOR:** Suddenly, he drops the paw.

**MR. WHITE:** Ahhh! It moved! It twisted like a snake! I swear it did!

**MRS. WHITE:** It couldn't have. It's just your imagination.

SERGEANT MORRIS

**HERBERT:** I don't see any money. (*He picks up the paw and puts it on the table.*) I guess it doesn't work.

**MR. WHITE:** There's no harm done. But it gave me quite a scare. Now let's go to bed and forget about magic for a while.

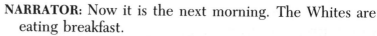

## SCENE 2

MR. WHITE

MRS. WHITE

**NARRATOR:** Now it is the next morning. The Whites are eating breakfast.

**MRS. WHITE:** Isn't it funny how in the light of day your night fears seem so foolish? That paw is really silly. How could it grant wishes? Even if it could, how could wishes hurt you?

**HERBERT:** The money could drop on your head.

**MR. WHITE:** That's not how it happens. The wishes are granted so naturally it seems the paw has nothing to do with it. It seems like a coincidence.

**HERBERT:** Well, save some of the money for me. I've got to get to work. So long.

**NARRATOR:** Herbert goes off to work and the day passes as usual. Later, as it's getting dark, Mr. and Mrs. White sit down to tea.

**MRS. WHITE:** Herbert will have a laugh when he gets home. How could a monkey's paw give us 200 pounds?

**MR. WHITE:** Well, the paw did move in my hand, like it was alive. I felt it. What's the matter?

**NARRATOR:** Mrs. White does not answer her husband. She is watching a man who is standing at the gate. Finally he comes to the door. As Mrs. White lets him in, she thinks of the 200 pounds.

**STRANGER:** I was asked to come here. I'm from Maw and Meggins.

**MRS. WHITE:** Maw and Meggins? That's where Herbert works! Is anything wrong? Has anything happened to him? What is it?

**MR. WHITE:** Now, sit down, Mother. I'm sure he hasn't brought bad news.

**STRANGER:** I'm sorry—

**MRS. WHITE:** He's hurt! He's hurt, isn't he?

**STRANGER:** He was badly hurt. But he's not in any pain.

**MRS. WHITE:** Thank goodness! Thank—

**NARRATOR:** She stops when she looks at the man's face. She realizes what he has said. There is an awful silence.

**MR. WHITE:** What—what happened?

**STRANGER:** He was caught in the machinery. He was killed instantly.

**NARRATOR:** Mr. White takes his wife's hands.

**STRANGER:** The company wanted me to give you their deep sympathy.

NARRATOR: There is no answer. The old woman is pale. Her husband is hardly breathing.

STRANGER: Maw and Meggins wish to give you some money. Your son was a good worker for them.

NARRATOR: Mr. White drops his wife's hand. He stares with horror at the Stranger.

MR. WHITE (*whispering*): How much money?

STRANGER: Two hundred pounds.

NARRATOR: Mrs. White screams as Mr. White faints.

## SCENE 3

NARRATOR: The Whites buried their son in the cemetery two miles away. As the days passed, they hardly spoke. They had nothing to talk about except sorrow. It is now a week after the funeral. The old man is awakened at night by his wife.

MRS. WHITE: The monkey's paw! The paw!

MR. WHITE: Where? What's the matter?

MRS. WHITE: I want it! Where is it?

MR. WHITE: It's downstairs. But why do you want it?

MRS. WHITE: Oh, why didn't I think of it before? It's so easy!

MR. WHITE: Think of what? What are you talking about?

MRS. WHITE: The other two wishes. We've had only one.

MR. WHITE: Wasn't that one enough?

MRS. WHITE: No! We'll have one more. Get the paw and wish for Herbert to be alive again.

MR. WHITE: My God! You're crazy!

MRS. WHITE: No I'm not. Hurry! Get it and wish.

MR. WHITE: You don't know what you're saying.

MRS. WHITE: The first wish came true. Why not the second?

MR. WHITE: It was just a terrible coincidence.

MRS. WHITE: Go and get the paw and wish.

NARRATOR: Mr. White goes downstairs in the dark. He feels his way to the table where the monkey's paw lies. He rushes back to the bedroom. His wife's face is terrible to see.

MRS. WHITE: Hurry! Wish!

MR. WHITE: It's foolish and wicked. The paw is evil.

MRS. WHITE: Wish!

MR. WHITE (*raising his arm*): I wish my son alive.

NARRATOR: The paw falls to the floor. Mr. and Mrs. White are silent. They wait until the candle burns out. Then they go back to bed. They can't sleep. A stair creaks. A mouse runs through the wall. Mr. White takes a deep breath. He takes the matches, strikes one, and goes downstairs for another candle. At the foot of the stairs the match goes out. There is a quiet knock at the front

HERBERT

STRANGER

door. Mr. White doesn't dare breathe. The knock comes again. He turns and runs back to the bedroom. A loud knock sounds through the house.

**MRS. WHITE:** What's that noise?

**MR. WHITE:** It's a rat. Just a rat.

**MRS. WHITE:** No, its Herbert! It's my son!

**NARRATOR:** She runs to the door. Mr. White stops her.

**MRS. WHITE:** Let me go! I forgot the cemetery is two miles away. That's what took him so long. I must let him in!

**MR. WHITE:** You can't let him in!

**MRS. WHITE:** You're afraid of your own son!

**NARRATOR:** There is a knock, and another. The old woman breaks free. She runs downstairs. Mr. White hears the chain on the lock rattle.

**MRS. WHITE:** The lock is stuck! I can't reach it. Come and help me!

**NARRATOR:** Mr. White is on his knees. He is feeling for the paw. If only he can find it before the thing outside gets in! The knocks are coming loud and fast. He hears his wife drag a chair to the door. She climbs on the chair. He hears the bolt creak back. At the same time he finds the paw and holds it in the air.

**MR. WHITE** (*whispering*): I wish my son back in the grave.

**NARRATOR:** Suddenly the knocking stops. The door opens. A cold wind rushes up the stairs. A long cry of sorrow from his wife gives Mr. White the courage to run downstairs. He goes out to the gate. The street lamp shines on a quiet, empty road.

# CLOSE UP

1. Working in a group of three or four, make up five questions about the key events or characters in the play. Exchange your questions with another group and answer their questions while they do the same with yours. Combine groups and discuss the accuracy of all the answers.

# WIDE ANGLE

1. Write a paragraph describing what you think the "thing" knocking at the door might have looked like. Include at least five details. Form a small group, trade descriptions, and choose the one that is most frightening.
2. Imagine that Mr. White does not find the monkey's paw in time. Working in a small group, rewrite the ending of the play, beginning with, "He hears the bolt creak back." Dramatize your ending for the class.
3. You are the drama critic reviewing the new ending to *The Monkey's Paw.* Write a paragraph-long review and "publish" it for the performers. (To help you focus, you may wish to refer to the Checklist for Re-seeing and Revision (p. 182).)
4. Pretend that you are a television reporter doing a feature on the White family's experiences with the talisman. To prepare for the program you decide to interview Sergeant Morris or Mr. White. Work with a partner to write up the interview, tape it, and play it for the class.
5. *The Monkey's Paw* was originally written by W.W. Jacobs as a short story. Check with your teacher or librarian to see if you have the story in a book at your school. Read the story. Which do you think is more effective in creating suspense—the play or the story? Make point-form notes on some of the differences and similarities between the two versions.

# THE VISITOR
*by Ian Serraillier*

A crumbling churchyard, the sea and the moon;
The waves had gouged out grave and bone;
A man was walking, late and alone . . .

He saw a skeleton white on the ground,
A ring on a bony hand he found.

He ran home to his wife and gave her the ring.
"Oh, where did you get it?" He said not a thing.

"It's the prettiest ring in the world," she said,
As it glowed on her finger. They skipped off to bed.

At midnight they woke. In the dark outside,
"Give me my ring!" a chill voice cried.

"What was that, William? What did it say?"
"Don't worry, my dear. It'll soon go away."

"I'm coming!" A skeleton opened the door.
"Give me my ring!" It was crossing the floor.

"What was that, William? What did it say?"
"Don't worry, my dear. It'll soon go away."

"I'm touching you now! I'm climbing the bed."
The wife pulled the sheet right over her head.

It was torn from her grasp and tossed in the air:
"I'll drag you out of the bed by the hair!"

"What was that, William? What did it say?"
"Throw the ring through the window! THROW IT AWAY!"

She threw it. The skeleton leapt from the sill,
Scooped up the ring and clattered downhill,
Fainter . . . and fainter . . . Then all was still.

# THE GLIMPSE
## *by Thomas Hardy*

She sped through the door
And, following in haste,
And stirred to the core,
I entered hot-faced;
But I could not find her,
No sign was behind her.
"Where is she?" I said:
—"Who?" they asked that sat there;
"Not a soul's come in sight."
—"A maid with red hair."
—"Ah." They paled. "She is dead.
People see her at night,
But you are the first
On whom she has burst
In the keen common light."

It was ages ago,
When I was quite strong:
I have waited since,—O,
I have waited so long!
—Yea, I set me to own
The house, where now lone
I dwell in void rooms
Booming hollow as tombs!
But I never come near her,
Though nightly I hear her.
And my cheek has grown thin
And my hair has grown grey
With this waiting therein;
But she still keeps away!

# CLOSE UP

1. List the words that the poet uses at the beginning of "The Visitor" to create an eerie, mysterious mood. Add to the list other words you think would be useful in creating such a mood.
2. Most people are afraid of ghosts and want to keep away from them. The man in "The Glimpse," however, buys the house where he saw the ghost and waits for her to return. Brainstorm with a partner the possible reasons for his unusual behaviour. Decide which of your explanations is most likely.

# WIDE ANGLE

1. Work in a group of four people to tape "The Visitor." One person will be the narrator; the others will play the man, the woman, and the skeleton. Vary the volume of your voices from whispers to shouts and add special effects if you wish.
2. Make a comic-strip version of "The Visitor." You can draw one frame of the comic for every stanza in the poem.

   **or**

   Choose one scene from "The Glimpse," illustrate it, and write an explanation of the scene. If you wish, use a computer graphics program or cartoon program for your comic or illustration.

# THE LADY WITH THE MISSING FINGER

*by Elma Schemenauer*

THE SKY was clear when the white-sailed ship set out from Halifax Harbour that bright morning in the early 1800s. But by afternoon the sun was obscured by a lead-coloured haze. Dark clouds gathered on the horizon and the wind moaned fretfully in the ship's tall masts.

Hurriedly the crew prepared to meet the storm, which soon burst upon them in terrible fury. Jagged streaks of lightning split the dark sky. The thunder crashed and rain descended in sheets. Suddenly, with no warning whatsoever, there was a sickening jolt as the vessel's wooden hull struck a submerged reef just off the coast of Sable Island. Seconds later the cold salt waters of the Atlantic were pouring in through her bottom, which had been scraped open on the hidden reef.

Within minutes it was all over. There was nothing left on the choppy grey surface but a few forlorn bits of floating wreckage. Sable Island, that Graveyard of the North Atlantic, had claimed yet another of its many victims.

The wrecked ship had sunk so quickly that her crew never had a chance to launch the lifeboats that could have saved both them and their passengers. There was only one survivor of the wreck. She was a beautiful young woman— a Mrs. Copeland, a doctor's wife from Halifax. Somehow she had managed to grasp a wooden hatch cover as it floated past her. Desperately she clung to it. At the same time, she craned her neck around to see if anyone else might be struggling in the water nearby. But as far as she could tell, she was all alone.

For hours the restless waves tossed the poor woman to and fro like a doll. Her fashionable white dress soon hung in tatters. Her long hair, which had been so carefully arranged, streamed out behind her in a tangled wet mass. Her lips turned blue. She was shivering so violently that she was afraid she would lose her hold on the hatch cover— her only link with life. At last she fell into a swoon. But her delicate hands never slackened their grip. Slowly the tide washed her makeshift raft in towards the Sable Island shoreline.

It was a Sable Island wrecker who found her. He lived with his family on the wind-swept sand bar, making a livelihood by picking up any goods of value that washed up on the beach from sunken ships.

Just at sunset the wrecker happened to notice the bobbing form of the white-clad woman in the water. As he watched, a huge breaker swept her in and flung her up on the wet sand. The wrecker ran down to where she lay and seized hold of her arm before the receding waters could drag her out again. Then he picked her up and carried her out of reach of the pounding surf.

He laid her on the sand in the shelter of a coarse clump of beach grass. Her eyes were closed and he couldn't tell whether she was breathing or not. "She's probably dead," he muttered to himself. "But I can't tell for sure. I'd better take her up to the house." He stooped to pick her up again. Suddenly his eye caught a bright flash of green on the third finger of her left hand. It was a huge emerald ring. His eyes popped as he examined the stone in the fading light. "That's a dilly, that is," he said to himself. "Why, it's probably worth a fortune!"

Greed now seemed to take possession of the man, overcoming any good intentions that he might have had in the beginning. He started to yank at the ring, trying to pull it off the woman's finger. But her hands, though small and delicate, were swollen from her long hours in the cold salt water. The emerald ring simply wouldn't budge.

In a frenzy the wrecker seized his hatchet and began trying to saw the ring off the woman's finger. At this, Mrs. Copeland struggled to her feet. She wasn't dead after all, but just unconscious. The man's rough treatment had jolted her back to her senses.

By this time the wrecker had only one thought in mind— to obtain the valuable emerald at any cost. And so he killed the poor woman. Then he chopped off her finger with the ring still on it, and put it in his pocket.

The man's wife was horror-stricken when she found out what he had done. The wrecker himself soon began to regret his rash action. He decided to leave Sable Island forever and move to Cape Breton with his family.

But even after leaving the scene of the crime, he couldn't forget the cold-blooded murder he had committed. Mrs. Copeland's ghost began to haunt him. When he was alone, she would often rise before his eyes, pointing the bleeding stump of her severed finger at him in an accusing way.

The wrecker kept the emerald for some time. Then one day when he was badly in need of money, he pawned it in a watchmaker's shop in Halifax. He left it with the

watchmaker in exchange for a loan of twenty shillings, intending to return for the ring when he was able to pay back the money.

About this time a number of other Sable Island wreckers were selling—among their other wares—a number of valuable pieces of jewellery. People on the Nova Scotia mainland started to wonder where all these expensive rings, necklaces, watches, and other personal belongings were coming from. Surely the Sable Islanders hadn't suddenly begun to find such rich booty simply lying on the beach. Perhaps the wreckers were finishing off weakened shipwreck survivors who managed to struggle to shore.

Government officials had no proof of this, since no one had actually witnessed any murders. But they felt that someone should be sent out to look into the matter. They chose Captain Edmund Torrens as their representative. Accordingly, Captain Torrens set off for Sable Island. But his ship, like so many others in those days, ran into a violent storm and was wrecked on one of the island's treacherous underwater reefs. Torrens and a dog were the only survivors.

They both managed to swim to shore, where the captain quickly put together a rough hut in the shelter of a sand dune. Then he and the dog set out to explore the island. One day they walked all the way to its eastern tip, a distance of over thirty kilometres.

The sun was shining. Puffy white clouds skimmed across the bright blue sky. The dog was bounding along the beach, chasing the sticks that Torrens threw for it. The captain was enjoying himself so much that he completely lost track of the time.

Suddenly he noticed that the sun was starting to go down. It cast an unearthly red glow over the wind-swept landscape that had seemed so friendly and pleasant just a few minutes before. Torrens began to think of the many dangers that might lurk among the dunes at night—bloodthirsty wreckers, giant rats, quicksand . . . With a start he realized how far he was from his shelter. He would never be able to retrace his steps and reach it again before dark.

He whistled for the dog. Then, with the animal trotting along at his side, he began to walk rapidly inland, looking for a safe place to spend the night. After a few minutes, he came upon a hut that had been built to shelter shipwreck survivors.

At-sight of the little wooden building, the dog stiffened. The hair on its back bristled. With a low growl, it sat down on the sand and refused to accompany Torrens a step farther. Cautiously the captain approached the rough-looking hut. He lifted the latch and tried the door, which swung inward, creaking on its rusty hinges. The place was quite dark inside, since there were no windows. But, as his eyes became accustomed to the dimness, Torrens saw that there was a fireplace in one corner.

He went out to gather some wood from among the wreckage along the beach. Soon he was back and had a bright fire blazing. The dog, however, still refused to come anywhere near the hut. Torrens himself began to feel increasingly uneasy inside, for some reason that he couldn't explain. He decided that, before he went to sleep, he would take a short walk inland. The dog went with him.

When they returned, Torrens entered the windowless building again. But the dog stayed outside. After a few moments, the animal started barking excitedly. Suddenly, through the gloom, Torrens noticed that there was someone sitting by the fire that he had kindled in the fireplace. It was a woman in a long white dress! She was completely engrossed in trying to dry her long tangled hair, which was dripping wet.

"Who are you?" asked Torrens in surprise. "What are you doing here?"

Slowly the woman lifted her head. She made no reply.

With a tragic expression on her face, she simply raised her left hand. Her ring finger was missing and only a bloody stump remained!

Torrens just stood there for a moment, not knowing what to do. Then his eye happened to fall on a box of medical supplies that had been left above the fireplace for the use of shipwreck survivors. He opened the box and offered to clean and bandage the woman's hand. But before he could do so, she slipped past him out through the open door. He followed her for a short distance. But then she disappeared into the night.

The captain was puzzled, to say the least. As he thought about what had happened, he began to suspect that the white-clad figure he had seen must have been a ghost. Nevertheless, he slept in the hut that night. Then, more out of curiosity than anything else, he returned to it again the following evening. He kindled the fire, just as he had done before. Again he went out for a walk. When he returned, the same woman was sitting beside the fire, trying to dry her hair, which was still dripping wet. This time Torrens recognized her as Mrs. Copeland, whom he had met in Halifax. "What can I do for you, Mrs. Copeland?" he asked gently.

Again, the woman remained silent. She merely raised her left hand, showing him the stump where her finger had been amputated.

"I see," said Torrens. "Someone killed you in order to steal your ring. Is that it?"

She nodded.

"I'll track down the murderer and see that he's punished!" cried Torrens. "Is that what you want?"

But the woman shook her head. It seemed that she had no interest in revenge.

"What can I do for you then, Mrs. Copeland?" asked the captain. "Shall I try to find the ring and return it to your relatives in England?"

The woman nodded vigorously.

Torrens promised to do everything he could to retrieve the missing emerald. The poor ghost seemed to be happy with this. She smiled and then slipped past him into the night.

Shortly afterwards, Torrens returned to the mainland to begin his investigation. He decided to call on the three best-known Sable Island wreckers, who had all left the island by this time.

When he reached the home of the one who was then living in Cape Breton, he found that the man had gone to Labrador. But his family invited the captain inside.

The wrecker's young daughter soon noticed the large ring that Torrens was wearing. He had bought it just a few days earlier, thinking that somehow it might help him to find Mrs. Copeland's emerald. It was a showy but inexpensive piece of jewellery.

"Your ring is lovely, Captain Torrens," remarked the girl.

"Thank you. I just bought it in Halifax," replied Torrens. "I'm really quite interested in rings of all kind."

"You should have seen the one my father took from the shipwrecked lady's finger when we lived on Sable Island," said the girl.

"Stop your chattering!" interrupted the girl's mother angrily. She turned to the captain. "My daughter made a mistake," she told him quickly. "Her father didn't take that ring from a lady. He got it from a Frenchman who had found it on the sand."

"I don't care how he obtained it," replied Torrens mildly. "But I'd like to see it if I may."

"We don't have it any more," snapped the woman. "My husband pawned it for twenty shillings at a watchmaker's shop in Halifax."

Torrens immediately went to Halifax. He found the watchmaker who had the ring and offered him twenty shillings for it.

"But this is a real emerald. It's worth many times that amount," protested the watchmaker. "Besides, the owner may still return for it. I have to keep it for him."

"This emerald doesn't really belong to the man who brought it to you," Torrens told him. "The real owner of the ring asked me to find it. Here, take your twenty shillings and give it to me."

"But what shall I say to the wrecker when he comes back?" asked the watchmaker.

"Tell him that if he wants any more money, he must bring me the finger that he cut off to obtain the emerald," replied Torrens sternly. With that, he picked up the ring, put it in his pocket, and strode out of the shop.

The captain returned the ring to Mrs. Copeland's relatives in England, just as he had promised. The wrecker was never brought to trial for the murder he had committed. But he was tormented by guilt for the rest of his life. People say he became so anxious and fearful that he couldn't even go outdoors after dark. As for Mrs. Copeland, some of the residents of Sable Island say that at times her ghost may still be seen, patrolling the wind-swept shores. She rises out of the mists with her long wet hair flowing out behind her. And she holds her left hand high to show the bloody stump of the finger that she lost so many years ago.

# CLOSE UP

1. Your teacher will divide the class into five groups. Each group is responsible for one of the following parts of the story:
   I    The Shipwreck
   II   The Murder
   III  Suspicious Jewels—The Government Investigates
   IV   Captain Torrens and the Ghost
   V    The Emerald Recovered
   In your small group, work on your section of the story until you are satisfied that you can all tell it in an exciting way. You may make point-form notes to help you when you join others who have not read your section. The teacher will then make new groups of five. Each group member will know how to tell a different part of the story; together, you will be able to tell the whole tale. Tape your group reading. You may wish to give your cassette to a nearby junior school for them to use at Hallowe'en.

# WIDE ANGLE

1. Find Sable Island, Halifax, and Cape Breton on a map of Nova Scotia. Ask your geography teacher or school librarian to help you find out why Sable Island is called "The Graveyard of the North Atlantic." Record the information in point form. After thinking through the information in a conference with a partner (see p. 176), summarize the information in a one- or two-paragraph explanation.
2. With the help of a partner, write a script of the conversation between the wrecker and his wife when he arrives home with the emerald ring. Role-play the scene for other students.
3. Pretend that you are a reporter for the *Halifax Gazette* and that you have interviewed Captain Torrens about his investigation of the case of the missing emerald. Write an article for the paper. Include a dramatic headline.

# KALEIDOSCOPE

1. View a ghost movie (e.g., *Ghostbusters*), and in a small group brainstorm five techniques the director used to scare the audience. Together, make a list of the elements of a typical ghost story and give examples from the movie.

2. Search for a ghost story. Check the library, ask a parent, a relative, a friend—anyone! In a group of four or five, read the stories aloud to each other. Make them as spine–chilling as you can. Choose the story that is the most scary and tape it using sound effects. Someone could design a poster to advertise the tape.

3. Not all ghosts rattle chains and scare people. Draw a chart using these headings: Story; Ghost; Ghost's Personality; Characters' Reaction to Ghost. Look over the selections in the cluster and fill in the chart. Remember that different characters react in different ways to the same ghost.

| Story | Ghost | Ghost's Personality | Characters' Reaction to Ghost |
|-------|-------|---------------------|-------------------------------|
|       |       |                     |                               |
|       |       |                     |                               |

4. Different cultures have different kinds of ghost stories. With two partners, find three kinds of ghosts or spirits from different parts of the world. Your social science teacher or librarian may be able to help. Share your findings with the class.

5. THE GHOST AND THE SKELETON
   A skeleton once in Khartoum
   Invited a ghost to his room.
   They spent the whole night
   In the eeriest fight
   As to who should be frightened of whom.

   *Anonymous*

   With a partner, write a ghost limerick. Compile all the limericks written by your classmates into a "ghostly anthology".

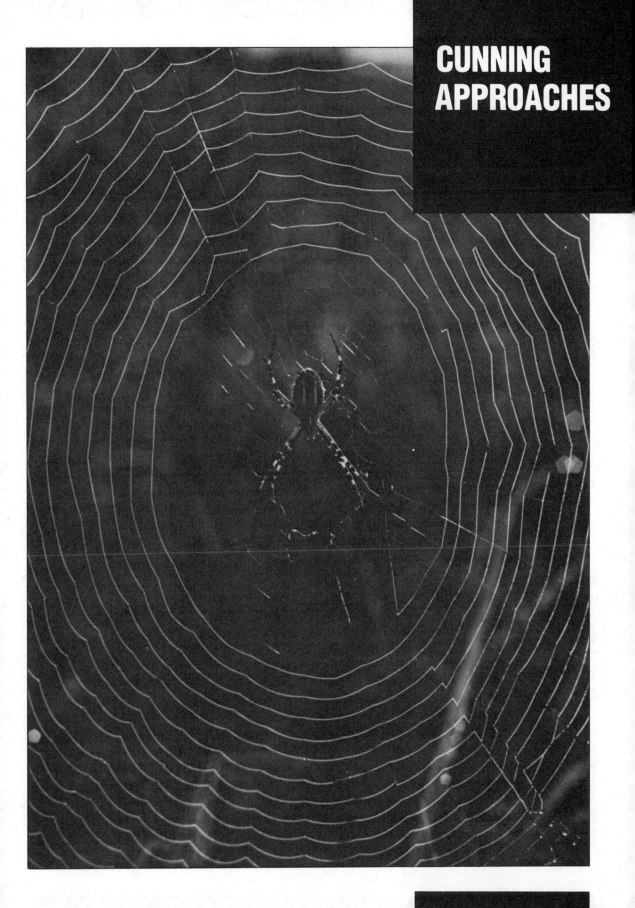

# *from*
# MY GRAND-FATHER'S CAPE BRETON

*by Clive Doucet*

THE STEADY whir of the cutting bar dominated the still, hot day. Our haying had begun, the tall grass coming down neatly to the ground, as the horses strained into their harness. Cutting hay was the toughest work I had ever seen Nellie and Donald do. The cutting bar was driven by the rotating wheels of the mower so the horses had not only to pull a rather heavy machine, but also provide the power to bring the grass down. It was heavy, continuous work that once begun couldn't be delayed. As long as the weather was fine you had to grind on. The two old horses had done it many times before and they knew the routine, heads down, pulling steadily, evenly. A grand team, they moved forward together step by step, with never a falter, like the old pros they were. But by mid-morning old Nellie was labouring more than she should have been. I was kind of worried about her. She seemed to be really struggling to keep up with her partner, her distended sides caked in white lather. It must have been on Grandfather's mind also because he stopped the mower and called to me, "Clive, can you run over to Gerard's and see if we can borrow his horse for this afternoon? I don't think Nellie's going to make it through the whole day." And he made a sign with his arms to indicate her distended middle. I nodded and set off for Gerard's place immediately.

It turned out as Grandpa had hoped. Uncle Gerard was using a tractor, a baling machine, and the like for his haying. His one remaining horse, a big grey-speckled fellow called Bill, was decorating a rough pasture by the sea along with a few cows. He watched me approach, strong and very full of himself. He kicked up his heels, and galloped to the other end of the pasture, not interested in my small bucket of oats and not at all fooled. He certainly was a powerful fellow, squat and built like a tank—quite different from the more rangy Clydesdales that Nellie and Donald drew their parentage from. I began to walk towards him once more rattling the bucket invitingly. Suddenly he turned and came charging straight towards me. My throat went dry. "I should have come out with Roland," was the one thought that flashed through my mind before the thundering monster stopped a few short yards in front of me. Then he advanced slowly and buried his head like a lamb in the bucket of oats. Once he had got a good start on the oats, I reached up for his halter. He didn't jump and I began to lead him cautiously to the barn. He came quietly, but I could feel the tensed spring in his step. If we could ever get this fellow hitched up, he was going to give old Donald a run for his money.

"Hi, Clive." I turned to see my cousin, Roland. "Need a hand?"

"No, I've got the bridle on. Anything I should know about him before I take him over to Grandpa's?"

"Just one thing. He kicks when you hitch him up to anything. Doesn't like to work much. Dad's going to sell him. Myself, I don't think you'll be able to use him."

"Maybe Grandpa will think of something. He's good with horses."

"O.K., but remember to warn him," advised Roland again.

"How about riding? Does he buck or anything like that?" I asked nervously.

"No, but he'll probably try and take the bit in his mouth and run." I looked at the big grey horse in bewilderment. It had never occurred to me that other horses might be different. Nellie and Donald were so well behaved.

"Don't worry Clive. You're right. Grandpa will probably settle him down. Dad says Grandpa speaks three languages—French, English and horse."

"That's fine, but in the meantime I'm liable to get killed."

"You can ride him, don't worry. Just run the devil out of him right at the start. That's what I do." Then he turned to go.

"Aren't you staying to watch the action?"

"No, I've got to get back."

"How's your haying coming along?"

"With luck we'll be finished by the middle of next week. Dad's promised to take me down to Chéticamp Beach on Sunday. Want to come?"

"Sure."

"O.K. See you around two."

"Easy for you to say," I said. Roland grinned and left me with Bill. We eyed each other appraisingly. I don't know who was more uneasy, the huge horse or me. Well, I had no choice. Old Nellie needed him. I eased onto his bare back from the porch railing. I could feel his muscles jumping underneath my legs like live wires. There was no question in my mind and less in Bill's—the second I gave him the chance, he was going to take off like an express train. I reined in on the bit until my arms ached, but he still sidestepped in something between a canter and a trot all the way down the lane. Things didn't look too promising for a safe journey home. There was a lot more of him than there was of me. At that moment, I'd settle for doing just as Roland had advised—point him in the right direction and hang on.

We turned the corner onto the highway. Bill was losing patience with the tight rein. I could feel it. He threw up his hind legs in a play-buck and I smashed my nose adroitly against the back of his neck. Bill didn't seem to notice but I did. I felt dizzy and slightly sick. Some blood dripped down on my trousers. I wiped my nose with my shirtsleeve, at the same time easing up on the reins. The big horse didn't miss the opportunity and sprang immediately into a tremendous headlong charge, his mane snapping into my face. The roadside flying along beneath me, sparks cracking up between his steel shoes and the pavement. I tried not to think about falling off onto the asphalt. The farm drew near. I pulled up on the reins. No response. I pulled up a little harder—no response. The big horse thundered on. Bill had the bit firmly clenched in his teeth. I was strictly a passenger. Grandfather watched from the mower as the big grey horse galloped all the way down to the Co-op where he began to slow down and finally loosened the bit from his teeth. I didn't waste the moment. I wheeled him around and we galloped back, considerably slower, towards the farm. Grandfather had the mower parked beside the barn and was in the process of unhitching the horses when we finally arrived.

"What happened?"

"Horse ran away with me."

"You O.K.?"

"Fine."

"How's the horse?"

"Sound, but crazy as a hoot. Roland says he kicks when you hitch him up." I slipped off the horse. Grandfather shrugged.

"What can you expect? He's a young horse and no one's ever taught him any manners. Can you take Donald and Nellie down to the stable and I'll see if I can fix something up for this young fellow?"

"Sure." I hurried the two old comrades down to their stalls, anxious to return and see what Grandfather was going to do. The old mare eased up to her manger with a sigh of relief.

When I got back, Grandfather had a pair of shafts hitched up to absolutely nothing at all. Just two shafts sitting on two barrels but the grey horse was all harnessed up as if he was going to pull something, somewhere.

"What's up?" I asked.

"We'll see in a minute," said Grandfather enigmatically. Then Grandpa backed up the grey horse between the two shafts. Nothing happened. "Try hitching him up," said Grandfather. "Stay well to the side." I nodded and, feeling somewhat foolish, proceeded to hitch his harness to the shafts. The big hind-quarters exploded in a devastating double kick but as the horse's feet met with absolutely no resistance, his legs extended more fully than he intended. His back hooves hung in the air for a second. The horse seemed to shudder with the effort of drawing them back under him, unbalanced and slowly fell forward onto his knees. For a moment he lay sprawled among the barrels and shafts before he stood up, unhurt but shaking and frightened.

"O.K.," said Grandpa, patting him gently on the neck. "Kick all you want, young fellow. We've got plenty of time. Let's unhitch him again, Clive." We unhitched him. "O.K., hitch him up on your side." We hitched both sides of the harness to the phony wagon once more. The young horse trembled a little around the hind end as we hitched him but he didn't kick. Grandpa smiled happily and said, "He'll do." We tethered him on the mow floor on a loose rein with a little hay to keep him occupied, and went to lunch.

Donald and Bill didn't match very well—one a golden chestnut, the other a silver-grey; one rangy, the other bulky. But they worked well together. The older horse steadied the younger one, while Bill helped Donald with some much needed pulling power. In the meantime Nellie swanned around the night pasture keeping quietly out of sight while her compatriots kept working until the grass began to dampen with dew.

It was two very large and very tired horses I led to the stables that night. To my surprise Grandfather was already snoozing in his rocker by the time I returned to the house. It was only eight o'clock. Usually we played checkers or something. I shouldn't have been surprised. Grandpa was seventy-eight years old and he had just spent almost ten hours bouncing around a baking-hot hayfield.

# FOCUSSING

1. Most people have animal stories to tell. In a small group, exchange stories about animals in your life. Choose your favourite story and write it down so that it could be read to a child. You may wish to illustrate it.

   **or**

   Think about the animal story you liked the best when you were a child. Write down what you remember of it. Look up the original story in the library, re-read it, and note any details you left out.

2. In your journal, describe the kind of animal
   a) you would most like to be and why; and
   b) you would least like to be and why.

3. There are many stereotypes or clichés about the characteristics and personalities of various animals. Often the stereotypes are misleading. Make a chart with a list of five animals. Beside each animal, write
   a) adjectives that are frequently used to describe the animal;
   b) the possible sources of the adjectives; and
   c) some facts that disprove the clichés.

| Animal | Common Adjectives | Source of Adjectives | Facts That Disprove |
|--------|-------------------|----------------------|---------------------|
| koala bear | cuddly, sweet, loving | television commercials | sharp and powerful claws, leathery snout, shy, dangerous when frightened |

You may want to construct your chart on a word processor and save it on disc. If you think of other examples as you work through the cluster, you can call up your chart and add the new entries. When you finish the cluster, print out your chart and share it in a small group.

# ANIMAL CRACKERS

*by Roger Bollen*

# THE FAR SIDE

*by Gary Larson*

"Okay, here we go! Remember, wiggle those noses, stuff those cheeks, and act cute — and no smoking, Carl."

# CLOSE UP

1.  The cartoon and the comic strip are funny because the artists have given human characteristics to animals. With a partner, decide which human characteristic each animal has, and then describe each animal's characteristic in a sentence or two.
2.  The title of this cluster, "Cunning Approaches," comes from "Polar Night," but it could apply equally well to both of the cartoons. Discuss how this is so with a partner and write a paragraph that expands on your points.

# WIDE ANGLE

1.  Create a cartoon or a comic strip in which you give an animal human qualities in order to create humour. You may wish to use an animal from one of the selections in this cluster. (If you have access to a computer, you could use a cartoon-making program.)

# THE TRAP
### *by William Beyer*

"That red fox,
Back in the furthest field,
Caught in my hidden trap,
Was half mad with fear.
During the night
He must have ripped his foot
From the cold steel.
I saw him early this morning,
Dragging his hurt leg,
Bleeding a path across the gold wheat,
Whining with the pain;
His eyes like cracked marbles.
I followed as he moved,
His thin body pulled to one side
In a weird helplessness.
He hit the wire fence,
Pushing through it
Into the deep, morning corn,
And was gone."
The old man looked around the kitchen
To see if anyone was listening.
"Crazy red fox.
Will kill my chickens no longer.
Will die somewhere in hiding."
He lit the brown tobacco carefully,
Watching the blue smoke rise and disappear
In the movement of the air.
Scratching his red nose slowly,
Thinking something grave for a long moment,
He stared out of the bright window.
"He won't last long with that leg," he said.
The old man turned his head
To see if his wife was listening.
But she was deep in thought,
Her stained fingers
Pressing red berries in a pie.
He turned his white head
Toward the open window again.
"Guess I'll ride into the back field, first thing.
Some mighty big corn back there this year.
Mighty big corn."
His wife looked up from her work,
Smiled almost secretly to herself,
And finished packing the ripe berries
Into the pale crust.

# CLOSE UP

1. Draw a series of sketches to show the events of the poem. Under each sketch, write the corresponding line of the poem.
2. Choose the description you like the most in the poem. Read the lines to a partner and explain why you like them. The Checklist for Making Positive Comments (p. 183) may help you be specific in your explanation.
3. Discuss with a partner why you think the poet decided to have the wife pressing bright red berries into a pie instead of doing some other chore. Write your answer in one or two sentences.

# WIDE ANGLE

1. Imagine that you are the fox, wounded and hiding in the deep corn. Write or tape the thoughts running through your head as you lie there. (See "On the Sidewalk Bleeding" on p. 62, which presents Andy's thoughts as he lies dying.)
2. Think of a time when you saw an injured animal. In your journal, describe the incident and record the feelings you had at the time.
3. Work with a partner and discuss what the woman might be thinking as she listens to the old man tell the story of the fox. Write a monologue in which her reactions and emotions are expressed. Tape your work if you wish.
4. Continue the poem for at least one stanza, telling what the farmer will do when he goes to the back field.

# POLAR NIGHT

*by Norah Burke*

A S THE HOT arctic summer drew to a close, till the magenta sun only slid along the horizon to sink again at once, the polar bear knew that a hard time lay ahead for her.

During the months of night, fifty degrees below zero, her cubs would be born. The great task of motherhood was already begun, the time soon coming when she would bury herself deep down under the snow to give birth. From then until the day when she and the cubs burrowed up into daylight again, she would not eat. She and they must live on what she had stored in her body during the summer, and on what she could catch and eat now. She must finish fattening herself up for the ordeal, and there was not much time left.

At the moment she was hunting along the edge of the ice, because where there was water there were seals, also fish, and the chance of a porpoise or walrus. As winter closed the roots and berries and lichen and seaweed of the polar islands into glass, the bears moved to the ice-edge for their food.

This was the arctic region, the area north of the limit of tree growth. The shores of Greenland, Siberia, Alaska, Canada bordered upon this spectral sea. It was a landscape of snow and old ice and new ice, of drifting pack ice, and berg ice from the glaciers, all in constant motion, lanes and pools of pure cobalt looking glass, opening and closing all the time in the pack. Where the old ice had been pushed up together in terraces, ice-eaves burned green and lilac underneath. In summer the skuas and ivory gulls and other birds made the air raucous with quarrels, but now all that the bear could hear was the wash of blue water against grinding ice.

Under the dark sky, on the white land, in the desolation of the arctic landscape, she was part of its white power, moving with a long swinging walk and huge fat yellow hairy snowman footfalls. Strong and dangerous, the largest of bears, able to swim forty miles out to sea if need be, she stalked her kingdom in which no natural enemy challenged her reign. Her feet, bristled underneath to give grip on the ice, carried her huge weight with a light and silent tread; while the low swinging head searched the ice all the time for food.

She was not clearly aware of what was happening in her body, but the instinct was there to love the unborn cubs, to prepare for them and protect them; she did not risk her body in careless adventures as she would at other times.

But food? Food—

Already the iron of winter was in the clean cold air, though she felt the cold only with her eyes and black nose and black lips, where the air stung her, and on the long pinkish grey tongue, moving all the time to prevent freezing, that slung in and out of her mouth among the large cruel teeth.

Suddenly, away down the ice field, where a dark blue lead showed in the pack, she saw a blackish slug on the ice—a seal. It was essential to catch it. In a moment she had decided on her approach, and slipped silently into the water to cut off its line of retreat. The ice rocked as her great weight left it.

The bear was as much at home in the water as on land—buoyant, swimming like a dog, but on top or submerged—and the water much warmer than the air on her face. Not wet, either. Inside the layer of fat and the shaggy oily watertight coat, she felt as dry as on land.

By a series of cunning dives and approaches, and keeping under the shoulder of ice, she got near to the seal. Breathing carefully, every nerve keyed to the task of silent approach, ready to spring—to dive—to slaughter, she slid nearer—nearer—

Suddenly the seal saw her. Terror convulsed its face. A moment of awful indecision—whether to plunge into the sea, its natural line of escape, and perhaps fall straight into her jaws, or to struggle across the ice to that other hole—

It swung away from her, humping madly along. The bear lunged up out of the water, onto the ice, onto the terrified seal.

The water slushed off her everywhere like a tidal wave. There was a flurry of snow and water and fighting seal. Its quick struggling body flapped under her as she slew it. Blood spurted onto the snow.

When the seal was dead, the bear attended first to herself, getting rid of the wet from her coat before it could freeze, although oil had kept off the frost so far. She shook, and the drops flew off in rainbows in all directions. She rolled and nosed along in the snow, wiping her flanks, her chin, and soon all was dry. A few hairs crisped up and stuck to each other with frost.

Now for the seal. She ripped up the body, turning back the skin and blubber, letting out a cloud of steam, and ate greedily of the hot crimson meat. Seal meat was her

favourite, full of flavour, a hot meal, not like the white icy flakes of cod.

Then, although the bear had no natural enemies, she stopped suddenly as she ate, lifted her head, looked, listened, scented. Blood dripped from her chin on to the snow.

There was nothing.

All the same she trusted her instinct and, leaving the rest of the meal, slipped into the water, where she could keep her cubs safe, where it was warmer, and easier to move.

Presently she saw upright seals coming along the shore. They were rather rare creatures, these, and dangerous for all they were so weak. The places where they lived had light and noise, and smelled full of good food. The she-bear often drew near the places, attracted by those smells. She hunted these land-seals too, and ate them when she could. They were not like the sea-seals, though. They wore seal fur, and their skins were rubbed with seal blubber, but there was a different taste inside.

They in their turn hunted bear, as the she-bear knew well. She had sometimes found the place of the kill, and seen the white empty skins hanging up by the camps, smelled the dark red gamy flesh cooking.

Now as she watched the approaching men, she considered whether to kill them, but the unborn life in her said get away. So she dived and swam and melted out of their radius.

In the next few days the bear gorged on fish and seal. No longer the hot rocks and scree of summer gave forth good-tasting moss and lichens or the sharp-fleshed berries and sweet roots. She dived into the cold blue ocean for her food.

But now the arctic day was over. In the pink twilight a snowy owl was flitting silently across the waste, moving south and south as life was squeezed out of the arctic desert by the polar night.

Then came the freezing of the sea. Crystals formed below the surface and rose, and needles of ice shot across from one to another, joining them together, thickening, hardening, adding more ice to the floes already many years old. The ice talked, grinding its teeth, sending out every now and then a singing crack. Curtains of coloured flame rippled in the sky. The polar night began.

Now the real cold came. Now the food disappeared, and old male bears grew lean and savage.

The she-bear chose her den.

There was a great raw range of decayed ice that had been

pushed up into mountains whose hollows were packed with snow. Icicles yards long hung on the south side from the summer, and behind this curtain of ice she found a great purple cave, carved in diamond and full of snow.

This was the place.

Her body was ready now for the ordeal. Thick fat, gathered from seal and halibut, lined her skin.

She burrowed down into the violet snow on the floor of the cave. It was so light that the wind of moving blew it about like feathers, and she could breathe in it. She burrowed deeper and deeper, while the snow sifted and fell in soundlessly behind her, till presently she was deep enough.

She curled and rolled herself round and round, pushing the snow, packing it, shaping the den. All the sides of it melted with her heat, then froze again into slippery walls. And the hot breath passed up through the way she had dug, melting the sides of the channel which also froze again and left a tube which would supply her with air until she came up in the spring.

Inside the snow and ice—inside her thick oily fur and the layer of blubber, she was warm, full fed, and sleepy. She slept and waited.

In the fullness of time, the first familiar pang of birth trembled in her stomach. Pain fluttered like a butterfly and was gone.

She stirred, lifted her head, rearranged herself.

It came again, stronger, longer.

She moved uneasily.

Then in long strong accomplishing strokes it was there—hard, forcing, contracting, out of her control. Moving to a crescendo. She grunted, tensed all her muscles, pressed, and gasped. Another spasm, and on the smooth strong river of pain, she felt the first cub come out.

A wave of relief relaxed her.

There he lay mewing, so wet and tiny, hardly alive, and she nuzzled him delightedly, starting to clean him up.

But now another spasm—the same long final one as before, though easier—and the second cub was born.

It was over now. She felt the diminishing contractions, the subsidence of pain, pulsing quieter.

Now to clean them up. She licked and licked them, turning them over, rolling and caressing them; then life strengthened in them as they dried, as they fed. She lay in bliss, feeling her own life flowing from her heart.

Meanwhile in the world above, the sun had returned, first a green glow, then a rosy one, then touching the topmost peaks, days before the first sunrise.

Deep in the snow cave, the bear knew it as the snow

grew luminous with the light pressing through.

One day she heard voices. The snow vibrated with footsteps, the ice ceiling cracked.

She rose, shook herself free of the cubs and stood ready in case the land-seals saw the warm yellow air hole that marked her den—in case one of them walked over her and fell in. . . .

She stood fierce, lean, ready, to defend her cubs, her heart pounding hot and loud as fever in her thin body.

Gradually the voices and the footsteps died away.

Presently it was time to come out into the world again. The cubs' eyes were open, their coats grown; they were walking, getting stronger every day. Now they must come out and face the world and swim and fight and catch seals. There was everything to teach them, and while they were still learning—still babies, they had got to be kept safe and fed. All this she had to do alone. Other years she'd had a mate to help her, but this time he was gone—lost—Those white skins hanging by the camps—

She began to tear her way out, the giant paws and black nails breaking open the ice walls of their den. The ice gave, snow fell in.

They climbed out.

Clean frozen air, dazzling with sun, hit them like the stroke of an axe. Light entered the brain in needles through the eyes. Only gradually, as the pupils contracted, did it become possible to see.

Under an iridescent sun-halo, the arctic landscape blazed white and navy blue. Everything hit them at once—light, noise, wind—the blast of a new world.

Down there was the water—

The mother bear plunged joyfully into the buoyant cleanness. All the dirt and staleness of winter were washed away. It was like flight. She plunged and rose and shook and plunged again in sheer joy. So fresh, so clean, the salt cold water running through her teeth—

Then she resumed the heavy duties of parenthood, turned to the cubs. They were sitting on the edge, squeaking with fright, and she began urging them to come in. They kept feeling forward, then scrambling back. Suddenly one ventured too far down the ice, and slithered, shrieking, into the sea, where he bobbed up again like a cork.

His brother, seeing this, plucked up courage and plunged in too, in one desperate baby-jump, landing with a painful *smack!* and blinking in the spray.

They found they could swim.

Presently she pushed them up on to the ice again where they shook and dried, and the next thing was food. She left them while she killed a seal, and the three of them ate it.

After that there were lessons, how to fish, how to kill. Living was thin at first, for three hunters cannot move as silently as one, but they got along.

Until the day when the land-seals approached them unseen from behind an ice ridge. The first they knew of it was an explosion, and one cub gasped and doubled up as he was hit. The bears dived for the water, even the wounded little one. He managed to keep up with them, and his mother and brother would die rather than desert him.

They all swam on, but slowly—slowly. Both cubs were still so small and *slow*, and they must hurry—

Blood ran in the sapphire water.

Other shots spattered beside them.

Anxiety roared in the she-bear's blood. Her heart was bursting. She pushed the cubs on, and turned to meet her enemies. Reared up on to the ice and galloped towards them, a charge that nothing could stop—not even death—if they'd stayed to face it, but they broke and ran.

The bear returned to her cubs.

The wounded one was sinking lower and lower in the water, breathing waves, and she managed to push him out at last onto distant ice. Then she licked him as he lay suffering in the snow, and his brother licked him too, whimpering with distress as he worked.

So that presently the blood stopped, and after a long time the suffering too. The cub sniffed the air. In the first real moment of recovery he consented to take food.

Pain went away from her heart.

Before them lay all the arctic lands, the snow in retreat. The floes, soft and friable from solar radiation, were being broken up by the waves. Plant life teemed in the water, the more open sea coloured bright green by diatoms. Millions of wild flowers studded the rocky scree. There was everything to eat at once—lichen and moss and roots and halibut and seals. Salmon swam the green water, and cod. Seaweed washed round the rocks. On the land there were hares and young birds.

The summer gathered to almost tropical heat. Snow water dribbled into pools. Icicles glistened with wet, dropped and broke like glass.

And the mother bear, in the snow, with her cubs did not know why she behaved as she did. There was pain and there was happiness, and these two things drove her according to unfathomable laws. When the summer ended, and the polar night began, she would do the same things over again, and her children after her.

# CLOSE UP

1. You have a friend who is an artist. She is going on a trip to the Arctic to paint landscapes. From the details in the story, list the paints she will need to take with her to capture the colours of the wilderness. Write a description of each colour and tell what she would use it for.

2. There are many conflicts in the bear's life. Fill in the following chart on each conflict in the order in which they occurred. One of the entries has been made already.

| Conflict | | |
|---|---|---|
| with Whom or What | Why | Outcome of Conflict |
| wintertime | harsh weather, lack of food | hibernation to survive |

3. Join with two partners to share the passages that, in your opinion,
   a) create the strongest pictures;
   b) are the most exciting; and
   c) are the most moving.
   Read these passages aloud to each other and discuss why you chose them.

4. Create a drawing of the she-bear that will be used in a science textbook in a chapter dealing with polar bears. In your drawing, highlight the ways in which her body is perfectly adapted to life in the Arctic.
   **or**
   Referring to the line "The She-Bear chose her den," and using the next five paragraphs for details, draw a diagram of the space she creates for herself. Point out all the important features of her den.

# WIDE ANGLE

1.  In "Polar Night" the "upright seals" are Inuit hunters. In a small group, research how Inuit hunting practices have changed in this century. (You might want to ask the assistance of your history or geography teacher.) Describe the changes in an oral presentation made to a group of students who have also read the story. Use a map and photographs of the area to illustrate your presentation.

2.  Many species of animals in the world today are in danger of becoming extinct. The following is a list of a few of them:

    | | |
    |---|---|
    | polar bear | white rhinoceros |
    | African elephant | cheetah |
    | snow leopard | gaur |
    | Grevy's zebra | Malayan tapir |
    | pygmy hippopotamus | Sumatran orangutan |

    a) Each group is responsible for a different animal. Go to the library to learn about it and find out why its numbers are decreasing. Brainstorm some strategies for the preservation of your animal, and then compose a radio or magazine advertisement to convince people to save the species.

    b) Draw or clip a picture of your animal and put it on a class poster of endangered species.

# KALEIDOSCOPE

1.  Work with a partner and read several poems about animals. Choose a few poems that both of you like. Make a booklet, give it a title, and illustrate it with drawings or photographs. Each of you should write your own animal poem to include in your booklet.

2.  Form a small group and view a movie in which an animal (or animals) is the main character. Your group should introduce the movie and show it for the class. Draw up some activities that the class can do after seeing it. You may wish to have them write a journal entry, draw a favourite scene, rewrite the ending, or compose a movie review, for example.

3.  Work in a small group in your resource centre. Each group member should find a myth about an animal. Summarize the story in point form and tell the story in your own words to your group. You may need to refer to your summary to help you tell your story.

4.  Arrange to interview someone associated with an organization in your community that works on behalf of animals. (You could go out to the organization or bring a speaker in.) Draw up a list of questions that you wish to ask. Tape your interview. Play the interview for a partner and explain two things that you learned from the person you interviewed. Try to answer any of your partner's questions.